THE NEW RUSSIAN
FOREIGN POLICY

THE NEW RUSSIAN
FOREIGN POLICY

Michael Mandelbaum, Editor

A COUNCIL ON FOREIGN RELATIONS BOOK

The Council on Foreign Relations, Inc., a nonprofit, nonpartisan national membership organization founded in 1921, is dedicated to promoting understanding of international affairs through the free and civil exchange of ideas. The Council's members are dedicated to the belief that America's peace and prosperity are firmly linked to that of the world. From this flows the mission of the Council: to foster America's understanding of its fellow members of the international community, near and far, their peoples, cultures, histories, hopes, quarrels and ambitions; and thus to serve, protect, and advance America's own global interests through study and debate, private and public.

From time to time books, monographs, and reports written by members of the Council's research staff or others are published as a "Council on Foreign Relations Book." Any work bearing that designation is, in the judgement of the Committee on Studies of the Council's Board of Directors, a responsible treatment of a significant international topic.

Council on Foreign Relations Books are distributed by Brookings Institution Press (1-800-275-1447). For further information on Council publications, please write the Council on Foreign Relations, 58 East 68th Street, New York, NY 10021, or call the Director of Communications at (212) 434-9400. Or visit our web site at www.foreignrelations.org.

Library of Congress Cataloging-in-Publication Data

The new Russian foreign policy / Michael Mandelbaum, editor.
     p.   cm.
  "Council on Foreign Relations books."
  Includes index.
  ISBN 0-87609-213-x
  1. Russia (Federation)—Foreign relations—1991– 2. Former Soviet republics. I. Mandelbaum, Michael.
DK510.764.N48   1998
327.47—dc21   98-4347
                                                        CIP

CONTENTS

FOREWORD

The Russia that emerged from the ruins of the Soviet Union is a new country that is conducting a new foreign policy. While the first post-Soviet years saw a generally pro-Western tilt in Moscow's international dealings, Russia's foreign policy has become less accommodating or predictable than it was. Moreover, Russia's military and political involvement in the Soviet successor states and, more recently, in diplomacy in the Gulf region suggest that the Kremlin will not allow itself to slip into irrelevance on the world stage.

This book, a product of the Council's Project on East-West Relations directed by Michael Mandelbaum, surveys Russia's external relations since 1992 and assesses the outlook for the foreign policy of Europe's largest country. The chapters offer an authoritative summary and treatment of Russia's relations with its neighbors and the rest of the world since the collapse of the Soviet Union.

Gary C. Hufbauer
Maurice R. Greenberg Chair, Director of Studies
Council on Foreign Relations

ACKNOWLEDGMENTS

This volume is part of the Council on Foreign Relations Project on East-West Relations, which is supported by the Carnegie Corporation of New York. The chapters in this volume were presented as papers at the Pieter A. Fisher Symposium on The New Russian Foreign Policy, held in Washington, D.C., on May 12 and 13, 1997. The views expressed are those of the authors alone.

The editor is grateful to all the people who attended the conference and all those involved in the production of this volume, especially Carolina Esquenazi-Shaio, who organized the symposium, and Patricia Lee Dorff, Tracey Dunn, and Sarah Thomas, who supervised the publication of the book.

Introduction:
Russian Foreign Policy
in Historical Perspective

Michael Mandelbaum

Andrei Gromyko, foreign minister of the Soviet Union from 1959 to 1987, once asserted that no international question of any consequence could be decided "without the Soviet Union or in opposition to it."[1] The thrust of Soviet foreign policy, during the years when Gromyko presided over it, was clear: an unyielding opposition to the West. As for its scope, Gromyko's assertion was smug but not wrong: Moscow may not have had the power of veto over any and all international issues, but its conflict with the West was certainly felt in every corner of the world.

In the wake of the collapse of communism in Europe, the foreign policy of the Soviet Union's successor state, Russia, is neither clear nor pervasive. Russian foreign policy is difficult to define. It is difficult, even, to detect. What are the international purposes of the new Russian state? Where and how will it seek to achieve them? Those questions are the subject of this book.

Russian foreign policy differs dramatically from Soviet foreign policy because the new Russia differs radically from the old Soviet Union. Russia's geography is different: It is smaller; what had been the western and southern provinces of the Soviet Union before 1992 are now independent countries. The Soviet Union was a multinational empire, with half its population non-Russian. The new Russia, by contrast, is a nation-state: 85 percent of its people are ethnic Russians. The Soviet Union was committed to implementing the precepts of an ambitious, elaborate ideology. In the new Russia, Marxism-Leninism in its Soviet form (and probably in any form) is dead. Last but, from the Western point of view, certainly not least, the Soviet Union possessed a huge military-industrial complex: a sizable fraction of its economy—perhaps as large as one-third—was devoted to military purposes. The new Russia's armed forces are less numerous and weaker, and its military industries much smaller, than their Soviet predecessors.

Because everything else has changed, it is hardly surprising that foreign policy has changed as well. To inform what are necessarily guesses about the future of Russian foreign policy, those making the guesses, including the authors of the chapters that follow, make use of historical analogies. The world in which post-Soviet Russian foreign policy will unfold may be new, but it is not unfamiliar. While extraordinary, the developments that produced this new world were not unprecedented, and the relevant precedents are useful in thinking about what will come next for Russia.

An obvious precedent for the end of the Soviet Union and its aftermath, a broad historical category into which these momentous events fit, is imperial collapse.[2] The Soviet Union was the last great multinational empire, the sole surviving member of the family of empires that once held sway over much of the planet and that, in the twentieth century, were weakened, then destroyed, by war.[3] The Habsburg and Ottoman empires were vanquished and perished in World War I. Britain and France were victors in World War II but were so enfeebled that they were not able to retain their imperial possessions, although they tried, fitfully, to do so: France fought substantial but losing wars in Indochina and Algeria.

The fate of the British and French empires is of limited value in predicting the future of Russian foreign policy because of two cardinal differences between them, on the one hand, and the Soviet Union on the other. Britain and France were nation-states that acquired empires. By contrast, the Soviet Union, and tsarist Russia before it, had no preimperial history as an ethnically homogeneous state. Russia did not acquire an empire: From at least the seventeenth century, it *was* an empire.[4] So the end of empire, traumatic as it was in many ways for the two Western European countries, could not have as large a psychological or political meaning for them as it has had for Russia. Nor did the end of the British and French empires coincide with a great political revolution and an economic depression, as was the case with Russia.

Moreover, Britain and France were separated from their imperial possessions by great distances, as in the case of Britain and India, or by bodies of water, like France and North Africa, or both. The two Western European powers could, in effect, resume life as nation-states without being obliged by geography to play a large ongoing role in the affairs of their former possessions. This was not possible for Russia, which expanded over land, not across water. After 1991 the option of disengaging and distancing itself from its former imperial possessions was not available; what were once Soviet provinces became Russia's nearest neighbors.

Like the Soviet Union, Habsburg Austria and Ottoman Turkey were land empires that lacked preimperial histories as nation-states. Their post–World War I experiences are thus of some relevance to Russia's post–Cold War future. But here a further distinction is in order. In two important ways the Soviet Union was like the Ottoman but unlike the Habsburg empire. Although they were multinational empires, the Soviet Union and the Ottoman state were dominated by one nation: the first by Russians, the second by Turks. This was not true of Austria-Hungary, where Germans were the leading nation but were a smaller percentage of the empire's population than the Russians and the Turks were in theirs. Moreover, by the twentieth century there was another German state that was more powerful, and was home to more Germans, than Austria-Hungary; there was no Russian state other than the Soviet Union and no significant Turkish state other than the Ottoman empire. Thus the independent Austria that emerged from the ruins of the Habsburg empire was tiny and in no position to be a significant force in European politics. By contrast, Turkey after 1919 and Russia after 1991 were and are large enough to play major roles in the international relations of the European continent.

One feature of post-Ottoman Turkey is not an encouraging precedent for post-Soviet Russia. Turkey's new borders were set, and its new national identity forged, in a bloody war with Greece between 1921 and 1922, a war that led, among other results, to a large-scale exchange of populations between the two countries in the first of what would be a dismal series of twentieth-century "ethnic cleansings." Happily, post-Soviet Russia has experienced nothing comparable—thus far. But two features of Europe after communism make for a potentially explosive combination: The Russian political elite is not yet fully reconciled to the sovereign independence of what were, for centuries, Russian and then Soviet provinces; and ethnic Russians in large numbers now live outside Russia not by choice but by the accident of history—what had been arbitrary and insignificant internal borders suddenly became international frontiers.[5] Comparisons with the multinational empires of the past thus suggest one of the central questions for the Russian foreign policy of the future: Will Russia try to re-create, in some form, the imperial domination over non-Russians that lasted so long and then disintegrated so rapidly?

If one feature of Turkey's postimperial history—war—highlights the worst case for post-Soviet Russia, however, another aspect of Turkish history points to the best of all possible outcomes. From what Turks call their war of independence emerged a new state with a new and decidedly non-imperial national ethos. Mustafa Kemal Ataturk, the father of modern Turkey, sought to make his country a European-style nation-state, indeed to make it part of Europe—a partially successful effort that continues to the present day.[6] This led Turkey to forswear reconquering the Christians to the west, or the Arab regions to the east, that had been part of the empire ruled for centuries from Istanbul. As it happens, Russia too emerged from the Soviet period with a foreign policy doctrine that not only forswore empire but that, like Turkey's, made becoming part of the West the highest priority of its approach to the rest of the world. But this initial foreign policy did not, at least in its original form, survive the first years of the post-Soviet era.

A NEW FOREIGN POLICY

The first postcommunist Russian foreign policy actually began in the Soviet period. It was an innovation of the last Soviet leader, Mikhail Gorbachev, the product of his "new thinking." It was developed in contrast—indeed in opposition—to the precepts that had guided relations between the Soviet Union and the rest of the world from the time of the Bolshevik revolution, precepts that Andrei Gromyko devoted his life to trying to achieve. Lenin and his successors considered the "international class struggle" between the communist and noncommunist camps to be the defining feature of international politics; Gorbachev rejected this staple of communist thinking and replaced it with the common interests that unite all peoples, foremost among them peace. He thereby changed the fundamental presumption of Soviet foreign policy from conflict to solidarity.

Where Soviet leaders had insisted that all countries once under communist rule had to remain communist—and launched armed interventions in Eastern Europe regularly after 1945 to keep communists in power there—Gorbachev asserted that every country had the right to choose its own international orientation and domestic political system. He thereby abandoned the rationale for the communist empire in Europe and, ultimately, for the Soviet Union itself. Not coincidentally, between 1989 and 1992, both disappeared.

Gorbachev concluded, finally, that in the nuclear age, national security had to be mutual: Neither the United States nor the Soviet Union, he said, could hope to gain a decisive military advantage over the other. This central conclusion, which Western leaders had publicly embraced earlier in the nuclear age, paved the way for agreements that dramatically reduced the arms that the United States and the Soviet Union had accumulated over four decades.[7]

The end of the arms race, of the Soviet empire, and of communism in Europe laid the foundation for a Russian foreign policy based on Gorbachev's first doctrinal innovation: cooperation with, and integration into, the West. This was the guiding principle first of Soviet, then of Russian foreign policy from 1987, when the reforms begun two years previously took a radical turn, to the end of 1993, when communists and nationalist xenophobes made strong showings in the December Russian parliamentary election.

After the end of the Soviet Union the new Russia began to steer, in economic, political, and cultural terms, a westward course.[8] The Western democracies proclaimed their enthusiasm for this goal. After 1991 the new Russia began to install a democratic political system and to create a market economy. Indeed, the threats the Russian leaders saw to their country were remarkably similar to those that concerned American officials: terrorism, religious fundamentalism, nuclear proliferation.

The Gorbachev-Yeltsin policy of unreserved cooperation with and integration into the West was not sustained. It was partly a victim of Russia's difficulties in the post-Soviet period: economic collapse, social disorder, and political confusion. Although these difficulties were mainly the consequence of the poisonous 70-year legacy of communism, many Russians blamed them on the West. The large sums of economic assistance promised by some Western governments, including the United States, were not delivered—although they would not have eliminated the postcommunist misery even if they had been. Western economic advisors made conspicuous contributions to the early economic policies of the Yeltsin government—although the postcommunist distress may well have been aggravated by the extent to which the Russian government *failed* to carry out their recommendations rather than by Moscow's having heeded their advice at all.[9]

Moreover, a neoimperial strain in Russian public opinion surfaced in the 1993 parliamentary election. It is not necessarily destined to guide Russia's relations with its neighbors; the countervailing forces, not the least of them Russia's continuing post-Soviet weakness, are formidable. But these sentiments are incompatible with what can be called the foreign policy of *perestroika* that Gorbachev and Yeltsin sought to conduct; and these sentiments came to carry enough political weight after 1993 to encumber Yeltsin's efforts to keep to the course that he and Gorbachev had charted.

The Gorbachev-Yeltsin foreign policy fell victim, as well, to the circumstances across Russia's new borders. Formal independence brought instability to the new countries to the south. Wars erupted in the Caucasus and Central Asia. Russia was drawn into several of them. Most spectacularly and disastrously, the Yeltsin government launched a military campaign to bring to heel rebels seeking independence for Chechnya, a predominantly Muslim region in the North Caucasus inside the borders of the new Russia. The Russian interventions in Georgia, in Armenia, in Tajikistan, and the bloody campaign the Russian army waged in Chechnya were not in keeping with the spirit of the new foreign policy.

They were certainly seen as incompatible with the foreign policy of *perestroika* in the countries of the West, notably the United States, in which Gorbachev and Yeltsin had placed such high hopes and where a welcome for Russia was central to their foreign policies. Russian military activities came in for considerable Western criticism. Western governments went beyond criticism: They announced plans to expand their Cold War military alliance, the North Atlantic Treaty Organization (NATO), to Central European countries that had once been part of the Soviet-dominated Warsaw Pact. The Russian political elite took this as a sign of indifference to Russian sensitivities at best and the beginning of a campaign to exclude, isolate, and humiliate the new Russia at worst.

Western governments asserted that NATO expansion was not directed against Russia, a claim made less convincing by the fact that the Central Europeans sought to join the Atlantic Alliance precisely because of their fears of the largest post-Soviet successor state.[10] For their part, the Russians believed that the war in Chechnya was an internal matter, that their military interventions to the south were exercises in legitimate self-defense, and that neither should affect their relations with the West. The result was a version—albeit a modest one—of the cycle of reciprocal misunderstandings known to students of international politics as "the spiral model,"[11] in which each side believes that what it is doing is legitimate, defensive, and altogether benign, but which is perceived by the other as improper, aggressive, and dangerous.

The political climate created by this cycle was not remotely as dangerous as the one in which the two nuclear superpowers had conducted their policies toward one another during the Cold War. Neither, however, was it hospitable to the strategic partnership with the West, and above all with the United States, on which Gorbachev and Yeltsin had counted. The deterioration in relations was not the consequence of ill-will or deliberate provocation. Nor was it exclusively the fault of one side or the other. Rather, the foreign policy of *perestroika* was overtaken, or at least temporarily submerged, by events. Five years after the end of the Soviet Union, cooperation and integration with the West ceased to be the unchallenged centerpiece of Russian foreign policy. What replaced it?

THE CHAPTERS

According to Leon Aron, the foreign policy of *perestroika* was replaced by a three-part doctrine that achieved surprisingly broad support, at least among that small fraction of Russians, most of them living in Moscow, who concern themselves with the world outside their country's borders. Russia must, they believe, be the dominant presence on the territory of the former Soviet Union, an influential participant in international affairs elsewhere, and the nuclear equal of the United States. It must, that is, be a regional superpower, an international great power, and a nuclear superpower.[12]

Aron suggests an historical analogy for the mood underlying this post-*perestroika* Russian foreign policy doctrine: Gaullism. As with France under the leadership of Charles de Gaulle, it has become a matter of principle for Russia to assert itself in international affairs wherever possible and to distinguish its own policies from those of the most powerful member of the international community—in both cases the United States. As with France, this Russian approach has psychological roots. It is a response, among other things, to wounded pride occasioned by a sudden, sharp loss of international status.[13] As in the case of France, Russia is seeking to lodge a protest against, although not to overturn, the international dominance of the United States. As Aron notes, Russian foreign policy could move from protest to outright opposition; but this would require a combination of developments that, from the perspective of the first six post-Soviet years, do not seem likely.[14]

Of the three arenas of post-*perestroika* Russian foreign policy, the third is the most important. Like most other countries most of the time, Russia's most intense relations are with the countries nearest to it. Moreover, post-Soviet Russia is weak. Like the Soviet Union, which was a one-dimensional international power, formidable in military terms only, it lacks the economic strength to pay a significant role in the world trading system. The new Russia may one day be, as China has become, an international economic force with which the world must reckon. But it is not one now and, unlike the Soviet Union, it lacks the military power that made Andrei Gromyko's boast about the pervasive Soviet role in international affairs a plausible one. Russia has inherited the Soviet nuclear arsenal, which is, of course, a source of influence. In other ways, however, Russia's presence is scarcely felt beyond its immediate neighborhood.

In that neighborhood, however—on the territory of the former Soviet Union—Russia's influence is considerable. Russia's neighborhood, moreover, is a large one. For the purposes of assessing post-Soviet Russian foreign policy, it is useful to divide it into two parts: the west, where Russia's neighbors are Ukraine, the three Baltic countries of Latvia,

Lithuania, and Estonia, and Moldova; and the south, where Russia borders on the countries of the Caucasus and Central Asia.

For all their considerable difficulties, the newly independent states to Russia's west are stronger, more coherent, and more stable than those to its south. The sense of political community and the capacity for effective governance are higher in Ukraine, and even more so in the Baltic countries, than in the Caucasus and Central Asia. The civil wars that erupted along the southern frontiers of the new Russia are not part of the political life of the new states to its west. In no small part for that reason, six years after the end of the Soviet Union, Russian troops were deployed throughout the south; they were not present to the west.

While Russia is far stronger than any of the other former Soviet republics that are now sovereign states, its margin of economic, political, and military superiority is greater over the new countries of the south than over those to the west. This is so for yet another reason: The newly independent states to the west feel a powerful attraction to the countries to *their* west, the countries of Western Europe. The southern newly independent states are not comparably attracted to their southern neighbors—Turkey, Iran, and Afghanistan. Russia's far west is Europe, which is one of the richest, most dynamic, and most powerful parts of the international system.[15] Its far south is the Middle East and southwest Asia, which carry less geopolitical weight.

Russians' attitudes differ toward the two parts of what they call their "Near Abroad"—a term that denotes their presumption of a special relationship with the newly independent countries that were once part of the Soviet Union. The countries to the west, especially Ukraine, are closer to Russia in cultural terms. Their languages are similar. Ukraine was part of a greater Russian state for three centuries, and it is difficult for most Russians to conceive of Kiev as the capital of a foreign country. The Russian sense of loss at Ukrainian independence is palpable.

By contrast, it is not at all difficult for Russians to see themselves as distinct even from the Christian (although not Slavic) peoples of the Caucasus—the Georgians and Armenians—let alone from the Muslims of Central Asia. No comparable sense of kinship draws Russia to the south. Rather, beyond a determination to gain a share of the the energy resources of the Caspian basin and a concern about the ethnic Russian population in the part of Kazakhstan that shares a border with Russia, the main Russian interest in the south is to keep the disorders there from spreading northward. The southern Near Abroad evokes in most Russians not a sense of loss but a feeling of threat.

Because the western Near Abroad is situated between Russia and Europe, Russia's relations with its western neighbors will go a long way to defining its relations with Europe and the United States. This has the potential to make it, as Sherman Garnett notes in Chapter 2, contested terrain. Particularly important will be relations between Russia and Ukraine, the bridge between Russia and Europe, relations that are bound to be difficult and delicate under the best of circumstances.[16]

Russia and Ukraine are the two largest and most powerful successor states to the Soviet Union. What is more, Ukraine was part of Russia longer than any of the others and has more ethnic Russians within its borders. For these reasons, of all the non-Russian successor states, Ukraine is the one whose independence has perhaps the least legitimacy in Russian eyes; Ukraine is therefore the likeliest object of a Russian effort to regain control of territories that were once part of the Soviet Union. As such, it is the test case of whether Russia will remain a nation-state or seek to become again a multinational empire. Relations with Ukraine will thus do much to define not only Russia's relations with the West but Russian national identity as well.

Its location between Russia and the West and the powerful, conflicting currents of politics, culture, and economics that are at play there make the western Near Abroad potentially contested terrain. An unhappy historical analogy suggests itself here: Central Europe between the two world wars. Like the Baltic countries and Ukraine after the Cold War, Poland, Hungary, and Czechoslovakia attained independence with the collapse of multinational empires in the wake of a great European and global conflict—in their case, World War I. The three found themselves caught between, squeezed by, and ultimately the victims of two powerful flanking neighbors: Germany and the Soviet Union. The Nazi-Soviet collusion and then conflict over the territory of the three countries touched off World War II.

Less is at stake for the United States and Western Europe in Russian policy to the south than in Russia's policies to the west. Russian military intervention to the west would trigger a new Cold War, or worse. This is not true of the south; and that is fortunate because to the south, as noted, Russia is *already* a military presence and plays a far more intrusive role than it does to the west. The Russian role to the south, as Rajan Menon observes in Chapter 3, is the product of two basic, timeless features of relations between sovereign states: proximity and asymmetry.

Because the two regions are close, Russia cannot ignore the Caucasus and Central Asia. Because the countries to its south are weak, Russia is almost bound to exert a degree of influence over them. This fact, however, gives rise to a wide range of possibilities. Historically, the strong have involved themselves in the affairs of the weak for a variety of reasons and have exercised the influence that their strength gives them in a number of different ways. The full spectrum of both motives and consequences is evident in post-Soviet Russia's role in the southern Near Abroad.

Russia was drawn there (or in some cases remained there after the collapse of the Soviet Union) partly out of an imperial reflex. But the Russian presence to its south also had the goal of staking out a share of the riches expected to flow from the exploitation of the local energy resources. Perhaps most important, Russian was present to its south in order to keep political turbulence—initially provoked almost nowhere by Russia itself but the product in some places, in the Russian view at least, of Islamic fundamentalism—from infecting Russia proper.

Once there, post-Soviet Russia sometimes has behaved in a heavy-handed manner, insisting on military bases in Georgia as the price of helping the Georgian government regain control of its territory and contributing, in Azerbaijan, to the ouster of leaders disliked by Moscow. But Russia has also, arguably, exercised a restraining influence to its south, stopping wars that otherwise would have continued.[17]

Because Russia has pursued a variety of policies, which have been animated by an array of motives, as Menon notes, a number of historical precedents are relevant to Russian policy to the south: the way Britain, by being constantly drawn into unstable locales, acquired its African empire at the end of the nineteenth century, according to historians Ronald Robinson and John Gallagher;[18] the sphere of influence France maintained in sub-Saharan Africa after the countries there attained formal independence in the 1960s; and even the role of the United States in Central America, with its recurrent military interventions, from the latter part of the nineteenth century onward.

The Russian government has, however, shown no sign of seeking to govern the countries to the south directly, as it did during the tsarist period, let alone of attempting to impose a particular kind of regime there, which was the pattern in the communist period. How then will Russia exercise its influence to the south? Historically, there is a tendency for the domestic political beliefs and institutions of the powerful to tend to shape their policies toward the weak. So Russia's relations with its southern neighbors will depend in part on what kind of country Russia itself becomes. And what Russia turns out to be will affect, and be affected by, its relations with the countries beyond the former Soviet Union, among which the Russian elite aspires to function as a great power. What Russia does to the south as well as what it does to the west will shape the terms on which it is part of the larger world.

For most Russians, "the world" still means, first and foremost, the West. That is the point of departure of Chapter 4, by Coit Blacker. His argument is that political and economic integration with the West, the aim of the original foreign policy of *perestroika*, is not only the most desirable goal for post-Soviet foreign policy, it is also the only feasible one.

The Gaullism of the post-1993 period, in this view, is to be understood, not only as a politically necessary but largely rhetorical response to domestic pressures, but also as a tactic designed to improve the terms under which Russia is integrated into the West. The relevant precedents for the new Russia are Germany and Japan after World War II, which were defeated, democratized, and integrated into the Western security and economic order, of which the United States was the chief architect and most powerful member.

The resumption of a foreign policy of integration would be, from many points of view, the best possible future course for Russia. And it may be the only viable course in the sense that any other would prove prohibitively expensive and thus impossible to sustain. But it is not the only *conceivable* course. The range of possibilities for the future of Russian foreign policy is, in fact, unusually broad.

SCENARIOS FOR THE FUTURE

The Western economic and political order, with Japan, North America, and Western Europe constituting its core, may be seen metaphorically as a magnetic field, pulling other countries toward it. Because this community of free-market democracies is both powerful and successful, other countries seek to join its organizations, observe its norms, and replicate its institutions. At least they seek to gain the benefits, especially economic ones, that those organizations, norms, and institutions have produced. The magnetic attraction of the Western order is not irresistible. But the capacity to resist it depends on a country's size and location. Belgium, for example, small and situated in the heart of Western Europe, is not well placed to adopt radically different political and economic practices from its neighbors. Russia is far larger and more distant, in both geographic and cultural terms, from the core of the Western order and so is much better able to resist its pull. Thus while Russia may turn out to be, in its own way, as western as Belgium, this is not foreordained. Other possibilities do exist.

One is that Russia will have *no* effective foreign policy because it will not have an effective national government. The trends that, if severely aggravated, could produce the disintegration of Russia as a unified state—hyperinflation leading to economic collapse, the fragmentation of the military, the rise of politically independent regional authorities—are already visible, although far from virulent enough to produce the disintegration of central authority. A historical precedent for a Russia of this kind is the chaos in China in the 1920s and 1930s, when different parts of the country were dominated by military leaders known as warlords who controlled independent armed forces.

A chaotic Russia is hardly desirable. While it would present no organized threat to any other country, the thousands of nuclear weapons within its borders would not be under the control of legitimate, competent, prudent authorities, a circumstance that would indeed pose a danger to other countries. Nor is chaos in Russia a likely scenario. Whatever its failings, the Yeltsin government has avoided the kind of wanton monetary indiscipline that would produce economic collapse. There is little appetite for secession in Russian regions other than Chechnya; instead, a number of them, such as heavily Muslim Tatarstan, have negotiated arrangements with Moscow that afford them considerable autonomy. While Russia is sufficiently disorganized and unstable to preclude the conduct of anything like the assertive global foreign policy over which Andrei Gromyko presided, it is unlikely to have no foreign policy at all.

Rather than no foreign policy, Russia could have several. It is part of three global neighborhoods—not only the West and the Middle East, but also, by virtue of its border with China and coastline on the Pacific Ocean, the Far East. The politics and economics of the three regions differ sharply. It would not be surprising, therefore, if Russian policies toward them should turn out to differ from one another. It is conceivable, for example, that Russia will conduct a policy of conciliation to the west, confrontation to the east, and neoimperial control to the south. Nor is a historical precedent required for a preview of a differentiated Russian foreign policy. Six years after the end of the Soviet Union, that *was* the pattern of Russian foreign policy. In none of Russia's adjacent neighborhoods did that policy follow, unambiguously, a single course. To the west, Moscow was not altogether conciliatory; to the south, it was not unambiguously imperial. And its relationship with its great neighbor to the east, while no longer marked by the undiluted hostility of the last two decades of the communist period, was not one of firm friendship either.

Sino-Russian relations are not fixed and, depending on the direction they take, could underpin a third kind of Russian foreign policy, one that seeks not to join but to oppose the Western order. Russian neo-Gaullism has elements of such a policy. Russia has displayed a friendlier attitude toward countries that the United States considers "rogue" states than Washington has thought appropriate—although so too have America's Western European allies.

Moreover, President Boris Yeltsin has held several highly visible meetings with his Chinese counterpart, Jiang Zemin. The United States and Western Europe have also sought good relations with China, but from the Yeltsin-Jiang meetings came conspicuous declarations of a common objection to "hegemonism," a reference to the pretensions of the United States.

A Russian foreign policy of opposition would go beyond rhetoric. Rather than a tactic to improve Russia's position in the world, it would be part of a strategy of assembling a coalition of the discontented. Such a coalition would not be likely to follow in the footsteps the Axis powers, Germany, Italy and Japan, whose aggressive pursuit of power, wealth, and territory was the cause of World War II. In the age of nuclear weapons, doing what they did—trying to overturn the existing international order by force—risks catastrophe for the entire planet. Nor would such a coalition replicate the communist bloc at the height of its power in the 1950s, when the Soviet Union and Maoist China were allies. What held that bloc together, a fully elaborated ideology that provided an alternative to Western political institutions and economic practices, is now missing. Marxism-Leninism is permanently discredited (in China as well as in Russia), and no substitute worldview is presently available.

For Russian foreign policy, however, there is a broad middle ground between the principled commitment to solidarity with the West that has been, if not rejected entirely, then at least temporarily suspended, and outright warfare—either hot or cold. Alone or together with other countries, Russia could frustrate the designs of the West in many ways: through its veto in the U.N. Security Council; by lax compliance or outright noncompliance with the rules of the international nuclear nonproliferation regime; by economic ties with countries that the West—or at least the United States—is trying to isolate.[19]

A suggestive analogy for a Russia in concert with other countries often if not always opposed to American international purposes is the loose association of Arab governments and movements that have resolutely opposed the state of Israel since the 1970s. They have little else in common, their relations with one another have sometimes been poisonous, and they have no real hope of destroying Israel. But they do share an adamant refusal to come to terms with it. A loose association of a disgruntled Russia and other countries with similar resentments might display something like the "rejectionist" attitude toward the West that the Arab irreconcilables have toward Israel.

To pose a major challenge to the West, a Russian foreign policy of rejection would require at least a limited partnership with China. Both are sufficiently large and self-contained, and culturally and politically distinct enough from the West, to resist the pull of the Western political and economic order. As the Yeltsin-Jiang statements attest, both harbor suspicions of the United States for real and imagined slights, which in both cases are fueled by the resentment that the powerful often attract. Both Russia and China, however, have evinced more interest in joining the Western order than in overturning or boycotting it. And even if both should become far more hostile to it, they would not find it easy to act cooperatively against it. Important issues divide them. Their common border is a potential source of friction. During the communist period, China claimed that large chunks of what was then the Soviet Union had been stolen from China by Russia at the zenith of Chinese weakness in the nineteenth century.

They are potential rivals for influence in the newly independent countries of Central Asia that were once Soviet republics, which are wedged between them. It was on the territory of these countries that the contest for influence between Russia and, from its base in India, Great Britain, was played out in the nineteenth century. This contest formed the backdrop for the plot of Rudyard Kipling's novel *Kim* and came to be known as "the Great Game."

There is another point of contention between the two large, formerly orthodox communist countries, and it is potentially the most serious one. Russia is an underpopulated country. China has an excess of inhabitants. A wave of Chinese immigrants has swept across the Russo-Chinese border into the Russian Far East since the relaxation of the strict border controls of the Soviet period.[20] This movement has aroused fears that the small number of Russians in the region will be swamped by an influx of Chinese through a peaceful, slow-motion invasion that will change the character of the Russian Far East.

Of all the possible scenarios for Russian foreign policy, the most desirable remains integration with the West. This is what both Russian and Western leaders regularly insist that they want. The foreign policy of *perestroika* may no longer dominate Russia's relations with the rest of the world, but it is neither entirely gone nor forgotten. And there are reasons to consider it not only a desirable but also, despite its post-1993 eclipse, a plausible path for Russian foreign policy. Those reasons are to be found in the historical experience with the greatest relevance for Russia's future: that of Russia itself.

RUSSIA AND THE WEST

It will surely be easier for Russia to be part of the West internationally to the extent that it is more like the West domestically, and here the course of Russian history provides paradoxical grounds for cautious optimism. There is a lively controversy about whether that history is, in its major features, more or less continuous since the sixteenth century, or whether it experienced a sharp break when the Bolsheviks seized power and installed a regime that governed according to the precepts of Marxism-Leninism.[21] But even if 1917 *is* seen as a radical turn in the course of Russian history, there remain major continuities over three centuries.

For most of that period Russia was the largest but also the least European of the European powers. Since the time of Peter the Great, who ruled from 1682 to 1725, Russia, under tsars and commissars, played a major role in the European state system. The other powers had to take it into account in the conduct of their affairs, and the other Europeans in turn influenced Russia's calculations. While never separate from Europe, however, compared with the countries to its west Russia was always distinctive in a number of important ways.

Like the rest of Europe, Russia was Christian—but Orthodox, not Catholic or Protestant. Like other European countries. its language was an Indo-European one, which used an alphabet rather than the ideograms of East Asia; but the alphabet of the Russian language was and is the Cyrillic, not the Latin, one. Like Europe in the nineteenth century, Russia's economy was largely agricultural, but until the second half of the century most of its laborers were serfs, not peasants; and in the nineteenth century Russia was slower to industrialize than Great Britain, France, or Germany. For most of the last century, few European governments were democratic. But the Russian tsar was not only an autocrat, he exercised something approaching absolute power, unchecked by countervailing groups, institutions, or rules.

Different from other Europeans and situated on the fringe of Europe though Russia always was, however, the degree of dissimilarity to the other Europeans, and the extent to which Russia was integrated into Europe-wide procedures and institutions, did vary over time.

Perhaps the high point of Russian similarity to, and integration into, the rest of Europe was the period after 1815. Tsar Alexander I was one of the leaders of the coalition that ultimately defeated Napoleon. His troops entered Paris in triumph, and he himself enjoyed considerable popularity throughout Europe. Conservative monarchs like him governed most of the continent. Russia was an integral part of the Concert of Europe, the informal series of understandings that brought a measure of order to continental affairs in the wake of the Napoleonic wars.

By contrast, Russia was probably most estranged from the rest of Europe after 1945. Ironically, this period was ushered in by a series of events uncannily reminiscent of those that had introduced the era of greatest solidarity. The Soviet Union was part of a coalition that defeated, at great cost, a would-be European conqueror, one with whom the Soviet authorities had at first been allied but who turned on the communist state and invaded and occupied a large part of its territory: Hitler was in this way a would-be successor to Napoleon. After 1945, however, the political and economic systems of the Soviet Union differed so radically from those of the European countries to its west that the continent was effectively divided for four decades. The Soviet Union did not belong to the international organizations that were established on the western side of what came to be known as the Iron Curtain.

The end of the Cold War, of communism in Europe, and of the Soviet Union itself have created the opportunity for Russia to become more European—more like the rest of Europe internally and more closely connected with it internationally—than at any time in the last two centuries.[22] These developments have had this effect because they have removed the obstacles to westernization at home.

The French Revolution of 1789 triggered social and political forces that led, with many twists and turns, to the spread of democracy over virtually all of Europe during the next two centuries. Democracy is, of course, entirely incompatible with tsarist and communist rule. Therefore, first the Russian and then the Soviet regime adopted as a central political purpose resistance to the infection, as they saw it, of democratic political ideas and practices from the West. In the nineteenth century, the tsar feared that the Poles he governed would demand the modest liberties that the Habsburgs permitted the Poles under their rule. In the twentieth century, the Soviet Politburo and its surrogates in East Berlin as well as the other Eastern European capitals were concerned that the citizens of communist Germany would demand the liberties enjoyed by the citizens of West Germany.

The barriers that they erected against the Western liberal ideas and practices have now crumbled. The tsars and the communists each professed a countervailing ideology. Opposition to democracy was based in both cases on principle: on the divine right of the Romanov dynasty to absolute power in the first case, and on the superior understanding of the imperatives of world history possessed by the leaders of the Communist Party in the second. Post-Soviet Russia has no such ideology. Liberal ideas may not be widely or deeply held there, but the commitment to illiberal ones in Russia is even weaker. Neoimperialist rhetoric is to be found in post-Soviet Russian politics, but it can scarcely be called a full-blown doctrine.[23] Nor does the government of the new Russia dispose of the means to suppress democratic impulses on which its predecessors could rely. The tsars and the communists built powerful governmental machinery for sealing their borders and crushing any and all opposition within them. The communist regime confronted a more democratic Europe than had the tsars, but it had a more powerful set of tools for resisting its influence, which it used more ruthlessly.

The contrast with the new Russia is stark. Six years after the end of the Soviet Union, the successor Russian government was weak, weaker not only than its tsarist and communist predecessors but considerably weaker than its Western counterparts. Incapable of doing what its predecessors had done—stifling independent political activity—it was also incapable of doing what Western governments routinely and necessarily do: collecting taxes and enforcing the law.[24]

Even when and if the Russian government achieves the capacity that other European regimes possess, moreover, it is unlikely to be able to exercise the degree of political control that its predecessors did, even if it were inclined to try. Any post-Soviet government will preside over a very different kind of country from the one that the tsars and the communists ruled. Russia is no longer populated largely by illiterate serfs and peasants. Fragmented and ignorant, the largely rural Russia of the past was, with the exception of occasional uncoordinated uprisings, far easier to bully and repress than the urbanized, literate Russia created under communism.[25] In the old Russia, the initiative for change rested with the ruler. From the time of Peter to the era of Stalin, change came from the top. That is no longer the case.[26] If rulers are less capable of blocking European ideas and practices than in the past, the Russian public is also now far better able to receive, absorb, and implement them.

Another reason that post-Soviet Russia can now be more like the rest of Europe than before is that it is no longer an empire. In the past, the requirements of empire often conflicted with the norms of democracy. Russian and communist rulers feared, rightly, that if granted liberty, the non-Russians they ruled would choose to leave the empire. Unwilling to permit this, the rulers were, as a result, unable to grant such liberties to Russians.

There is a final reason that it is easier than ever before for Russia to be like the rest of Europe. Europe is a safer place for Russia—and for all other countries—than ever before. For virtually all of its recorded history, the defining rule of Europe's international politics was the law of the jungle. Every power had to be prepared to defend itself. The constant and pressing need for self-defense lent itself to the centralization of political power, the better to muster and deploy military force; and this trend was particularly pronounced in Russia. To be sure, the world beyond its borders was not solely responsible for the oppressive character of Russian governments until the last decade of the twentieth century. The failure of political liberalism in Russia is a long and complicated story, sometimes dreary, sometimes tragic, sometimes both. But during the nineteenth century and into the twentieth, efforts at liberal reform were repeatedly derailed by the need to attend to real or perceived foreign threats.

A dangerous international environment is not, of course, an insurmountable barrier to liberal politics; if it were, liberal politics could scarcely have made any headway whatsoever in Europe.[27] Moreover, the degree of danger in Europe varied over time. From the middle of the eighteenth century to the defeat of Napoleon in 1815, war was a constant feature of European public life. From 1815 to the Crimean War in 1854, the continent was relatively peaceful. But from the middle of the nineteenth century to the end of the twentieth, Russia was threatened almost continuously, at least in the eyes of its rulers.

In the wake of the Cold War, that too has changed. The international relations of Europe proceed according to new, different, and radically more promising norms.[28] This change is important for Russia's internal development and even more so for its foreign policy. It creates the opportunity for Russia not only to be more fully a part of Europe, but to be part of a Europe that is far more benign than ever before.

The domestic political norms of Europe changed, by fits and starts, over two centuries, from autocracy to democracy. The international norms in the western part of the continent changed just as dramatically, and in a far shorter period after 1945, from rivalry to cooperation. The post–World War II reconciliation between France and Germany is the core of, and model for, this new Europe. There is no historical precedent for such a Russian relationship with any neighboring country. But then, there is virtually no pre-1945 precedent for such a relationship *anywhere* in Europe. That kind of international relationship is now, however, normal west of Russia. And it is a pattern that, were Russia to follow it, would provide a stable, comfortable, useful framework for its post–Cold War foreign policy. Russia would then be part of a community of peaceful, democratic, economically integrated nation-states. This would mean the expansion of what has come to be known since 1945 as "Europe" far enough to the east to include Russia. If the question that broaches the worst future for Russian foreign policy is "Will Russia be an empire?" the one that frames the best scenario for the Russian future is "Will Russia become part of the West?"

Becoming part of the West would not be easy. Russia would have to become much more like the countries of Europe in political and economic terms than it is now. The new Russia would have to create and sustain the kind of relationship France and Germany have developed over the last half century, and to create and sustain it not only with France and Germany but also, and most importantly, with Ukraine. Russian-Ukrainian relations, with all their difficulties, would have to be more like those between the United States and Canada (in the twentieth, not the nineteenth, century) and less like the post-1947 relationship between India and Pakistan.[29]

Even if Russia can make the changes necessary to fit comfortably into the Western community, the rate at which it can do so, and thus the pace at which it can proceed westward, in political and economic terms, are unknowable. Nor are such changes the only requirements for anchoring the new, postcommunist Russia in the West. Not only must Russia be ready and willing to enter the gates of the West, the West must be ready and willing to receive Russia. This condition is less easily fulfilled than the rhetoric of Western governments suggests.

The rhetoric is welcoming. Of course, Western leaders assert, Russia is welcome in their ranks. Nothing is more important, no project has a higher priority among the advanced capitalist countries, than integrating Russia into the West. The actual *policies* of the Western countries, however, are at variance with the rhetoric. In the wake of the Cold War they asserted the continuing centrality of two Cold War–era international organizations: NATO and the European Union (EU). These, they said, would define the borders of the West. They then proceeded to propose adaptations to the two that had the effect of excluding Russia.

In 1997 NATO invited three Central European countries to join its ranks and promised membership to a number of other countries, including some that had once been republics of the Soviet Union, but not to Russia. Whatever the merits, if any, of the scheme for NATO expansion, it did not—indeed could not—have the effect of smoothing Russia's path westward.[30]

In 1991 at a meeting at Maastricht, the Netherlands, EU members agreed to deepen their economic relations; the centerpiece of this effort was to be the creation of a common European currency during the following decade. While it was far from certain that all the existing members of the European Union would qualify for the common currency, there was no chance whatsoever that Russia could conceivably do so for decades, if ever.

The motives for NATO expansion and the Maastricht accords were diverse, and not necessarily anti-Russian. (Part of the motivation for NATO expansion, however, was decidedly anti-Russian.) But whether intentionally or not, the two initiatives had the anti-Russian consequence of defining post–Cold War Europe in a way that ensured that Russia could not belong to it.

This Western approach to Russia was not, as during the Cold War, one of active, principled hostility. Indeed, the two major Western initiatives were not, on the whole, aimed at Russia at all. On the basis of the NATO and EU initiatives, however, neither could the Western approach to Russia be described as one of active embrace. Six years after the end of the Soviet Union, the door to the West was not closed to Russia; but neither was it flung wide open. Postcommunist Russia was not, in any case, yet in a position to walk confidently through that door. When and if it is ready to do so, however—and indeed even before that—Russian foreign policy would not, and will not, be determined by Russia alone.

Notes

1. Quoted in Seweryn Bialer, *Stalin's Successors: Leadership, Stability and Change in the Soviet Union* (New York: Cambridge University Press, 1980), p. 237, n. 5.
2. The often-cited parallel between Russia and the United States, most notably drawn by Alexis de Tocqueville in *Democracy in America,* is not relevant to post-Soviet Russia. There are, to be sure, marked similarities between the two. Both were, and are, countries of continental scope. Both expanded from their original areas of settlement in the nineteenth century, the United States westward, tsarist Russia to the east. Both subjugated the indigenous people they encountered in the course of expansion. But there was a crucial difference. The United States did not incorporate territories with large numbers of people of non-European ancestry: The parts of Mexico that became American, for example, were settled by relatively few Mexicans. In the course of Russian expansion to the east and south, by contrast, large non-Russian populations came under the control first of the tsars and then of the communists. The native American population was too small, relative to the European-descended Americans, to affect the basic political character of the country. Thus, while Russia was an empire, the United States was not.
3. Russia remains a multinational state; and in China, Han Chinese govern Tibetan Buddhists and Central Asian Muslims without their consent.
4. Roman Szporluk, "The Russian Question and Imperial Overextension," in Karen Dawisha and Bruce Parrott, eds., *The End of Empire? The Transformation of the USSR in Comparative Perspective* (Armonk, NY: M.E. Sharpe, 1997), p. 70. That volume explores in depth the similarities and differences between the Soviet Union and other empires.
5. An estimated 25 million ethnic Russians suddenly became members of a national minority in an entirely new country. Many then emigrated to Russia. Many more, however, especially in the two neighboring countries with the largest Russian populations—Ukraine and Kazakhstan—stayed put.
6. There are some striking parallels between Ataturk and Boris Yeltsin. Both emerged from the old regime to dominate the politics of the new successor state.

Each sought to make his country more Western. It is too soon to assess Yeltsin's success in this endeavor; and, with the increasing attraction of Islamic politics for many Turks, that also may be true, six decades after his death, of Ataturk.

7. On Gorbachev's "new thinking," see Coit D. Blacker, *Hostage to Revolution: Gorbachev and Soviet Security Policy, 1985–1991* (New York: Council on Foreign Relations, 1993), pp. 63–65; and Robert Legvold, "The Revolution in Soviet Foreign Policy," *Foreign Affairs,* America and the World, 1988/89, Vol. 68, no. 1 (1989), pp. 82–98. On the significance of the arms treaties, see Michael Mandelbaum, *The Dawn of Peace in Europe* (New York: Twentieth Century Fund, 1996), chap. 5.

8. For a fuller discussion of this issue, see below, pp. 169–72.

9. On this point see, for example, Anders Aslund, *How Russia Became a Market Economy* (Washington, DC: The Brookings Institution, 1995), especially chap. 8, and Aslund, "Social Problems and Policy in Postcommunist Russia," in Ethan Kapstein and Michael Mandelbaum, eds., *Sustaining the Transition: The Social Safety Net in Postcommunist Europe* (New York: Council on Foreign Relations, 1997), chap. 3, pp. 124–46. See also Richard Layard and John Parker, *The Coming Russian Boom: A Guide to New Markets and Politics* (New York: Free Press, 1996), chap. 4.

10. Michael Mandelbaum, *NATO Expansion: A Bridge to the Nineteenth Century* (Chevy Chase, MD: Center for Political and Strategic Studies, 1997), p. 13.

11. See Michael Mandelbaum, *The Fate of Nations: The Search for National Security in the Nineteenth and Twentieth Centuries* (New York: Cambridge University Press, 1988), chap. 5.

12. See below, pp. 25–38.

13. On the relevance of Gaullism to Russia (and China), see Michael Mandelbaum, "Westernizing Russia and China," *Foreign Affairs* (May–June 1997).

14. See below, pp. 42–51.

15. In political and economic terms, Russia's "west" also includes the United States and Japan, although each is geographically closer to the eastern borders of Russia.

16. See Mandelbaum, *The Dawn of Peace in Europe,* pp. 134–40. See also Alexander J. Motyl, *Dilemmas of Independence: Ukraine after Totalitarianism* (New York: Council on Foreign Relations, 1993), chap. 4; and Sherman W. Garnett, *Keystone in the Arch: Ukraine in the Emerging Security Environment of Central and Eastern Europe* (Washington, DC: Carnegie Endowment for International Peace, 1997), chaps. 2 and 3.

17. See below, pp. 125–47.

18. Ronald Robinson and John Gallagher, *Africa and the Victorians* (Garden City, NY: Doubleday Anchor, 1968. First published, 1961).

19. In September 1997 a consortium of Russian, Malaysian, and French energy companies signed a contract with Iran that not only contradicted the American policy of trying to isolate the Islamic republic economically and politically but also violated an American law against large-scale economic dealings with Tehran.

20. The numerical estimates range widely. A reasonable guess is several hundred thousands.

21. The classic statement of the argument for continuity is Richard Pipes, *Russia under the Old Regime* (New York: Charles Scribner's Sons, 1974). An

eloquent presentation of the argument that the 1917 revolution led to a radical break may be found in Martin Malia, *The Soviet Tragedy* (New York: Free Press, 1994).

22. Precedents from Russian history are relevant here. On several occasions lost wars discredited the regimes responsible for them, creating opportunities for change that were not available previously. For example, the Russian defeat in the Crimean War led to the abolition of serfdom. The defeat in World War I paved the way for the Russian Revolution.

23. "Today, the neoimperialist blowhards in Russia do not bother to justify their claims against the newly independent states with anything more than vague references to Russia's perceived interests." S. Frederick Starr, "The Fate of Empire in Post-Tsarist Russia and in the Post-Soviet Era," in Dawisha and Parrott, eds., *The End of Empire?* p. 253.

24. See Stephen Holmes, "Cultural Legacies or State Collapse? Probing the Postcommunist Dilemma," in Michael Mandelbaum, ed., *Postcommunism: Four Perspectives* (New York: Council on Foreign Relations, 1997), pp. 22–76.

25. For an appreciation of the political implications of the social changes of the second half of the twentieth century, published during the Gorbachev era, see Moshe Lewin, *The Gorbachev Phenomenon: A Historical Interpretation* (Berkeley: University of California Press, 1988).

26. It was ceasing to be the case in the late Soviet period. See S. Frederick Starr, "The Changing Nature of Change in the USSR," in Seweryn Bialer and Michael Mandelbaum, eds., *Gorbachev's Russia and American Foreign Policy* (Boulder, CO: Westview Press, 1988), pp. 3–36.

27. It is worth noting, however, that historically, the most democratic European power—Great Britain—was the one least threatened by the others, thanks to the natural protection afforded by the English Channel.

28. See Mandelbaum, *Dawn of Peace in Europe,* chaps. 4–6.

29. On these analogies see ibid., pp. 138–39.

30. For a critique of the policy, see Mandelbaum, *NATO Expansion.*

CHAPTER ONE

The Foreign Policy Doctrine of Postcommunist Russia and Its Domestic Context

Leon Aron

Until 1993 Russian foreign policy unfolded within the framework inherited from the Mikhail Gorbachev–Eduard Shevardnadze "new political thinking" (1987–90). Strengthened by the collapse of the one-party state in August 1991, *perestroika* diplomacy,[1] as Russian scholars would later label it, seemed invincible as the Soviet Union's and Russia's massive geostrategic retreat continued to generate enthusiastic reviews and a rhetoric of unlimited goodwill in the West.

With the advent of what President George Bush called the "new world order," the radical democrats then in effective control of the Russian government expected the shared ideals of democracy and human rights not only to fill the deep divisions left from half a century of Cold War and to harmonize Russian interests and those of the "civilized world" (as capitalist democracies often were referred to in the Russian media), but also to blunt and, eventually, extirpate ancient ethnic animosities on the territory of the former Soviet Union.

This idyll began to unravel in the late spring and early summer of 1992. The declaration of independence by the Dniester Republic, a Russo-Ukrainian ethnic enclave in Moldova; the citizenship restrictions imposed on ethnic Russians in Latvia and Estonia as Russia prepared to withdraw troops from these newly independent nations; the Russian vote for the U.N. Security Council's resolution imposing economic sanctions on Serbia, which supported Bosnian Serbs in the civil war against their Muslim and Catholic neighbors; and, soon, civil wars in Tajikistan and

Georgia coalesced into a background against which the fragility of a democratic "new world order" became manifest. Just as plain was the fact that, with respect to Russian immediate interests, its new responsibilities, and new potential threats to its security, there was precious little that the "civilized world" could (or would) do to help.

This sudden realization gave rise to an intense debate within the Russian elite on the objectives, priorities, and tactics of their foreign and security policies. The combatants were the "internationalists," residing mostly at the Ministry of Foreign Affairs, and "neopatriots" or "derzhavniks" (from the Russian word *derzhava,* "a great state") in the Supreme Soviet and in the presidential administration. The first group was led by Andrei Kozyrev. State Counselor Sergei Stankevich emerged as the self-appointed spokesman for the "derzhavniks."

The "internationalists" advocated a conciliatory, noninterventionist, even isolationist stance in the Near Abroad (a shorthand description of the former Soviet "republics" as distinct from the world outside the U.S.S.R.'s borders, the Far Abroad) and support for—if not, in fact, alliance with—the United States in world affairs. In each of the three crises that unfolded at the time in the Dniester Republic, the Baltic states, and Bosnia, the "internationalists" counseled (and, in the case of Kozyrev, pursued) gradualism, negotiations, accommodation, and solidarity with the U.S.-led "civilized world."

The "derzhavniks" insisted on a more active defense of Russia's "vital national interests" in the Near Abroad, such as the transfer of Soviet nuclear weapons to Russia, the settlement of border disputes, and defense of ethnic Russians in the post-Soviet diaspora. They also insisted on recognizing force as a still-valid instrument in international relations. To them, the unconditional, knee-jerk support for the United States, which they said the "internationalists" practiced, was unbecoming to a great power.[2]

Surprisingly, given the temperature of the debate, a consensus began to emerge very quickly, with two sides contributing to the development of a common position. By the second half of 1993, Kozyrev was credited with abandoning the initial "radical superdemocratism" for "postimperial pragmatism," which took into consideration the "national interests of Russia," its status of a nuclear superpower, and its "regional responsibilities."[3] In its turn, by the end of 1993 and beginning of 1994, the "national-patriotic opposition" had significantly tempered what a Russian observer called "imperial restorationism."[4] In the rhetoric of its leaders, references to Russia's "calling" and "mission" gradually were replaced with invocations of "national interest."[5]

The taking of stock, which occurred in 1993, signaled the emergence of a post-*perestroika* foreign policy of Russia. It seemed at the time that this was the first step in the construction of a broad, post–Cold War doctrinal consensus within the Russian foreign policy establishment.

The goal of this chapter is to revisit the Russian foreign policy doctrine, which this author described in 1994.[6] By definition, such a task includes a review of the key elements of the 1993 consensus to determine if they had been incorporated, amended, or transcended as well of the changes in the domestic political context in which Russian foreign policy is formed. We also shall examine issues that could only be adumbrated in 1993; chief among them is the operational meaning with which Russian policymakers and policy commentators filled the strategic outline developed in 1993.

"CONSENSUS-93"

A long policy memorandum was forwarded by Foreign Minister Andrei Kozyrev to the chairman of the Committee on Foreign Relations of the Supreme Soviet, Yevgeny Ambartsumov, in January 1993 (*Kontzeptzia vneshnei politiki Rossiiskoy Federeratzii*)[7] and signed (in a leaner version) into law by President Yeltsin three months later after extensive reviewing and redrafting in the Security Council (*Osnovnye polozhenia kontzeptzii vneshnei politiki Rossiiskoy Federatzii*).[8] The *Concept, Kontzeptzia*, and the *Main Tenents, Osnovnye polozhenia,* formalized a revolutionary shift in Russia's national security priorities that occurred between 1987 and 1993. First, the national tradition of the unchallenged domination of national security and foreign policy priorities over those of domestic economic, political, and social development had been reversed.[9] For the Kremlin, economic progress and democratic stabilization emerged as the key objectives to which the country's external activity was to be subordinated. Second, the Russian state, whose emergence coincided with Russian colonial conquests, had been "decoupled" from the Russian empire after more than four centuries during which the two were inseparable.

Gone too was the messianic component ("Third Rome," "panSlavism," "world socialism"), which for centuries was a guiding principle of foreign policymaking. The process of "secularization" of Russian foreign policy, its "liberation" from the "special spiritual mission"[10]—which started at the end of the nineteenth and the beginning of the twentieth centuries and was interrupted by the reign of communist "internationalism" between 1917 and 1989 (when Moscow accepted the demise of socialist states in Eastern Europe)—finally appeared to be prevailing. For the first time since 1914, Russia was not at war—real, Cold, or "class"—with anyone.

Coinciding with economic revolution and the demise of the U.S.S.R., relentless decreases in defense expenditures and reduction in manpower under Yeltsin undermined militarism as a key and defining feature of the Russian state. On the ground, meanwhile, a historically unprecedented—peaceful and voluntary—contraction of the empire was taking place, with Yeltsin surrendering two centuries' worth of imperial conquests from Peter to Alexander II and returning Russia to the early eighteenth-century borders: without the areas now occupied by Ukraine, Belarus, and the Baltic states in the west and the Caucasus, Crimea, and Central Asia in the southeast.

The emphasis of *Osnovnye polozhenia* was unmistakably domestic and inward-looking. Of the nine "vitally important interests" of Russia, only two pertained to the world outside the former Soviet border.[11] Two other "interests" consisted of strengthening all manner of ties with the newly independent states on the formerly Soviet territory and protecting the rights of Russian speakers there.

The rest of the country's "vital interests" were strictly domestic: "securing state and territorial integrity"; "maintaining stability and strengthening constitutional order"; "overcoming domestic crisis through deep socioeconomic and political reforms"; "securing a stable progress in the economy and respectable standard of living for the people"; and providing "environmental protection."

The overarching primacy of domestic economic, social, and political development determined the rest of the Russian foreign policy agenda. First, global superpowership, greatly weakened by the German unification and the retreat from east-central Europe, was surrendered. (At the time, a group of leading foreign policy experts titled their report "Etap za globl'nym" ["The phase after global"]).[12] A 1993 survey of the foreign policy establishment found that 55 percent of those polled saw Russia as one of the world's great powers, with only 4 percent insisting on the restoration of superpower status.[13]

Second, since neither economic progress nor transition to viable democratic statehood was deemed possible without economic and political rapprochement with and stability in the so-called Near Abroad, the post-Soviet "space" was declared the most important area of Russian foreign—as well as security—policy. That area (which Foreign Minister Andrei Kozyrev declared "unique, *sui generis* geopolitical space, to which no one but Russia could bring peace")[14] was effectively declared off limits to the "third" states.

The core of the foreign policy doctrine, as it emerged in 1993, rested on a tripartite vision of Russia and a corresponding national strategic agenda: Russia as regional superpower, Russia as a world's great power, and Russia as the nuclear superpower.

The general agreement on Russian behavior in the world coincided with the emergence of consensus regarding the world itself. Little remained of the exuberance that only two years earlier greeted the enunciation of the new world order. Russia still was a nuclear superpower, to be sure, but a superpower lonely, isolated, and confronted with dangers that its nuclear might was helpless to mitigate.

As they surveyed their country's geostrategic environment in 1993, even the solidly democratic liberal experts from an elite Moscow research institute found the landscape very bleak. "The changes in the system of international relations did not create a benign international environment for Russian domestic transformation," they contended, "but, on the opposite [produced] one that is, on the whole, hostile and engenders challenge after challenge."[15] For the first time since World War II, they insisted, rather implausibly, that the "very survival" of Russia was "under question."[16]

The strategic implications of the postimperial contraction were deeply disturbing. "Cut off" from northern Europe and Poland by the Baltic states and from southeastern Europe by Ukraine, and threatened by the instability on its southern border, Russia, in this analysis, had very few friends and no reliable allies—in the Near or Far Abroad.[17] Ethnic Russians or Russian speakers in the Near Abroad were seen as subjected to "apartheid" (in the Baltic states) and even, potentially, to "genocide" (in Central Asia).[18] The country's "territorial integrity" was in danger from separatists inside Russia, aided and abetted by their ethnic brethren in the contiguous areas across new borders. The North Caucasus, home of the Chechens, the Ossetians, and the Ingush, among others, was the prime example of this tendency.[19]

Finally, despite Russia's self-assigned mission of serving as "the key factor of Eurasian stability," containing the growing "pressures" from the south and east and acting as a giant protective zone for Western Europe,[20] the West was perceived as doing everything possible to "weaken" Russia as a competitor on the world market (especially in the area of arms trade and space technology). More alarming still, the West was "tempted" to "finish off Russia" as a great power.[21]

Skewed (or even paranoid) as this vision might have seemed to a foreign observer at the time, its main postulates, *mutatis mutandis*, appeared to have been accepted by most of the Russian political class and, as such, were to influence the country's foreign policy for years to come.

RUSSIA AS A NUCLEAR SUPERPOWER

Global nuclear superiority, shared with the United States, is the area of the Russian foreign policy consensus most impervious to domestic and international politics and least prone to challenge and evolution. As long as the country's conventional capability undergoes a painful contraction and transformation (and as long as the general view of the outside world, sampled earlier, remains unchanged), the importance of the nuclear arsenal as deterrent, in addition to its enormous symbolic cachet as Russia's sole remaining claim to equality with the United States, is not likely to diminish.

Furthermore, with Ukraine, Kazakhstan, and Belarus having surrendered their nuclear weapons to Moscow, Russia's inheritance of the Soviet Union's nuclear might helps immeasurably its claim to the regional superpowership. In the words of Russia's first deputy minister of defense:

> Russia remains a nuclear superpower. The nuclear potential of Russia (strategic and tactical) is, in some respects, more important for Russia's security now than in the past when we had large conventional forces. The Russian nuclear umbrella is important for the security of practically all the former republics of the Soviet Union, even though their present leaders may not be aware of it [*sic!*]. Russia's nuclear forces play a key role in the collective security of the CIS [Commonwealth of Independent States]. The nuclear shield created by the efforts of scientists and industrialists ensures the peace that we need in order to carry out reform. . . . Under international agreements, the Russian strategic forces nuclear forces are not at present targeted. But when necessary they can be quickly retargeted.[22]

Perhaps to blunt the impact of stark evidence of Russia's conventional weakness as Moscow was preparing to concede defeat in Chechnya, top national security officials not only vigorously reaffirmed the centrality of the nuclear deterrence for the country's defense but suggested a major modification of the post-Soviet nuclear doctrine: the use of nuclear weapons against a conventional attack (the "first strike").[23]

After his appointment the then minister of defense, Igor Rodionov, repeatedly stressed the maintenance of nuclear deterrent as the "first priority" of a new Russian military doctrine—made especially urgent by the planned expansion of NATO.[24] At the same time, Security Council Secretary Ivan Rybkin announced that as part of the same revised military doctrine, Russia "reserved the right to use nuclear weapons in response to a conventional weapons attack."[25] Three months later, in the beginning of May 1997, the first-use policy was incorporated in a new national security doctrine.[26]

Rodionov's departure from the ministry did not signal any diminution of the enhanced importance of the nuclear deterrent. The man who replaced him, General Igor Sergeev, is on the record as extolling the role of nuclear weapons "in conditions when the weakened general-purpose forces find it difficult properly to fulfill the deterrence task."[27] He stressed their indispensability in maintaining "the strategic nuclear balance" and in ensuring that no one have "any illusions of achieving a unilateral advantage over Russia."[28]

Russia's nuclear superpowership is, finally, the best advertisement for an industry that, alongside gas, oil, and gold, accounts for most of the country's export earnings: missile technology and nuclear energy know-how. For economic (as well as strategic) reasons, Russia is likely to pursue this trade, despite the friction the exports to Iran, India, and Pakistan cause in its relations with the United States.

At the moment, the only potential threats to Russia's status as a nuclear superpower are drastic reductions mandated by radical arms control on the one hand and the general impoverishment of the military-industrial complex on the other. Yet, given the virtual absence of domestic challenges to any of the four crucial benefits of nuclear superpowership— deterrence at a time of conventional weakness, parity with the United States, the regional military superiority, and export revenues—one can confidently predict that Russia will not surrender it through piecemeal arms control reduction, no matter how much lip service it pays to a "nuclear-free world," and will continue to exempt at least its key sustaining structures from the debilitating penury that engulfed its defense sector.

RUSSIA AS A GREAT POWER

The Russian political and foreign policy establishments appear more united today on both strategy and tactics of conduct in world affairs than they were in 1993. This broad convergence of views across the political spectrum was confirmed by the reaction to the appointment of Yevgeny Primakov. The new foreign minister was found acceptable, indeed welcome on both sides of the ideological divide that separates Yeltsin and his supporters from the communist-dominated opposition. He remains the only senior minister on whom Boris Yeltsin and the communist leader Gennady Zyuganov continue to agree.

The reason for such a remarkable unanimity became obvious at the new foreign minister's first press conference, when he promised that

Russian foreign policy would reflect the "country's status as a great power" and, at the same time, seek "equal, mutually beneficial partnership" with the West.[29] Primakov's words reflected the consensus regarding Russia's position and behavior in the world outside the former Soviet borders.

He claimed that his vision was informed by sober "realism" and a great deal of hard-headed pessimism, which had come to replace the inflated expectations of a uniformly benign new world order.[30] The end of the global ideological and military confrontation and competition of the Cold War did not result in a "stable and predictable world" and proved "insufficient" to neutralize the old and new "threats and risks": terrorism, nuclear proliferation, and regional conflicts, whether in Europe (the former Yugoslavia), the post-Soviet Transcaucasus, or post-Soviet South Central Asia.[31] "Stability and balance" in world affairs were no longer around the corner but, instead, would take "decades of strenuous efforts" by many states to achieve.[32]

Reflecting suspicion of the United States (which is among the keystones of the new consensus), the new foreign minister welcomed a "tendency" toward a "multipolar world" and pledged resistance to a "new division" between the "leaders" and the "led" in world affairs.[33] He endorsed, instead, an "equitable" partnership with the West, promising to defend Russian interests "more vigorously and effectively," while avoiding confrontation.[34] He said he supported the United States and its allies in the former Yugoslavia and the Middle East, but staked out and pledged to advance Russia's "own position,"[35] critical of certain aspects of these efforts and of the severity of economic sanctions against Iran, Iraq, and Libya,[36] which had resulted in major revenue losses for Russia.

After Primakov's first year at the helm (January 1996 to January 1997), Russian analysts concluded that, contrary to expectations, his arrival did not change the direction of foreign policy by "180 degrees." Instead, he adjusted it by "90 degrees," smoothing altercations with the "West" by the reiteration of Russia's "unwillingness" to precipitate the "confrontation of the cold war."[37] Or, as Primakov himself put it in early 1997, his was a "middle course" between the "extremes of Soviet anti-Westernism" and Kozyrev's "pro-Western romantic approach."[38]

Such a "middle course" reflects broad public sentiment. In June 1966 almost two-thirds of Russians (61 percent) agreed that the United States was "utilizing Russia's current weakness to reduce it to a second-rate power and producer of raw materials," and in April 1996 a huge majority (85 percent) believed that "Russia must do its utmost to ensure that its military might is not inferior to that of the U.S." At the same time, virtually everyone (91 percent, April 1996) thought it "important" for Russia to "cooperate with the U.S. and other Western countries."[39]

In terms of historic precedence and models, Russia's behavior on the world scene today fits quite comfortably into what might be called the Gaullist paradigm: a host of strategic objectives and tactical measures deployed to obtain by other (mostly symbolic) means that which used to flow from the abundance of tangible military-political assets. Charles de Gaulle was said to seek "nothing less than an independent France returning to great-power status" and a place of honor in the post–World War II settlement.[40] In the aftermath of the Cold War, these seem to be Russia's goals as well.

In addition to vocal and occasionally shrill criticism of the United States, this "independent foreign policy" included policies and gestures, which in the context of the Cold War could not but be found in Washington objectionable, if not outright hostile: de Gaulle's flirtation with the Soviet Union in the early 1960s; or the adoption, in the aftermath of the Six Day War, of a Middle East position opposite to that of the United States; or the rallying against the superpower "hegemony" and the "power of the dollar."

The imperatives of today's world, as they appear to Russia, inevitably lead it to challenge the United States. As de Gaulle said to Harry Hopkins, "America's policy, whether it was right or not, could not but alienate the French."[41] Most Russian politicians and policymakers view American rhetoric as a "disguise for hegemony," as did de Gaulle, and, like him, they prefer a "multipolar world" to a one dominated by the United States.[42]

But, as with France, the tweaking, the shouting, and the occasional— and painful—kick in the shins must not be confused with "anti-Americanism" of the kind that was practiced by the Soviet Union of yesteryear or, say, the Iran of today. This crucial distinction derives from a fundamental commonality between de Gaulle's France and Yeltsin's Russia: Their opposition to the United States was, and is, informed neither by ideology nor by revisionism.

Gaullism, according to a classic account, was a "stance, not a doctrine; an attitude, not a coherent set of dogmas."[43] De Gaulle's "ideology" contained little beyond a "determination to give France the greatest possible role in a hostile world."[44] He sought to restore France's grandeur (which, to him, was the "opposite of resignation to a passive role in the world")[45]—but within the existing international order.

Russia's world policy unfolds in a very similar framework. While peevish and truculent, thus far it has been decidedly nonrevisionist: It may bemoan the unfairness of the score, but it does not intend to change the rules of the game. It continues to welcome the end of the Cold War even though it meant its fall from world superpowership.

Under Yeltsin, Russia's "opposition" to the U.S.-led "West" has been pragmatic and self-limiting. As such, it is not likely to be either relentless or antagonistic but, rather, selective and calculated.[46] So far Moscow has refrained from steps that would take it beyond the Gaullist model of international behavior and into a consistent pursuit of strategic objectives inimical to the truly vital U.S. national interests. When U.S. policy positions are communicated firmly and unambiguously by the United States (especially at the highest level), Moscow is likely to concede (as in the case of the NATO expansion that does not cross the former Soviet borders) and even extend cooperation (as in Bosnia).[47]

While, as we shall see shortly, other aspects of the original doctrine came under strain, the renunciation of globalism and messianism in Russian foreign policy appears to have become the least contentious area of the national consensus. The new national security doctrine adopted in the beginning of May 1997 identified major dangers as emanating from social and economic instability, not external threats. Accordingly, the document, which was never published, reaffirmed the priority of domestic economic progress over defense from external military dangers as the key to Russia's well-being.[48]

Previewing the official adoption of the doctrine, the secretary of the Security Council, Ivan Rybkin, affirmed the "priority of political, economic, informational means of ensuring national security" over traditional military instruments. "It has been traditionally assumed that at the heart of the national security were physical survival of society, the preservation of sovereignty and unity of the state . . . But real security of the state also includes the creation and maintenance of the necessary conditions for a dignified existence for its citizens, preservation of national culture, spiritual values, environment and civil rights."[49]

In a detailed exposition of the country's national security needs and problems, published shortly after the new doctrine was adopted, Deputy Chief of the General Staff General Valery Manilov was quite direct in confirming the abandonment of global ideological ambition. While Russia was "a state possessing nuclear weapons and all the other necessary parameters [*sic*] . . . to aspire to the role of superpower," such aspiration, according to Manilov, was not likely to be realized: "Having suffered for more than seventy years from the absence of democracy, Russia consciously and voluntarily renounces any claim to serve as a role model of social development for all humanity."[50]

Paradoxically, it is the strength of nonrevisionist consensus regarding Russia's behavior on the world scene that might account, in part, for the unanimous and intense hostility toward NATO expansion felt by the Russian elite across the entire political spectrum. Rather than a direct and immediate military threat, the move is perceived as a negative verdict on Russia's ultimate quest for overcoming a historic handicap and rejoining the "civilized world" as a defeated but nonrevisionist military power—as Germany and Japan did 50 years before. The NATO decision is seen as a rejection of Russia even when, after 75 years of relentless ideological revisionism and subversion, it tries to play by the rules.

RUSSIA AS THE REGIONAL SUPERPOWER

Since 1993 Russian policymakers have confirmed repeatedly that the maintenance of Russia's regional superpowership remained the most important objective. A decree on Russian strategy on the territory of the former U.S.S.R., which Boris Yeltsin signed on September 14, 1995, called the Near Abroad a "priority area" because of "vital interests" that Russia had in the area's "security, economics and defense of Russians living abroad."[51]

A year later, in an interview on the eve of the second tour of presidential elections, Yeltsin was asked what he would "include in the sphere of Russia's foreign policy interests." Promptly stating that the "whole world is the sphere of Russian interests," Yeltsin went on to name "broader and stronger cooperation between CIS countries" as the first of the three top priorities ahead of relations with the "West" and China.[52] In his first press conference in January 1996, Yevgeny Primakov listed his own "four priorities" of Russian foreign policy, the first three of which pertained to Russia's position in the region. (The last one had to do with "the spread of weapons of mass destruction.")[53]

In the intervening years, the division between (mostly) right-center democratic "internationalists" and (mostly) left-center nationalist "derzhavniks" among the foreign policy elite has become obsolete. Virtually everyone in that group is a "derzhavnik" (or a "realist," or a "liberal nationalist") now.

Although the shift toward "realism" among the "democrats" in and out of the government began as early as 1992, it was the success of Vladimir Zhirinovsky's Liberal Democratic Party of Russia (LDPR), which placed first in the party list vote in December of 1993, that proved a powerful catalyst. The poll highlighted the depth of postimperial trauma and made obvious the danger of ceding the issue to the populists and the left—

together with the political capital that could be earned from a robust and unabashed rhetoric of advocacy of Russian national interests in the Near Abroad.

In May 1996 *Nezavisimaya Gazeta*, which since 1992 has served as a kind of Democracy Wall for the Russian foreign policy establishment, published a very long *Theses* by the Council on Foreign and Defense Policy, Russia's most prestigious nongovernmental organization in the area of national security strategy. Billed as "nonpartisan" and signed by leading foreign policy and defense experts, scholars, legislators, journalists, and entrepreneurs, the "report" attempts a comprehensive review of Russia's strategic posture vis-à-vis the post-Soviet states.[54]

While confirming the key postulates of "Consensus-93," the report extended and refined the original agenda and rendered it more muscular. Russia, the authors postulated, had several "vital interests" in the Near Abroad and must deploy all means necessary (including force) to protect them.

As in the initial 1993 compendiums (the *Kontzeptzia* and the *Osnovnye polozhenia*), first among such interests were the "maintenance of liberty, increase in prosperity of the citizens of Russia" and the preservation of the country's territorial integrity and independence.[55] (The "strategic goal," the authors reiterated later, was "economic, political and spiritual renaissance and rise of Russia."[56] The other "vital interests" consisted of preventing states from "dominating" the territory of the former U.S.S.R.; securing "unhindered access" to "strategic resources" (which include transportation routes and ports); averting local wars and "large-scale armed conflicts" in the newly independent states; preventing "mass violation of human rights of ethnic minorities, especially of ethnic Russians," in the Near Abroad; and "securing the closest possible political, economic and military union with Belarus, Kazakhstan, and Kyrgyzstan."[57]

This posture appears to reflect public opinion. Russians seem to define national security concerns almost exclusively in terms of economic, social, and political well-being.[58] For instance, presented with a list of "threats to national security" and asked to choose "the most serious" one, an overwhelming majority (71 percent) chose economic deterioration, or crime and corruption, or "politicians' struggle for power." When asked to name the "most serious problem facing the country," 63 percent named the economy and corruption, while less than one-half of 1 percent referred to the traditional national security issues ("military weakness, threat of war, etc.").

The consensus on the strategic priority of regional superpowership must not obscure serious rifts concerning tactics and implementation.

Here the agreement is far more tenuous, nuanced, strained, and politically conditioned than in the case of Russian behavior in the world outside the former Soviet territory.

This difference relects the contrasting domestic contexts. Russia's conduct of world diplomacy is virtually an exclusive province of political and foreign policy elites. The country's interests in the world outside the Near Abroad and its behavior there belong to an outer ring of domestic politics. Very distant from the everyday existence of millions of Russians, the country's policymaking in the Far Abroad offers few, if any, inviting investment opportunities for political capital. An intensely inward-looking society, preoccupied with domestic affairs, Russia has left world politics to the experts and columnists. (Even such an extensively publicized issue as NATO's eastward expansion has remained—much to the chagrin of foreign policy and media elites—an esoteric concern.)[59]

By contrast, Russia's position in the region, tied as it is to essential economic and social realities, remains very much a domestic political issue. From 1992, the Near Abroad has been an attractive platform for ambitious domestic players such as Sergei Stankevich, who sparred with Andrei Kozyrev over the Dniester Republic and ethnic Russians in the Baltic states; Alexander Lebed, who was launched into national politics as the commander of 14th Army, which "defended" the Dniester Republic; and, of course, Vladimir Zhirinovsky in the 1993 parliamentary campaign. In the 1995 legislative elections, the Congress of Russian Communities, on top of whose party list was Lebed's name, made Russian diaspora in the Near Abroad a key issue in its platform. And the Russian parliament rarely missed a chance to score points—whether by constant goading of the Kremlin to adopt a tougher stance in the negotiations with Ukraine (between 1993 and 1997)[60] or by the March 1996 resolution nullifying the Belavezh Accords that formalized the dissolution of the Soviet Union.

The maintenance of the regional superpowership involves two complementary and overlapping but distinct sets of tasks. One is centered around preventing the deterioration of Russian geostrategic posture anywhere in the "post-Soviet space." The other seeks to improve this posture wherever possible. The modes of implementation differ markedly: defensive, reactive, uniform, and relatively simple for the former group of chores; and proactive, creative, dynamic, and selective (but also more complicated and protracted) for the latter one.

There seems to be little disagreement regarding the first, "defensive," set of objectives and tasks. These include preventing forces viewed as hostile to Russia (first and foremost, Islamic "fundamentalists") from coming to power; averting massive instability on the Russian border and forced migration of millions of ethnic Russians into Russia; and the thwarting of economic and developmental choices perceived as disadvantageous (for instance, the export routes of Azerbaijan's oil and Turkmenistan's gas that would bypass Russia).

Both the public and the elite appear also to be accepting the traditional set of postcolonial tools and techniques deployed in support of these tactical objectives: providing economic and military assistance to friendly regimes and reducing such assistance to ones deemed insufficiently accommodating;[61] protecting economic and military assets by increasing the dependency of the regimes in question on Russia, including, in the case of Georgia, by training and supplying ethnic secessionist insurgencies in Abkhazia and South Ossetia; peacekeeping and peace mediation; and the patrolling of former Soviet borders. As long as they do not entail sizable casualties, these projects are largely ignored by the public; the occasional protests are confined to a small human rights community and a handful of courageous and ambitious journalists.

It is when we move from the maintenance of the status quo to its improvement that the consensus begins to fray. Today, as in 1993, everyone seems to consider a significant amelioration of Russia's domestic and regional conditions unimaginable without a closer "integration" with newly independent states. Yet the ways in which such integration ought to proceed is a matter of intense dispute. The tactics of "integration" are riddled with political fault lines.

The majority of pro-regime foreign policy experts inside and outside the government view integration as a long and laborious process, unfolding in a virtually open-ended time framework. The correct sequencing involves economic integration first and "political-military" integration much later. In this vision, long-term, patient, and gradual increases in economic cooperation and compatibility result in incremental political integration. The proponents of this mode compare it to the European Union.

The advocates of the alternative model of "integration"—the communist-led Popular-Patriotic Union of Russia (NPSR in its Russian acronym) most prominent among them—insist on the rapid political integration with the Near Abroad (especially with Belarus and Ukraine) regardless of economic costs. "No price, or almost no price, is too high for the Russian elite to pay to . . . unite with Belarus," wrote an anonymous author (or authors) of yet another foreign policy charter published in *Nezavisimaya Gazeta* in 1996.[62]

Behind the disagreements regarding the time frame, sequencing, and cost lies a fundamental divergence and clash between two conceptual models of integration and two tendencies in Russia's behavior in the region. One might be called "postcolonial" (closer to the French—assertive, muscular and activist—policy in the Francophone Africa than to that of Britain's) and "economic." The other is best described as "imperial" and "ideological." Ultimately, the first tendency, for all its high- and heavy-handedness, is nonrevisionist, and the second is.

The aforementioned *Theses* provides the most detailed exposition to date of the "postcolonial" stance, which is the Kremlin's official policy. In this paradigm, the progress toward integration, no matter how vital, must be framed by the cost. Given the "limited political, economic and military means" and the preoccupation of the country's citizens and leadership with "domestic matters," the authors expect the "nostalgia" for the Soviet Union to be accompanied by "a rather broad unwillingness of Russians to pay for the restoration of the Union."[63]

Post-Soviet integration is a "long and uneven" process, and the policymakers must be wary of attempts to "expedite it by force": Such attempts are "doomed" and, in the end, would backfire by slowing down the process.[64] Even in the case of Belarus, which is strategically extremely desirable as Russia's "bridge to the West" and which, officially, is fervently pro-integrationist, the objective ought to be limited to no more than a "confederation" within "one or two years."[65]

The most effective means of integration will not be some spectacular military alliance but "a successful economic development of Russia itself," the beginning of economic growth, and the continuation of political and market reforms. "Only an [economically] powerful and dynamically developing Russia will be able to create a gravitation field for another 'in-gathering of lands' on a strictly voluntary basis."[66]

Thus far, the bulk of the Russian political class has shown little enthusiasm for long-term state-building (or rebuilding) in the region. "It is not in the Russian interests," state the *Theses*, "to give political and military commitments left and right and then follow up on them by striving to save an ally. The range of such commitments must be limited by our capabilities and our own interests."[67]

Again, the cautious approach to integration parallels societal concerns. The Russians are almost evenly divided on accepting some of the burdens of regional superpowership. While 51 percent agreed that "Russia has a responsibility to maintain order throughout the former Soviet Union," 45 percent disagreed. Asked about the deployment of Russian troops in Tajikistan, 47 percent supported it and 40 percent opposed.[68]

With the unpopular war in Chechnya very much on its mind, Moscow is reluctant to take on new open-ended commitments in the region. Thus it continues to resist Georgian demands for Russian policing of the return of ethnic Georgians to the Gali and Ochamchira districts ("raions") of Abkhazia and appears to want to settle, once and for all, the civil war in Tajikistan, the only CIS nation where Russian regular troops were engaged in combat. This weariness with long-term and expensive commitments in the Near Abroad distinguishes Russian policy both from traditional imperialism and, a fortiori, from its Soviet variety.

In devising and implementing policy vis-à-vis the Near Abroad, both the Russian foreign policy establishment and the government have largely adhered to what four years ago this author called the Grand Compromise:[69] an implicit strategic understanding between Russia and the new states by which the latter surrender a measure of independence (but by no means the independence itself) in exchange for economic,[70] political, and, in some cases, military assistance by Moscow. While "near," the post-Soviet states are recognized as "abroad."

Since 1993 the Grand Compromise has proven viable and, in some cases, evolved in a series of quite explicit "grand bargains" struck by Russia and the more vulnerable of the post-Soviet nations. First, there were countries at war that sought to maintain control over a newly acquired territory, as in Armenia[71] or to save a fragile state mortally threatened by ethnic secessionism and civil strife, as in Georgia[72] and Tajikistan. Another group consisted of the states most Russified and thus most threatened by Russian irredentism (Kazakhstan).[73] Finally, there were those most dependent on Russian exports and imports (Belarus, Kazakhstan, and Kyrgyzstan) and on expertise by resident ethnic Russians in the leadership of industry and armed forces (Kazakhstan and Kyrgyzstan).[74] These countries (minus the deeply ambivalent Georgia) have formed the pro-integrationist core of the CIS.[75] (The other, "anti-integrationist," pole of the CIS consists of countries that are at peace, relatively free of secessionism and external threat, comparatively stable politically and with a strong sense of national identity, and in possession of alternative, to Russia, sources of economic viability: Azerbaijan, Ukraine, and Uzbekistan. Georgia's "heart," without a doubt, is with this group; its mind, as well as skin and stomach, is with the "integrationists.")

The proponents of the postcolonial and imperial models of integration have much different uses for the Grand Compromise. For the "postcolonialist" it is a major, long-term mechanism of maintaining the regional superpowership that allows probing for weaknesses, exploiting the partners' troubles to the full, and taking advantage of every opening,

but stopping at the violation of the basic ground rules: political sovereignty of the CIS nations and their independence from Russia.[76] The imperial model, on the other hand, presupposes modalities that would
subject the Grand Compromise to an enormous stress and, likely, scuttle
it altogether: heavy involvement in domestic politics of the CIS nations,
destabilization of the recalcitrant regimes by any means available (including secessionism), and the deployment of a "heavy economic stick,"
including boycotts and disruption of trade routes and labor markets.[77]

It was precisely because of an unusually direct collision of the two
concepts and the two policymaking tendencies that "reunification" with
Belarus has acquired, in the eyes of the political elite, the status of a por-
tentous test. As Russia stands to gain little economically from such a
"union" (and risks losing a great deal by merging with the premarket and
inflation-ridden economy), and because at the time of signing Belarus was
a semidictatorship run by an erratic and increasingly brutal president, any
steps toward a real union would signify the administration's adoption of
the "ideological" model of integration.[78]

As a result, the reaction to the signing in Moscow on April 2, 1997,
of a Russo-Belarussian Treaty highlighted some fundamental political
cleavages. Gennady Zyuganov hailed the agreement; Alexandr Lebed
called it "premature"; and Sergei Yushenkov, a prominent legislator from
Russia's Democratic Choice Party, warned that the integration with Belarus "could do even more damage to Russian political and economic interests than the war in Chechnya."[79]

The "party line" was just as sharply drawn inside the government.
Supporting the treaty were the then minister for CIS affairs, Aman Tuleev
(the only member of the communist-led opposition in the cabinet); the
deputy prime minister, Valeri Serov; Yevgeny Primakov; and Sergei
Shakhrai (Yeltsin's representative to the Constitutional Court). The critics,
who "expressed concern about the economic consequences" of the affair,
included the leading economic reformers: First Deputy Prime Ministers
Anatoly Chubais and Boris Nemtsov; Economics Minister Yakov Urinson;
and the then chairman of the State Property Committee, Alfred Kokh.[80]

The champions of imperial and postcolonial approaches to regional
superpowership also differ profoundly over the role of the 25-million-
strong Russian diaspora in the CIS states. The former view ethnic
Russians and Russian speakers as a potent tool to be deployed fully and
without hesitation in pursuit of tactical advantages in the "post-Soviet
space." In this strategy, the Kremlin ought to at least threaten an irredentist option, which includes "politization" of the Russian diaspora and
even a "massive redrawing of borders" to join to the metropolia the areas

populated by ethnic Russians (for instance, northern Kazakhstan and eastern Ukraine.)[81]

The postcolonial camp approaches the "irredentist option" with a great deal of weariness, which, thus far, has been shared by the Kremlin. Here the regime appears to be operating within a pragmatic cost-benefit framework, perhaps suspecting (rightly) that the effort to engage ethnic Russians was likely to destroy the Grand Compromise as the cornerstone of the present strategy in the Near Abroad.[82] Accordingly, Moscow's diaspora policy has been reactive, defensive, and steering very much clear of "politicization." (A student of this subject called Moscow's policy "muted and restrained.")[83]

The "dual citizenship" affair seems emblematic of this attitude. In 1993 both Yeltsin and Kozyrev began to tout the idea of Russian citizenship for ethnic Russians in the Near Abroad. The issue found ready and enthusiastic support in the Duma and for a while became one of the most publicized aspects of Russian public diplomacy in the CIS. (The Duma Committee on CIS Affairs even announced that it would oppose ratification of Russia's treaties with those CIS states that refuse the dual citizenship.)

Yet after encountering fierce resistance from the CIS states (primarily Ukraine), Moscow began to retreat. In the end, the Russian government abandoned the policy and, with it, "a very important instrument of the Russian policy of hegemony and dominance."[84] Since then, from a blanket national policy backed with ultimatums, the issue of ethnic Russians in the "post-Soviet space" has turned into an item of multilateral negotiations with individual CIS nations; and, as such, has been removed from the strategic map.[85]

Here too Moscow's policy appeared to agree with public opinion. While strong majorities or pluralities of voters across the entire political spectrum did not believe the dissolution of the Soviet Union to be "a good thing"; while an even larger proportion felt that ethnic Russians in the former republics were "treated unfairly" and that the government should be "concerned" with the violation of their rights, only Zhirinvsky's constituency was firmly for the "expansion" of Russia's borders "to include ethnic Russians in the Near Abroad.[86] Responding to the suggestion that ethnic Russians there should "give their allegiance to the states where they live and not to Russia," again, only those who intended to vote for Zhirinovsky disagreed (barely), while even Zyuganov's voters agreed.[87]

In 1997, following Yeltsin's recuperation from heart surgery and illness in March, several developments appear to point to the ascendancy of the more moderate and cautious postcolonial tendency, to which demilitarization of the conflicts in the Near Abroad always had been central.

Russia actively sought to end all the major armed disputes in the region—in Tajikistan, Moldova's Predniestrovie, Georgia, Nagorno-Karabakh—and defuse tension in relations with some its neighbors. Only in the case of Nagorno-Karabakh did Moscow fail to make at least some progress.[88]

In June 1997 the Dushanbe regime, supported by Moscow, and the Tajik opposition ended the five-year-old civil war by signing, in Moscow, a Russia-sponsored Peace and National Reconciliation Accord, which mandated the opposition's immediate inclusion in the government. Primakov and his first deputy, Boris Pastukhov, reportedly continued mediation until the final agreement was reached two hours before the signing ceremony.[89]

In April and May Primakov shuttled between Chisinau and Tiraspol, the capital of the self-proclaimed Dniester Republic, which "seceded" from Molodova in 1992. In the second half of May, Moldova's president, Petru Lucinschi, and the head of the Dniester Republic, Igor Smirnov, signed, in Moscow, a "memorandum" that effectively confirmed Moldova's sovereignty over Predniestrovie. The signing was attended by the presidents of Russia and Ukraine, which, as co-guarantors of the agreement, agreed to provide peacekeepers and oversee the implementation.[90]

In May and June Moscow mediated between Georgia and Abkhazia within a framework of a seven-point "interim protocol" drafted by the Russian Ministry of Foreign Affairs. In June Abkhaz President Vladislav Ardzinba spent two weeks in Moscow negotiating with Primakov, Yeltsin's Chief of Staff Valentin Yumashev, Security Council Secretary Ivan Rybkin, and Defense Minister Igor Sergeev. Several weeks later President Yeltsin reportedly drafted a "more comprehensive" peace agreement for Ardzinba and Shevardnadze to sign. The new document, according to Shevardnadze, stipulates "broad autonomy" for Abkhazia "within a unified Georgian state." On August 14 Ardzinba, for the first time, traveled to the Georgian capital of Tbilisi for discussions. At the end of August Yeltsin publicly praised Primakov for "breaking the deadlock." On August 25, in his weekly radio address, Shevardnadze also "expressed his appreciation" of Primakov's effort in arranging for Ardzinba's visit to Tbilisi. Two weeks later First Deputy Foreign Minister Boris Pastukhov mediated talks in Abkhazia, the capital of Sukhumi, between the Abkhaz leadership and high-level Georgian officials.[91]

On September 5 and 6 Russian Prime Minister Viktor Chernomyrdin met in Vilnius, the capital of Lithuania, with the presidents of Estonia, Latvia, and Lithuania. At the conclusion of the negotiations, the heads of the three Baltic states announced that they would "soon" sign border agreements with Russia.[92] The talks marked a major departure from

Moscow's previous position, which tied the normalization to the end of what Russia insisted was the "violation of civil and political rights" of ethnic Russians in the Baltic states.

Yet by far the most important step toward postcolonial normalization was the May 31 Treaty of Friendship, Cooperation, and Partnership between the Russian Federation and Ukraine, signed by Yeltsin and Kuchma in Kiev. The two nations undertook to "respect each other's territorial integrity, confirm[ed] the inviolability of existing borders, . . . mutual respect, sovereign equality, a peaceful settlement of disputes, non-use of force or its threat. . . ."[93]

The treaty was unprecedented in the history of Russia's relations with its weaker neighbors. Moscow gave up two centuries of sovereignty over Crimea,[94] where ethnic Russians are an overwhelming majority, and with it the city and naval base of Sevastopol, the legendary site of Russian military valor and heroism during the 1854–55 Crimean War and World War II (June 1942). After almost six years of bitter dispute, the battleships of the formerly Soviet Black Sea Fleet were recognized as Ukrainian property. Half of the fleet was to be rented by Russia, along with several of Sevastopol's docking bays, with rent payment subtracted from Kiev's debt to Moscow.

Given the technical complexity of the issues, the enormous stakes in national pride, and the disturbing record of similar divisions in separate statehoods (Britain and Ireland, India and Pakistan, Serbia and Bosnia), the Russo-Ukrainian normalization, if it holds, is truly remarkable. With Kiev as the birthplace of the first Russian state, no other part of the Soviet Union is as central to Russian national identity as Ukraine. In no other instance was the tempering of Russia's imperial ambition put to a harsher test than by a trial by an independent Ukraine.

In a larger scheme of things, normalization of relations between Europe's largest and its sixth most populous state will be just as critical to the stability of the post–Cold War order on the continent as Franco-German rapprochement, engineered by de Gaulle and Konrad Adenauer in 1958 was for Europe after World War II. Within the domestic context of Russian foreign policy, the Treaty of Kiev was a signal victory of a more restrained tendency in the assertion of Russian regional superpowership.

THE LONGEVITY OF THE DOCTRINE: CHALLENGES AND STABILITY

The present-day Russian foreign policy doctrine emerged in a very distinct, perhaps unique, context of Boris Yeltsin's leadership, economic and military weakness, and protodemocracy. Such a combination is not likely to be sustainable even in the medium run. Will the country's doctrine change with the inevitable passing of this context?

The most obvious source of change comes from a set of variables that together might be called "regime" challenges, generated from within the political elite and the government. In addition to the departure of Yeltsin (a hugely important factor by itself), the regime challenges may be categorized as institutional, ideological, and populist.

The most obvious of the institutional threats emanates from the Russian military and its industrial base. If the Kremlin, in conjunction with free-market revolution and tight anti-inflationary budgets, continues to pursue a nonrevisionist foreign policy without global aspirations and messianic fervor, then, in the absence of a clear external threat, the armed forces and defense industry inherited from the Soviet Union cannot be sustained in their current size. It is quite certain that both the generals and the managers will continue to question, oppose, and lobby to change such a policy. What are the chances of their success?

As always, the most reliable measure of an institution's strength and efficacy is the share of resources it is given and the treatment its top representatives are accorded by a country's political leadership. By these criteria, the decline of the Russian military has been spectacular. "Reduction" is a palpably inadequate word for the depredation and strangulation visited by the Yeltsin regime on its only recently all-mighty army.

Between 1992 and 1996, the Russian defense expenditures declined from between 15 to 25 percent of the GNP to less than 5 percent. In absolute terms, the decrease in the military spending from 1992 to 1995 was at least 45 percent.[95] Still, as the government implemented emergency across-the-board spending cuts in summer 1997, the defense sector again was the target of choice: The already meager spending there was estimated to shrink by as much as 20 percent.

The number of troops fell from around 3.8 million in January 1992 to, at most, 2.5 million in October 1996, a reduction of 34 percent.[96] On July 16 President Yeltsin signed several decrees that mandated a reduction of the armed forces by 500,000 men, to 1.2 million. The abolition of the draft and an all-voluntary armed force of 600,000 was promised to be implemented between the years 2000 and 2005.

The budgetary devastation has been paralleled by an equally graphic loss of the army's political clout. Between June 1996 and June 1997, backed with a fresh electoral mandate, an often very sick president fired two ministers of defense, two chiefs of the general staff, and several senior generals, including commanders of paratroop and space forces. In the case

of Minister Igor Rodionov, insult was added to injury when the state television showed him standing at attention as the president berated him at a
session of the Defense Council.

To point out an obvious, and precipitous, weakening of the institutional position of the Russian military is not to dismiss it entirely as an
institutional actor. It has been capable of conducting major operations
allegedly without the knowledge or consent of the political leadership:
assistance to the Abkhaz separatists and a massive transfer of weapons to
Armenia. Yet, at least within the next decade, it is hard to imagine the
Russian military significantly shaping policy beyond the borders of the
former Soviet Union.

Barring a direct military threat or a return to authoritarianism and
a state-run militarized autarky, whatever additional institutional weight
the Russian military might regain, its sway will be more than matched
by that of new and powerful institutional players whose interests are already quite different from (indeed, often opposite of) the armed forces
and the VPK (the military-industrial complex). These ambitious new-
comers are the banking and export-oriented sectors of the Russian
economy.

In most general terms, *Osnovnye polozhenia*, quoted in the beginning
of this chapter, established a connection between the core foreign policy
agenda and economic development by proclaiming "securing a stable
progress in the economy and respectable standard of living for the people"
a central objective of Russian foreign policy. Since then the state of the
economy and Russia's economic integration in the world have become an
integral and central part of the national security doctrine elucidated by the
top officials: Ivan Rybkin listed "political risk" that diminishes foreign
investments among major threats to the country's security.[97]

Top officials in the Ministry of Defense emphasized "a modern and
effective economy" as one of the "most urgent tasks" and "highest priorities for Russian foreign policy," and the reform of the national economy is one of "Russia's fundamental national goals."[98] Moreover, the
same officials considered the opening of the Russian economy to world
competition and foreign investment as key prerequisites for a successful
economic transition and "stable economic growth."[99]

Political ascendance of the internationalist wing of the Russian business elite became apparent in the aftermath of the 1996 presidential election. After Yeltsin's historic March 7 "State of Russia" address to the
Federal Assembly, which precipitated the overhaul of the government and
launched what became known as a "second economic revolution," one
could begin to discern signs of the growing influence of financial and

export-oriented sectors of the economy in the formulation of the country's economic and security relationship with the outside world.

In July 1997 President Yeltsin signed a profit-sharing decree that allowed foreign investment in several oil, gas, iron, and gold extraction sites in exchange for a percentage of the resources extracted in the future. At the same time, foreign investors were permitted to bid for up to 25 percent of major privatized enterprises, with the share of foreign ownership promised to increase in future auctions.

Simultaneously, Russia intensified its quest for membership in the World Trade Organization (WTO), which would clearly benefit the financial and export-oriented sectors of its Russian economy and, just as obviously, damage uncompetitive domestic industries (especially food production, automobile, textiles and clothing) by facilitating cheaper imports of far superior quality.

The appointment of the mogul Boris Berezovsky as deputy secretary of the National Security Council on October 29, 1996, announced the arrival of a new category of institutional actors at the heart of Russian policymaking. Given Berezovsky's contribution to Yeltsin's reelection, any office below that of first deputy prime minister was, undoubtedly, his for the asking. That Berezovsky chose the council and was given the job might indicate the new elites' interest in claiming (and obtaining) more direct venues for influencing international economic and security policy formulation and implementation than had been available to them until then. (Berezovsky's departure a year later left the precedent intact.)

Preceded by the two years of strident protests, Moscow's relatively muted reaction to the expansion of NATO and the signing of the Russia-NATO Founding Act were widely attributed to an enhanced leverage of "internationalist" magnates. Reporting from Moscow on the day Boris Yeltsin and Bill Clinton signed the act, a *Washington Post* correspondent quoted a "Western diplomat": "What we are seeing is the influence of Chubais and the financial elites. They are not interested in confrontation with the West, and they want to avoid remilitarization of the economy."[100]

To such a major export-oriented company as giant natural gas monopoly Gasprom, which counts Prime Minister Viktor Chernomyrdin among its alumni and most active lobbyists, the trade-off between political complications stemming from NATO's decision and the maintenance of the status quo in relations with the West was quite acceptable. "Why are you guys so concerned about the enlargement of NATO to the East?" a Gasprom executive was quoted asking a leading Russian foreign policy expert. "I can assure you that the enlargement of NATO to the East will be more than compensated for by the enlargement of Gasprom to the West."[101]

At the time of the signing of the Russo-Chechen peace accord on May 12, 1997, many Moscow observers claimed privately that Yeltsin had been successfully lobbied by Russia's mammoth LUKoil company to settle the conflict. LUKoil needed peace to secure the flow of oil across Chechnya from the Caspian oil fields to the terminals in the Russian Black Sea port of Novorossiisk. Since 1992 LUKoil had been a major partner in the Azerbaijani International Operating Company (AIOC)[102] and the Caspian Pipeline Consortium, in which LUKoil, Mobil, and Chevron pooled resources to build a pipeline from the Tengiz oil field in Kazakhstan.[103]

The political economy of Russian foreign policy is likely to be influenced also by the growing economic and political diversity of Russian regions. It seems quite plausible that the voting and lobbying record of regional governors, in their *ex officio* capacity as deputies to the upper house of the Russian parliament, the Council of Federation, will begin to reflect the division between relatively advanced, export oriented, gas and oil producing areas (center, northwest, the Urals, northern Siberia, western Siberia, and the Far East) on the one hand; and agricultural, "rust belt," light industry, and coalmining regions, which stand to lose from the opening of the market and decline of the military-industrial complex, on the other hand (north, central-west, and central-south Russia, the Lower Volga, and south Siberia).

One must not, of course, exaggerate what was aptly called the "economization" of Russian foreign policy.[104] We are still very far from the point when what is good for LUKoil will be considered good for Russia. It would, indeed, be quite ironic if an analysis of the domestic context of Russian foreign policy that notes the growing influence of internationally oriented capitalists succumbs to the same vulgar Marxism that the Soviet ideology once used to predict the "eventual victory of socialism."[105]

History has shown again and again that the existence of an internationalist business elite does not preclude aggression, militarism, or even an evolution toward autarky. In direct confrontation, economic rationale invariably is overcome by fear, hatred, perceived military threat, wounded national honor, or messianic fervor. Still, the interests of the politically ascendant economic internationalist elites and entire regions are a novel and important addition to the domestic context of Russian foreign policy and must be taken into account.

Contrary to what was widely expected in the late Gorbachev era, virtually all revisionist impulses have shifted from the increasingly marginalized right to the communist-led "popular-patriotic" left, which has become the main provenance of xenophobia, militarism, and revanchism.

These political quarters are a source of what might be called the "ideo-logical" threat to consensus on Russian foreign policy doctrine.

Epitomized by the communist-sponsored March 15, 1996, Duma Res-olution nullifying the December 1991 Belavezh Accords, which legalized the dissolution of the Soviet Union, the symbiosis of the hard-line socialism and an increasingly hard-line foreign policy stance was epitomized by Zyu-ganov's denunciation of NATO expansion at a communist-sponsored May Day (1997) rally in Moscow. The leadership of the communist faction in the Duma labeled the NATO-Russia Founding Act "treason."[106]

Even in the medium run, despite the shrillness and determination of its purveyors, the opportunities for "ideological" revision of the current for-eign policy doctrine are tightly circumscribed by the Communist Party of the Russian Federation's (KPRF) less than sanguine political prospects. The results of the 1996 presidential election (in which a near-total turnout of Zyuganov's voters still failed to prevent a 14-point victory for Yeltsin) and the steady erosion of the communist electoral base because of the age of its core constituency decrease the ability of the "national-patriotic" left to con-test the fundamentals of the doctrine. Meanwhile, the constitutional re-straints on the Duma's policymaking role in national security and foreign affairs blunts the influence of the communist-led plurality in the legislature.

In the long run, a far more effective challenge may come from what can be called the "populist" appeals to injured national pride and pa-triotism. The combination of the growing openness of Russia's politi-cal process and the highly personal mode of political mobilization, characteristic of young democracies, invites exploitation of the post-imperial trauma of outside from any more or less permanent ideologi-cal divisions.

The threat is mitigated somewhat by the growing moderation and sophistication of the Russian electorate since the first post-Soviet elections in 1993. The decline of Vladimir Zhirinovsky, who professed nothing less than a global revanchism, is the most vivid testimony to this evolution.

Zhirinovsky's two most obvious successors in the populist field are General Alexandr Lebed and Yuri Luzhkov, the mayor of Moscow. After the failure of the Congress of Russian Communities (which placed the fate of ethnic Russians in the Near Abroad at the center of the electoral plat-form), Lebed moderated his position and played a key role in ending the Chechen war. Luzhkov, on the other hand, appears to be testing the political power of a nationalist appeal with his periodic statements on Sevastopol, which he intends to keep a "Russian city," and the denunci-ation of the Russian-Chechen peace agreement in Khasavayurt, which he called a "bomb under the Russian Constitution."[107]

Yet even if the "populist" challenge is victorious (that is, the challenger is elected president), it, like a far less probable success of the left's "ideological" opposition to the current doctrine, is unlikely to overcome both elite and popular resistance to any (much less all) of the key changes that would signal the abandonment of the reigning paradigm: (1) the restoration of the dominance of external and military factors over domestic and economic progress in the definition of national security and prosperity; (2) the substitution of nonideological pragmatism for "ideological" foreign policy with traditional messianic overtones; (3) a shift from mostly regional to mostly global ambitions; and (4) replacement of the acceptance of post–Cold War geopolitical realities with revisionism.

For such an overhaul to occur, the "regime" challenges will have to coincide with a set of changes affecting the geostrategic situation of Russia: the country's overall economic strength; external threats to its security; and consensus on national priorities and purposes.

Here the likeliest development is significant improvement in Russia's economic performance: stabilization, revival, and growth. The most obvious corollary of such a scenario will be the end of the institutional debility of the Russian armed forces. As the economic situation improves, the Russian defense sector is bound to become, first, viable and, then, perhaps, dynamic again. Conventional strength will again become a factor in foreign policy planning and the military a powerful institutional player (scenario 1X, Table 1–1).

While such a development would without doubt make Russian foreign policy more muscular, it would not, by itself, render its focus global and its thrust revisionist. For the same economic upturn is likely to enhance the political influence of the "internationalist" business elites and regions, whose institutional priorities are largely inimical to those of the military-industrial complex. Similarly, the same economic revival is likely to blunt the effectiveness of both "ideological" (communist) and "populist" appeals by improving the well-being of their core intended recipients: state employees, industrial workers, and pensioners.

Thus the success of the transformation of the Russian foreign policy doctrine within the "economic progress" + "renewed military strength" + "populist"/"ideological" takeover scenario is more likely if the sequencing of these developments is modified to resemble the historically familiar post-Weimar pattern: an authoritarian takeover ("ideological" or "populist"); a sharp increase in defense funding; temporary but sharp defense-driven economic growth; and, finally, a revisionist foreign policy

Table 1–1. Challenges to the Russian Foreign Policy Doctrine

"Regime" Variables	*"Geostrategic" Variables*
X. "Institutional" (military)	1. Economic growth
Y. "Ideological"/"authoritarian"	2. Perception of external threat
Z. "Populist"/"authoritarian"	3. National priorities

Scenarios and Probabilities
(from least probable to more probable)

1X
YX1 or ZX1
Y13X, 213X
13X, 12X

(scenarios YX1 or ZX1). While possible, this scenario presupposes a dramatic change in Russian domestic politics. Judging by the public opinion data, it will meet with such a formidable resistance that in today's Russia, its implementation would require something very close to a Stalinist revolution from above.

In a somewhat more plausible course of events, a successful "regime" challenge ("populist" or "ideological" authoritarianism) and a markedly improved economic performance are accompanied by sweeping changes in national priorities that would make remilitarization politically feasible (Y13X or Z13X). There is a contemporary model for the combination of an authoritarian regime, rapid economic growth in the private sector, a very significant increase in military expenditures, and nationalism: today's China.

If Russia is to implement the "Chinese option" without an authoritarian takeover, the support for which has been steadily diminishing and is now confined to a distinct minority, the success of this scenario is predicated either on a rapid evolution of the national *Weltanschauung* away from the individual pursuits and domestic economic progress, so overwhelmingly prevalent today, and toward grand communal and global projects; or on a very significant deterioration of the country's geostrategic position: 13X or 12X scenarios. While the former eventuality seems, at this writing, quite remote, the latter development is rather easy to chart. Its most proximate sources are Chinese military modernization and China's increasingly assertive behavior in the region immediately adjacent to Russia's "sphere of influence," and the expansion of NATO toward the borders of today's Russia.[108]

While plausible, a fundamental transformation of Russian national foreign policy doctrine in response to the policies of either China or NATO is by no means assured. In the case of China, the century-old popular hostility could be rekindled rather easily. However, within the neo-Gaullist consensus in Russian foreign policy both the antiregime left and proregime center-right are united in wishing to use Russia's relationship with China as counterweight to the perceived U.S. "hegemony" and as a bargaining chip in relations with Washington—in addition, of course, to China's place of honor among the markets for Russian weapons and military technology. Thus, barring a direct and immediate military threat, even Chinese policies objectively detrimental to the Russian geostrategic posture (such as an aggressive economic and political penetration of the Far East and Central Asia or militarization of the border with Russia) may not be sufficient to foster a thoroughgoing revision in Russian foreign policy.

In NATO's case, the first barrier is widespread and obvious ignorance or lack of concern. There has been no automatic connection between the elite's opinion and the public's reaction. Moreover, Yeltsin masterfully split the elite opposition into the "irreconcilables" on the left and those who accepted the regime's strategy of containing the adverse consequences through the Founding Act.

For NATO to become a credible threat of necessary proportions, it must be incorporated into a successful "populist" campaign eager to exploit the issue. In this context, coinciding with the run-up to Russia's year 2000 presidential campaign, the final stages of NATO's eastward enlargement might play precisely such a role: first, by providing a candidate with an ideal issue on which to attack proregime contestants (be he Boris Nemtzov or Viktor Chernomyrdin) and then, in case of victory, making him a hostage to his rhetoric.

Undoubtedly sensing the issue's populist appeal, General Lebed, who until the May 27, 1997, NATO-Russia Paris summit was among the most restrained of the leading Russian politicians with regard to NATO expansion, turned into a critic when the NATO-Russia Founding Act was signed. Russia, Lebed declared, was "the losing side" which had "signed the act of its own capitulation"; he also accused NATO of "aggressive intentions."[109]

Not yet daring to antagonize Yeltsin by venturing into the highest presidential policymaking domain, Luzhkov praised the NATO-Russia agreement as helping "contain" NATO.[110] Yet he is almost certain to inject the issue into his presidential campaign.

There are obvious limitations inherent in an attempt to capture policymaking patterns within an unfolding revolution. Instead of institutionalized choices and solidified behavioral patterns, one has to deal with fluid and frequently contradictory tendencies, markers and broken lines, instead of well-trodden paths, and rely on anticipation rather than direct examination.

Yet, with all the deficiencies and inevitable tentativeness inherent in the results of such an exercise, the results warrant at least two conclusions. First, for all the inconsistencies, the emergent patterns in Russian foreign policy point to the existence of some fairly well established priorities, which together justify the name "doctrine." Second, such a doctrine is rooted in a rather broad and stable national consensus: the priority of the domestic/economic over external/military definitions of national security, of regional over global concerns and interests, and of pragmatism over "ideology" and messianism. This consensus translates into the tripartite strategic agenda: nuclear superpowership; regional dominance; and the acceptance of a diminished global status and, with it, the engagement in the world as one of the great powers.

Steadiest in the areas of nuclear superpowership and behavior on the world scene, this consensus grows considerably weaker where the maintenance of regional superpowership is concerned. While "integration" is accepted as the overarching objective, the concepts and the corresponding policy tendencies—postcolonial/economic and imperial/ideological—differ vastly. The choice of one over the other depends on the results of political competition between their proponents.

Yet in addition to most of the political elite, the current doctrine appears to have a much broader constituency, as public opinion surveys consistently demonstrate. Domestic economic and social problems are perceived as far more dangerous to the country's security than external military threats. Mistrust of the "West" and resentment of the United States coexist with the desire for cooperation. And regret over the dissolution of the Soviet Union fails to overcome the wariness of long-term military entanglements in the Near Abroad and of playing the "irredentist" (ethnic Russian) card.

Such sentiments extend the durability of the doctrine beyond the "regime" factors (of which Boris Yeltsin's leadership is by far the most important) and even beyond the country's current economic and military strategic weakness. Effective challenges to the key principles of today's Russian foreign policy doctrine, while possible, will require a powerful coincidence of both regime and geostrategic developments. For that reason, the success of such challenges can be neither easy nor quick.

Notes

I am grateful to Ms. Lisa Bustin (Research Assistant, American Enterprise Institute) and Mr. Soren Johnson (Intern, American Enterprise Institute) for their help in the research of this article.

1. V. B. Benevolenskiy, A. D. Bogaturov, Yu. P. Davydov, K. V. Pleshakov, and A. Yu Shumikhin, *Etap za global'nym. Liberal'nyi natsionalizm vo vneshney politike Rossii* (After the global stage. Liberal nationalism in Russian foreign policy) (Moscow: Rossiyskii Nauchnyi Fond, 1994), p. 7.

2. For an analysis of the fateful debates in spring-summer 1992, see Leon Aron, "The Battle for the Soul of Russian Foreign Policy," *American Enterprise* (November–December 1992), pp. 10–16.

3. Viktor Tretiakov, "Prezident El'tsin: dva goda u vlasti" (President Yeltsin: Two years in power), *Nezavisimaya Gazeta,* June 11, 1993.

4. B. Mezhuev, "The Notion of 'National Interest' in Russian Social and Political Thought," *Polis,* no. 1 (1997), p. 16.

5. Ibid.

6. Leon Aron, "The Emergent Priorities of Russian Foreign Policy," in Aron and Kenneth Jensen, *The Emergence of Russian Foreign Policy* (Washington, DC: United States Institute of Peace, 1994), pp. 17–34.

7. Unpublished document in the author's possession, Moscow, January 25, 1993.

8. Unpublished document in the author's possession, Moscow, 1993.

9. In a 1818 memorandum to Alexander I, the great Russian historian Nikolai Karamzin wrote: "The first duty of the sovereign is to preserve the internal and external unity of the state. Solicitude for the welfare of social classes and individuals must come second." Quoted in Adam Ulam, *Russia's Failed Revolutions* (New York: Basic Books, 1981), p. 13.

10. Mezhuev, "Notion of 'National Interest,'" pp. 13, 14.

11. One postulated "securing a reliable defense from any forms of external threat through the maintenance of a sufficient military potential of Russia and the existence of a stable system of international relations," and the other "protection of the rights and interests of citizens and organizations of the Russian Federation abroad."

12. Benevolenskiy et al., *Etap za global'nym.*

13. "Vneshnyaya politika Rossii—1993. Analiz politikov and ekspertov" (Russian foreign policy—1993. An analysis by politicians and experts), *Polis* 4 (1993), p. 217. The survey, which was conducted by the All-Russian Center for the Study of Public Opinion and two German research organizations, Sinus and the Friedrich Ebert Foundation, included "parliament, political parties and groups, scholarly centers and institutions and the press."

14. Andrei Kozyrev, "Rossia fakticheski v odinochku neset bremia realnogo mirotvorchestva v konfliktakh po perimetru svoikh granits" (Russia, in fact, is carrying alone the burden of peacekeeping in the conflicts along its border), *Nezavisimaya gazeta,* September 22, 1993.

15. Benevolensky et al., *Etap za global'nym,* p. 23.

16. Ibid., p. 24.

17. Ibid., p. 42.

18. Ibid., pp. 25–26.

19. Ibid., p. 25.

20. Inevitably, the new mythology was buttressed by the invocation of past suffering: a Russia that, at the cost of national catastrophe, "saved medieval Europe by exhausting and absorbing the Mongols." Ibid., p. 27.

21. At the time one also was "tempted" to dismiss this view as mild paranoia so typical of Moscow salons. Yet at least with respect to the arguments advanced by some of the proponents of NATO's eastward expansion, the pessimists proved quite prescient. Henry Kissinger, for instance, continued to call a democratic Russia, led by an anticommunist regime, an "adversary" ("Whoever heard of a military alliance," Dr. Kissinger demanded to know, "begging with a weakened adversary?") William Drozdiak, "Poland Urges NATO Not to Appease Russia," *Washington Post,* March 17, 1997.

22. Andrei A. Kokoshin, *Reflections on Russia's Past, Present, and Future* (Cambridge, MA: Harvard University, Strengthening Democratic Institutions Project, June 1997), p. 31. Kokoshin was appointed Secretary of the Security Council in March 1998.

23. During the Cold War, the Soviet Union rhetorically committed itself to the "no-first-use" doctrine.

24. See, for instance, Igor Rodionov, "What Kind of Defense Does Russia Need?" *Voyennoye Obozrenie,* November 28, 1996; Oleg Blotsky, "Rodionov—Russia will not be able to economize on the Army in 1997," interview with Igor Rodionov and Natalya Kuznetsova, "Military Reform in Russia," (*Nezavisiamaya Gazeta,* December 16, 1997.

25. Ivan Rybkin's interview in *Rossiiskaya Gazeta,* February 11, 1997.

26. See, for example, David Hoffman, "Yeltsin Approves Doctrine of Nuclear First Use If Attacked," *Washington Post,* May 10, 1997.

27. Igor Korotchenko, "Russian Strategic Missile Forces May Build Up Powers," interview with General Igor Sergeyev, *Nezavisimaya Gazeta,* December 17, 1996.

28. Ibid.

29. *OMRI Daily Digest,* January 15, 1996.

30. Evgeny Primakov, "Na gorizonte—mnogopolyusnyi mir (A multipolar world is on the horizon), *Nezavisimaya Gazeta,* October 22, 1996.

31. Ibid.

32. Ibid.

33. Ibid.

34. *OMRI Daily,* March 6, 1996.

35. In this regard, Primakov follows the explicit wish of his boss who, long before Primakov's appointment, wrote in his memoris: "Understanding the importance of cooperative actions, we would not want to look too docile, too manageable—much less to actually be so. Such a behavior damages our authority, the trust in our policy, and the balance of forces in Europe and the world." Boris Yeltsin, *Zapiski Prezidenta* (Moscow: Ogonyok, 1994), p. 220.

36. Primakov, "Na gorizonte . . ."

37. Dmitriy Gornostaev, "Perviy god diplomatii Primakova proshel bez provalov i proryvov" (The first year of Primakov's diplomacy has brought neither failures nor breakthroughs), *Nezavisimaya Gazeta,* January 9, 1997.
38. *OMRI Daily Digest,* January 9, 1997.
39. Richard Dobson, "Is Russia Turning the Corner? Changing Russian Public Opinion, 1991–1996 (Washington, DC: USIA [R-7-96], September 1996), p. 72 (Table 43), p. 71 (Table 42), and p. 70 (Table 41). The polls were commissioned by the United States Information Agency in October 1995, April 1996, and June 1996.
40. Stanley Hoffmann, *Decline or Renewal. France since the 1930s* (New York: Viking Press, 1974), p. 94.
41. Ibid., p. 192. The present-day French gripes, listed by Stanley Hoffmann in a recent article, are indistinguishable from Russia's litany of American sins (especially if one substitutes "post-Soviet states" for "Central Africa"): "The U.S. has tended to become the scapegoat of French national unhappiness. . . . The U.S. is accused of violating other states' sovereignty by passing laws preventing trade with them. It manipulates international organizations—the GATT, the World Trade Organization, the U.N. Secretariat—and it excludes others from vital decisions, such as the expansion of NATO or the Middle East peace process, even when, as in Dayton, or in the Washington ceremony of September 1991 that followed the Oslo breakthrough between Israel and Arafat, the terms of the agreement had been worked out by others. The U.S. is suspected of wanting to replace France in Central Africa; it is denounced by French diplomats and politicians alike as a triumphalist, unilateralist, and imperialistic power." Stanley Hoffmann, "Look Back in Anger," *New York Review of Books,* July 17, 1997, p. 46.
42. Again, the French perception of the United States in the 1950s and 1960s was very similar to the Russian attitudes in the second half of 1990s: "a hegemonial nation, slightly drunk with power, and [resorting], like all empires, to moralistic window dressing of the naked *animus dominandi.* Hoffmann, *Decline or Renewal,* p. 337.
43. Ibid., p. 217.
44. Robert O. Paxton, "De Gaulle and His Myth," *New York Review of Books,* April 23, 1992, p. 19.
45. Hoffmann, *Decline or Renewal,* p. 191.
46. This modus operandi is exemplified, par excellence, by the leading liberal "derzhavnik," Vladimir Lukin, chairman of the Committee on International Relations of the State Duma, who combines the tough rhetorical stance vis-à-vis the United States with a keen awareness of dangers inherent in overstepping the limits.
47. Of course, Russian foreign policy has not yet passed the crucial test of Gaullism: unequivocally siding with the U.S.-led "West" on issues of vital importance, as France did in the confrontation over Berlin in 1961, in the Cuban missile crisis, or in condemning the Soviet invasion of Czechoslovakia—or as Gorbachev did in the case of Operation Desert Storm.

48. See, for instance, "Russia, Refining Security Policy, Seeks Compromise with NATO," *New York Times,* May 8, 1997; David Hoffman, "Yeltsin Approves Doctrine of Nuclear First Use If Attacked," *Washington Post,* May 10, 1997.
49. Ivan Rybkin, "O kontseptsii natsional'noy bezopasnosti Rossii" (On the Russian national security concept), *Nezavisimaya gazeta,* April 29, 1997.
50. Valery Manilov, *The National Security of Russia* (Cambridge, MA: Harvard University, Strengthening Democratic Institution Project, June 1997), p. 20.
51. *OMRI Daily Digest,* September 18, 1995.
52. Interview to Interfax, June 30, 1996, via Foreign Broadcast Information Service Sov-96-127, July 1, 1996, p. 4.
53. *OMRI Daily Digest,* January 15, 1996. Primakov's first official trips were to Ashkhabad and Kiev. To the latter capital he soon dispatched as ambassador one of Russia's most distinguished diplomats, Yuri Dubinin, who once headed the country's embassy in Washington. Meanwhile, he waited a month before scheduling a meeting with U.S. Secretary of State Warren Christopher.
54. Sergei Karaganov and Vitaly Tretiakov, Working Group Chairmen, "Vozroditsia li Soyuz? Budushchee postsovetskogo prostranstva. Tezizy Soveta po vneshnei i oboronnoy politike" (Will the Union revive? The future of the post-Soviet space. Theses of the Council on Foreign and Defense Policy) *Nezavisimaya Gazeta,* May 23, 1996.

    Among those who signed the report were members of the State Duma Alexei Arbatov (deputy chairman of the Defense Committee), Vladimir Averchev (secretary, Committee on Foreign Relations), Irina Khakamada, Ivan Rybkin, and Sergei Shakhrai; scholars, experts and journalists Sergei Karaganov, Vitaly Zhurkin (director, Institute of Europe), Evgeny Kozhokhin, Alexei Pushkov (member of the Board of the Russian Public Television, ORT), and Vitaly Tretiakov (editor of *Nezavisimaya Gazeta*); entrepreneurs Arkady Volsky, Lev Vainberg, Sergei Yegorov (president of the Association of Russian Banks), Petr Zolotarev (head of the Analytical Center of the Ministry of Defense), and Vladimir Stepanov (president of the Moscow Industrial Association).
55. Karaganov and Tretiakov, "Vozroditsya li Soyuz . . ."
56. Ibid. The similarity with de Gaulle's favorite goals of *rassemblement* and *élever* is uncanny.
57. Ibid.
58. The precedence of the domestic and Near Abroad contingencies over the traditional dangers from the West appears to be shared by experts whose political home is considerably to the left of the authors of the Theses of the Council on Foreign and Defense Policy. Thus, after devoting well over half of a long article to bemoaning the deterioration of the Russian geostrategic situation because of NATO's eastward expansion, Zyuganov's principal foreign policy advisor goes on to state that the "greatest threat" to the country's security comes from

within the post-Soviet space and Russia itself. He lists "interethnic conflicts" and "separatist tendencies"; organized crime; and the "untoward tendencies" in the economic relations between Russia and the CIS nations, including the vulnerability of Russia's economic leadership to the competition with "developed Western states"; and the increasingly precarious access to the "transportation and communication structures" in the Near Abroad. Similarly, recommending urgent "preliminary measures" to bolster Russia's national security, the same author lists ten steps of a domestic economic and political nature before moving (in the last two planks) to the military-industrial complex and armed forces. Alexei Podberiozkin, "Vyzovy bezopasnosti Rossii" (The challenges to the securing of Russia), *Sobodnaya Mysl'*, no. 12 (1996), p. 67–69.

59. Polled in October 1996, barely over four in ten Russians had an opinion about NATO expansion (32 percent said it would be "bad" for Russia and 11 percent said it would be "good"). The majority were either "uninformed" about the issue or did not know whether the expansion "would be good or bad for their country." (USIA, "Russians and Ukrainians Differ in Their Views of NATO and the U.S.," *Opinion Analysis*, January 24, 1997.

60. The anti-Ukrainian sentiment was expressed until a few months before the signing of the Russo-Ukrainian treaty in May 1997. Thus, in October 1996, the Duma passed a resolution affirming that Sevastopol had always been a "Russian city." In late December 1996, the upper house of the Russian parliament, the Federation Council, called on President Yeltsin not to negotiate with Ukraine about the Black Sea Fleet until a special commission examined the "status" of Sevastopol.

61. The September 14, 1995, decree makes assistance they received from Russia contingent on the CIS states' positions on "integration." (See, for instance, Victor Gomez, "A Russian Grip on the CIS," *Transitions*, February 23, 1996, p. 52.) Reversing the position of his predecessor (Kozyrev refused to resort to economic sanctions), Primakov declared that Russia ought not be "afraid" to apply economic sanctions to the Baltic states in order to "liquidate discriminatory policies against the Russian-speaking population. The minister "reminded" Estonia (with which Russia refused to sign a border treaty until the issue of "discrimination" was resolved) that 60 percent of Estonian national income came from processing and reexporting Russian raw materials and goods. Dmitry Chernogorskiy, "Rossiyskaya diplomatia vybirayet rezkuyu tonal'nost'" (Russian diplomacy opts for a tough tone), *Nezavisimaya Gazeta*, January 11, 1997.

62. "SNG: Nachalo ili konets istorii" (CIS: The beginning or the end of history?), *Nezavisimaya Gazeta*, March 26, 1997).

63. Karaganov and Tretiakov, "Vozroditsia li Soyuz? . . ."

64. Ibid. The chairman of the Committee on Foreign Relations of the Russian legislature, Vladimir Lukin, personifies the democrat-

"derzhavniks," tough but cautious integrationists. By his own admission he had opposed a military solution in Chechnya, wished his country victory once the war started, and helped negotiate the 1996 Khasavayurt peace agreement by "softening" the Russian position. He continues to hope "to combine the freedom of Chechnya with the territorial integrity of Russia" and to see Russia "unlearn thugishness and the haughtiness of force." Ilya Mil'shtein, "Interview with Vladimir Lukin," *Novoye Vremia,* no. 45 (1996), pp. 12–14.

65. Ibid.

66. Ibid. Perhaps taking this line of argument a bit too far, Boris Nemtsov, the then-governor of Nizhniy Novgorod, suggested in February 1997 that Russian businesses ought to be encouraged to buy up property and business in Sevastopol (a predominantly Russian city and naval base, which is now part of Ukraine), thus "restoring historical justice by capitalist means." *OMRI Daily Digest,* February 20, 1997.

67. Ibid.

68. Dobson, "Is Russia Turning the Corner?" p. 66 (Table 37) and p. 67 (Table 38).

69. Aron in Aron and Jensen, *The Emergence of Russian Foreign Policy,* pp. 26–27.

70. Russia's gross national product (GNP) exceeds that of all the CIS nations together by one-third and is four times the size of the combined GNP of the new Central Asian nations. Yuri Aleksandrov, "Integratsia kak poslednyaya stadia dezintegratsii" (Integration as the final stage of disintegration), *Novoye Vremia* 11 (1997), p. 17.

71. In a 1996 survey, commissioned by the U.S. Information Agency, 94 percent of Armenians viewed Russia favorably, while three in ten felt threatened by "possible Russian efforts to recreate the Soviet Union." Reflecting, most likely, the satisfaction with Russia's role as the de facto guarantor of Armenia's territorial gains in the war with Azerbaijan, 86 percent of the respondents expressed either a "great deal" or "fair amount" of confidence in Russia's ability to "deal responsibly with problems in the Caucasus"—a significant increase since 1993 (61 percent) and 1994 (75 percent). "Armenians Like the U.S. Fine, But Look Primarily to Russia," *Opinion Analysis,* USIA, Office of Research and Media Reaction, July 3, 1996.

On April 29, 1997, the Armenian parliament by an overwhelming majority ratified a treaty that allowed Russia to keep a military base in Armenia. Four months later, in Moscow, Presidents Yeltsin and Levon Ter-Petrosian signed a 25-year Treaty of Friendship, Cooperation, and Mutual Assistance between Russia and Armenia, the first such agreement between post-Soviet Russia and its neighbors.

72. Perhaps the most conspicuous of the "bargains" was struck with Georgia. In October 1993, after Georgia's defeat in separatist Abkhazia and major setbacks in a civil war against the ousted President Zviad Gamsakhurdia, with his army near collapse,

Eduard Shevardnadze appealed for Russian military assistance in exchange for Georgia's entry into the CIS, membership in which it had until then resisted.

Responding to the domestic critics, who charged that Georgian independence had been "compromised for good," Shevardnadze acknowledged the "blow to Georgian statehood" but, reportedly, countered that he "had no choice." (Lee Hockstader, "Rebels Retreating in Georgia. With Russian Help, Shevardnadze's Government Retakes Territory," *Washington Post,* November 8, 1993.)

Three months after Russian marines, tanks, and advisors ensured Shevardnadze's victory over Gamsakhurdia, Boris Yeltsin traveled to Tbilisi to sign a treaty of "Friendship, good neighborly relations and mutual assistance." Commenting on Russian assistance, Shevardnadze said that although many nations had offered aid with "inspectors and instructors," none agreed to supply weapons for the "rebuilding of Georgian armed forces. Except for Russia, no one has the ability to help us in this matter." ("Eduard Shevardnadze: 'Prezidentu khvatilo muzhestva . . .'" [President had enough courage . . .], an interview with *Moskovskie Novosti,* February 6–13, 1994.)

In return, Russia received bases in the Black Sea port of Batumi and on the border with Turkey. "From a country that until recently had no treaty relations with Russia at all," wrote a Russian observer, "Georgia is about to become the CIS nation most saturated with Russian troops." (Mikhail Shevelev, "Gruzia: ne vreden Sever dlia menia" [Georgia: North is not bad for my health], *Moskovskie Novosti,* February 6–13, 1994.)

Two years later Georgia insisted that maintenance of Russian military bases be contingent on Russia's restoring Georgia's "territorial integrity," that is, control over Abkhazia and South Ossetia. (Liz Fuller, "Is Russia's Peacekeeping Force in Abkhazia a New Casus Belli?" *RFE-RL Newsline,* April 29, 1997.) After the mandate of the Russian peacekeeping troops in Abkhazia expired on January 31, 1997, Shevardnadze pleaded with Moscow to renew it, to expand the area of deployments throughout the Gali and Ochamchira districts, and to assume the responsibility of policing the return of ethnic Georgians there. He threatened to leave "Russia's sphere of influence" unless Moscow agreed to "restore Georgia's sovereignty" over Abkhazia and South Ossetia.

73. According to Nigmatzhan Isingarin, the first deputy prime minister of Kazakhstan, his country is the "most Russified state in the entire CIS": Ethnic Russians constitute 35 percent of the population, and 30 percent of all marriages are ethnically mixed. Ekaterina Sytaya, "Dogovor ob uglublionnoy integratzii rabotaet" (The agreement on a deeper integration is working), *Nezavisimaya Gazeta,* November 24, 1996.

74. In Kazakhstan and Kyrgyzstan, ethnic Russians were estimated in 1993 to constitute "more than 70 percent" of those employed in the

sciences. Igor Zevelev, "Russia and the Russian Diasporas," *Post-Soviet Affairs* 12, no. 3 (1996), p. 278.

75. In March 1996 Belarus, Kazakhstan, Kyrgyzstan, and Russia signed the largely symbolic Treaty on Deepening Integration in Economic and Humanitarian Spheres.

76. Thus far, Russia's control over even the most vulnerable CIS members is nowhere near the United States' dominance of Central America in the 1950s and 1960s or the French influence in Francophone Africa today.

77. The difference between the two approaches is akin to one between twisting arms and cutting them off. Much as outside observers may (and do) find both operations equally reprehensible, the actual choice makes a great deal of difference to the arms' owner. Hence the quite audible sigh of relief with which the news of Yeltsin's 1996 reelection was greeted in all the CIS capitals.

A detailed menu of "imperial" stratagems is offered in "SNG . . ." At the time of publication, rumors in Moscow attributed the authorship to Andranik Migranian, a member of the presidential council and a leading imperial strategist. Following a relentlessly grim analysis of Russia's geopolitical situation, the "report," as the newspaper billed it, urges a "decisive involvement" of Russia in the "state-building" process in the CIS nations, the use of "all economic, military and ethno-demographic means" available to prevent the advent of "anti-Russian and disintegrationist forces" in the leadership. "Only energetic actions (including destabilization of the domestic political situation in the regions where the anti-integrationist forces are especially strong" can thwart the process of "slow but sure" exit of the new states from the Russian sphere of influence.

Thus, regarding the Central Asian states, alongside the deployment of a "hard economic stick," the paper recommends the threat of the removal of the Russian troops from Tajikistan, which would "inevitably" lead to the state's disintegration and, given the "inherent instability" of the region, collapse of Kazakhstan and, eventually, Uzbekistan as well. Russia is advised to use this option as a means of pressure to "effect a gradual reorientation" of the Central Asian states to Russia.

In the Transcaucasus, where Azerbaijan and Georgia allegedly serve as "key links in the anti-Russian axis" and where Russia is threatened with an expulsion with "no possibility of return," the paper calls for a "threat of destabilization" of both states as the only hope of "averting" the "consolidation" of anti-Russian forces in the leadership. The suggested measures include an end to the "blockade" of Abkhazia, "stimulation" of secessionist tendencies in the Georgian region of Adzharia, and the "strengthening of ties" between South and North Ossetia.

Not surprisingly, Ukraine received the most detailed attention. To "exclude the threat of Ukraine's turning into a *place d'armes* of anti-Moscow intrigues," Russia must administer a "hard therapy." A suggested course of action includes, for instance, "severely limiting" the access of Ukrainian workers to the Russian labor market; insisting on the repayment of Ukrainian debt to Russia and switching Russo-Ukrainian trade from barter to cash (which would, in effect, mean the end of such commerce); denying to Ukraine "economic infrastructures of Russia" and the export and import routes through the Russian territory; and, finally, a gradual "economic blockade [of Ukraine] along the US-Cuban lines." Although a "breakup of Ukraine," at which these and other measures aim, might create "problems" for Russia, such an outcome still would be "better than a permanent challenge of [a hostile] Ukraine."

78. For an excellent analysis of the political and economic context of Russian-Belarussian "unification" by its scholarly opponent, see Arkadiy Moshes, "Nesvoevremennoye gosudarstvo" (A badly timed state), *Moskovskie Novosti,* January 19–26, 1996, and "Vozvrashenie na zemlyu" (The return to earth), *Moskovskie Novosti,* March 9–16, 1997. "Modern history offers no examples of forging a stable political organism by two states which were not [first] integrated economically . . ." Moshes writes in the latter piece. "It is absolutely unnecessary to create a unified state in order to export Russian diesel engines [to Belarus] and bring back sour cream."

79. *OMRI Daily Digest,* April 3, 1997.

80. *OMRI Daily Digest,* April 2, 1997. Yeltsin's attempt to satisfy both sides resulted in a watered-down and largely declarative treaty. Charged with an impossible task of reconciling both models of integration, the president's foreign policy advisor, Dmitry Ryurikov, predictably failed and lost his job.

   In less than half a year the relationship between Moscow and Minsk began to deteriorate sharply. First, in September, First Deputy Prime Minister Boris Nemtsov declared that the "unity" between Russia and the premarket and impoverished Belarus is just as impossible as united "economic systems" of North and South Korea or Florida and Cuba. *RFE/RL Newsline,* September 29, 1997. A week later, in retaliation for the jailing of a Russian journalist in Belarus, Boris Yeltsin refused to grant permission for the plane of Belarussian President Alyaksander Lukashenko to enter Russian air space.

81. "SNG . . ." See also Vadim Pechenev, "Rossiyskaya vneshnyaya politika po otnosheniyu k stranam SNG i Baltii" (Russian foreign policy vis-à-vis the CIS and the Baltic states), *Nezavisimaya Gazeta,* November 20, 1996.

82. The many—and enormous—risks inherent in the "politization" of the Russian diaspora must be quite apparent to Moscow's policymakers. There is, to begin, an almost certain migration to Russia of hundreds of thousands, perhaps millions of ethnic Russians forced to leave their host states as a result of the backlash that such a policy inevitably would engender. Once in Russia, impoverished and unemployed, the Russian *pieds-noirs* would likely join the "popular-patriotic" opposition, as their French predecessors who were forced

to flee Algeria did in the 1960s. Second, should the "politization" deteriorate into violence (as it probably would), Russia might face a military rescue operation whose scale would be completely beyond its present capabilities. As Andrei Kozyrev wrote in 1992, Russia "could not send a military helicopter for every Russian-speaking boy or girl in Moldova." (Aron, "Battle for the Soul of Russian Foreign Policy," p. 14.) This dictum remains one of the very few policy-making guidelines from the Kozyrev era surviving (if unheralded) in Russia foreign policy today.

83. Zevelev, "Russia and the Russian Diasporas," p. 265.
84. Ibid., p. 272.
85. The dual citizenship treaties with Russia had been signed only by Turkmenistan and Tajikistan. Kazakhstan, Kyrgyzstan, and Belarus seem forever frozen on the verge of signing.
86. Zhirinovsky's voters approved of this proposition by 44 to 24 percent. Yeltsin's voters disagreed (37 to 27 percent), as did Yavlinsky's (45 to 27 percent), Chernomyrdin's (57 to 13 percent), and Yegor Gaidar's (41 to 30 percent). Even Zyuganov's supporters were split almost evenly: 38 percent for and 34 percent against. Stephen Whitefield and Geoffrey Evans, "Support for Democracy and Political Opposition in Russia, 1993–1995," *Post-Soviet Affairs,* 12, no. 3 (July-September 1996), p. 235 (Table 9).
87. Ibid. Chernomyrdin's supporters were split evenly (34 and 34 percent).
88. Liz Fuller, "Solution to Abkhaz Conflict Continues to Prove Elusive" and "Abkhazia and Georgia Rule Out Violence and Further Concessions," *RFE/RL Newsline,* July 10 and August 18, 1997; and *RFE/RL Newsline,* August 26, 1997.
89. Arkady Dubnov, "Peizazh posle tseremonii" (The landscape after the ceremony), *Novoye Vremia,* no. 26 (1997), p. 16.
90. In September 1997 Russian Deputy Prime Minister Valerii Serov brokered a follow-up meeting between Smirnov and Lucinschi in Chisinau. The two sides agreed to draft an economic treaty between Chisinau and Tiraspol and to continue negotiations at weekly meetings.
91. Prodded by Pastukhov, the sides made "some progress" toward the resolution of the key issues that obstruct the settlement of the conflict: the repatriation of ethnic Georgians who fled Abkhazia during the 1992–93 war and the delineation of areas of responsibility between federal (Tbilisi) and Abkhaz authorities. *RFE/RL Newsline,* September 11, 1997.
92. See Paul Goble, "The Spirit of Vilnius," *RFE/RL Newsline,* September 8, 1997.
93. Articles 2 and 3 of the Treaty of Friendship, Cooperation and Partnership Between the Russian Federation and Ukraine, *RIA/Novosti Daily Review,* June 16, 1997.
94. Part of Russia since 1783 (the year Catherine the Great wrestled it from the Ottoman empire), the peninsula's nominal jurisdiction was

transferred to the Ukrainian Soviet Socialist Republic by Nikita Khrushchev in 1954. Ethnic Russians are 68 percent of the population; ethnic Ukrainians, 26 percent; most of the rest are Crimean Tatars.

95. Celeste A. Wallander, *The Economization, Rationalization, and Normalization of Russian Foreign Policy* (Washington, DC: Aspen Institute, 1997), p. 7. A leading Russian expert's far more dramatic estimate lists the decrease in expenditures between 1990 and 1996 as follows: organization and maintenance, 2.5 to 4 times; procurement and military construction, 9 to 12 times; and research and development, 10 to 11 times. Sergei Rogov, "Military Reform and the Defense Budget of the Russian Federation," Center for Naval Analyses, CIM 527, August 1997.

96. Rogov, "Military Reform and the Defense Budget," p. 39, estimates the 1996 troop level to be as low as 1.7 million.

97. Rybkin, "O kontseptsii . . ."

98. See, for example, Andrei A. Kokoshin, *Reflections on Russia's Past, Present, and Future,* pp. 40, and First Deputy Chief of the General Staff, General Valery Manilov, p. 10.

99. Kokoshin, "The National Security of Russia," p. 40, 41, and Manilov, "The National Security of Russia," p. 17.

100. David Hoffman, "For Yeltsin, Business Prospects Outweighed NATO Threat," *Washington Post,* May 27, 1997.

101. Ibid.

102. With 10 percent of the AIOC shares, LUKoil, along with Azerbaijan State Oil Company, is the fourth largest of the 12 investors behind Amoco, Unocal, and British Petroleum but ahead of, among others, Exxon and Pennzoil. Laurent Ruseckas, "Caspian Oil: Getting Beyond the "Great Game," *ACE* 9, no. 2 (February 1997), p. 5. For details of "pipeline politics," see Chapter 3.

103. See, for example, Robert O. Friedman, "Russian Policy Making and Caspian Sea Oil," *Analysis of Current Events* 9, no. 2 (February 1997), pp. 6–7; and Duygu Bazoglu Sezer, "From Hegemony to Pluralism: The Changing Politics of the Black Sea," *SAIS Review* (Winter-Spring 1997), p. 19.

According to some observers, the Russian invasion of Chechnya had been prompted, in part, by the necessity to "secure the pipeline route once and for all." Ghia Nodia, "Ethnic Conflicts and Oil Politics in the Caucasus," *Analysis of Current Events* 9, no. 2 (February 1997), p. 9. The importance of the transit of the Caspian Sea oil via Chechnya was underscored by the first deputy prime minister personally negotiating with the Chechen head of the Chechen state oil company (YUNKO); in the end, he secured an agreement.

104. Wallander, *The Economization, Rationalization, and Normalization of Russian Foreign Policy,* p. 1 and passim.

105. Nor can we forget that, in addition to nuclear and missile technology, conventional weapons are among the most lucrative Russian exports, projected to bring $5 billion in 1997. Ibid., p. 9.

106. Gennady Zyuganov called the Russia-NATO Founding Act "an act of unconditional surrender," while the chairman of the Duma Security Committee, Communist Viktor Ilyukhin, denounced it as "another example of the betrayal of Russia's interests." *RFE/RL Newsline,* May 30, 1997, and May 16, 1997.
107. *RFE-RL Newsline,* May 5, 1997.
108. Those who believe, rightly, that to any objective observer the potential danger to Russia from NATO's enlargement to the east cannot possibly be compared to that emanating from China's military buildup must remember that the Russians are not objective observers. This would be a case ready-made for the application of the "Thomas Theorem"; the great sociologist Robert Merton liked to remind graduate students at Columbia University if people believe something to be real, it is real in its consequences.
109. *RFE/RL Newsline,* May 27, 1997.
110. Ibid.

CHAPTER TWO

Europe's Crossroads: Russia and the West in the New Borderlands

Sherman W. Garnett

Belarus, Estonia, Latvia, Lithuania, and Ukraine occupy the critical space where an expanding Europe and the post–Soviet Union meet and overlap. Because of this crucial fact of political geography, Russian policy toward these states will define, in large measure, both its policy toward Europe as a whole and how the states of the former Soviet Union, including Russia, fit in. History has given Russia a long-established set of interests in the region, particularly the habit of seeing it as a vital security zone in which it must predominate. Belarus and Ukraine are each in its own way vital to Russia's attempt to fashion a workable integrated community on the territory of the former U.S.S.R. The stakes for Russia in the region are enormously high.

The states of this crucial space, however recent their independence, also bring long-held views of Russia, both as a partner and a threat. The stability of these states and of their relations with Russia and each other is clearly of importance to Europe. They have become an important frontier for an enlarged North Atlantic Treaty Organization (NATO) and an enlarging European Union.[1] These Western institutions will continue to be a magnet for the Baltic states and Ukraine, and thus a potential irritant for Russia in the region. Russian, Western, and local state interests crisscross and overlap this region, creating possibilities for both cooperation and misunderstanding.

This crisscrossing and overlapping of geopolitical zones occurs at a relatively favorable point in history. There are few signs of the return of old-fashioned strategic rivalry, such as defined interstate competition in this region for centuries. No power in the region is so strong as to dominate it. No single state dominates the region the way the Russian or Soviet empires did. Russian power has contracted. For the next decade and beyond, even if it wanted to, Russia cannot restore itself to anything like the strategic posture of the Soviet Union or the Russia from Catherine to Nicholas II. While Russia is the largest and strongest of the regional actors, it no longer simply dominates the scene. Its current troubles have opened up a large breathing space for the states of the region. Even the smallest and weakest of the parties have room to maneuver.

The region has not seen such low levels of usable military power in decades. Indeed, there are hard feelings and deeply held suspicions among all the actors, but nothing approaching the strategic rivalry of the Cold War. In fact, despite the suspicions and accusations, Russia and its neighbors have managed to fashion at least some of the building blocks of long- term bilateral and regional stability. There are good examples of multilateral efforts to find solutions to difficult problems, particularly the negotiations of Russian troop withdrawals from the Baltic states and the removal of nuclear weapons from Belarus and Ukraine.

It would be wrong, however, to conclude that these positive foundations are unshakable. Russia has undertaken important internal reforms and its power is constrained, but many Russians see their country facing prolonged strategic isolation, and they are not happy about it. In addition, no other state or institutional actor in the region can be described as a status quo power. All are to some extent discontented with the way things are. The Baltic states are anxious about Russia's long-term intentions and want full membership in all of Europe's key institutions. The current regime in Belarus, particularly its president, wants integration with Russia and has consistently put itself in opposition to the emerging European order, both by its internal politics and foreign policy. Ukraine wants to change the long-term basis of its relationship with Russia and expand its options for full participation in Europe. NATO's decision to enlarge into Central Europe and its potential enlargement into the former U.S.S.R. itself have irritated Russia and made the countries of this region uncertain as to their basic foreign and security policy. Even if further expansion is delayed, NATO's movement to the edge of the region is part of a larger expansion of Western interests and activities to the edge and on into the former U.S.S.R. Historically, a near-universal discontent with the status quo and lack of consensus about what should replace it has been a source of friction and instability in Europe.

The institutional structures and established rules of the road that define security in Western Europe are weakly developed or untested in this region. Such structures exist, especially the East-West arms control agreements of the past two decades that set limits on Europe's conventional and nuclear forces, establish provisions for transparency, and provide consultative arrangements. Other initiatives of more recent vintage—NATO's Partnership for Peace, Nordic-Baltic security cooperation, the U.S.-Russian-Ukrainian trilateral agreement, and the Commonwealth of Independent States (CIS)—have yet to be tested or lack legitimacy among some or all of the states of the region. The vast reductions in conventional and nuclear forces that have taken place as a result of the collapse of the Warsaw Pact and subsequently the Soviet Union also distinguish the current situation from the past. However, any frictions that emerge in the region will put correspondingly greater stress on the less completely developed security structures of this part of Europe, where institutions like NATO are lacking.

The forces that will determine the shape of the region and of Europe itself are already in motion. They include a constrained Russia, looking simultaneously for a wider role in Europe and a predominant one close to home, the five quite diverse states of the region, and a variety of Western states and institutions. It is the thesis of this chapter that these forces will not be harmonized easily and troubles will emerge but that a shipwreck can be avoided. The important positive trends just discussed ensure that the near future will not see the repetition of the destructive geopolitical rivalry of the past, but wise policy on all sides must nurture these trends and prevent misunderstandings, irritation, and the increasing alienation of Russia, the states of the region, and the West from one another. Only such a policy will ensure that the old rivalries remain dormant.

A CONSTRAINED RUSSIA

The first and most obvious influence on the region is a constrained Russia. The Russian Federation is by far the largest and strongest of the area's states, but it is no longer able to dominate its weaker neighbors. Russia continues to labor under the enormous strain of its internal political and economic transformation. These internal problems severely limit Russian resources and distract the attention of the Russian leadership and general population from foreign policy.

Russia's economy is barely half that of the former U.S.S.R.'s. Privatization has removed vast resources from state control. However imperfect the reforms, the demands of the global economy now exert real influence on Russia's choices. A diverse set of economic interests has arisen within Russia that likewise alters the definition and pursuit of

Russian interests. The other traditional pillar of state power, the military, is on the verge of ruin. "The current situation in the Russian army," stated a February 1997 Council on Defense and Foreign Policy report, "can be described only as an accomplished catastrophe of the armed forces, which will develop into a *national catastrophe* very soon, unless society and the state at long last begins working to prevent this threat in a responsible manner and through concerted efforts."[2] Although in May 1997 Yeltsin brought in a new defense minister and gave him broad support to carry out long-delayed reforms, the effort is immense and still barely under way.

The Russian foreign and security policy apparatus is unreformed, fragmented, and chaotic. President Boris Yeltsin's reemergence from months of convalescence in January 1997 restored needed momentum and direction to Russian foreign policy, but the problems of making and implementing that policy run deeper than the health and vigor of the president. In fact, the very indispensability of Yeltsin in reaching an accommodation over NATO enlargement and expanding Russia's relationship with NATO reveals basic institutional weaknesses. Without Yeltsin there would have been no NATO-Russian Founding Act.[3]

Beyond Yeltsin's health and staying power, the major problems remain institutional, particularly the weakness of state structures devoted to foreign and security policy. Ministries and departments are poorly coordinated when it comes to the real review and implementation of decisions, although the national security council and other coordinating mechanisms exist. Since January 1996 Russia has replaced its foreign minister once and defense minister and national security advisor twice. It has formed two separate policy coordinating mechanisms, issued new regulations for the National Security Council, and created a Defense Policy Council. These actions have been much more a confirmation of continued chaos at the top than its remedy. As Yeltsin complained, "fecklessness and indifference, lack of responsibility and incompetence in deciding state problems" remain the hallmarks of state power.[4] This system, particularly its mechanism for making and implementing foreign policy, is chaotic and fragmented beyond the frictions and differences of interest and opinion that characterize a normal state. This problem is not a permanent one, but it profoundly affects Russia's ability to pursue a consistent policy now and in the near future. It particularly affects the ability of the Russian bureaucracy to follow through on policy initiatives and international agreements made by Yeltsin and the senior Russian leadership.

There are other political changes at work of a more positive character, although they also present a near-term challenge to a decrepit national security system. The number of interests and actors involved in the making and implementing of Russian foreign policy is growing. These include new business, regional, and financial interests that are oriented on economic, not security, issues. These powerful economic interests are making their presence felt on issues of great importance to them, particularly regional trade, investment, and infrastructure questions. Their desire to do business and do it efficiently could become an important force for moderating the dominant geopolitical and historical approaches to foreign and security policy. However, currently these groups exercise this influence through their powerful informal positions in Russian politics, not through an organized policy process. Absent a settled state structure, they are just as likely to distort Russian policy for their individual interests as to moderate it. In the Western borderlands, the most important of these new interest groups probably are energy, industrial banking, and export groups—so-called financial industrial groups—that have sought to control key aspects of the energy, industrial, and trade infrastructure there.

While the making of Russian foreign policy has become more chaotic and fragmented, the views of the foreign policy community itself have become more uniform and assertive. This community is not yet an accurate reflection of the new interests and actors described earlier. It still dominates the foreign policy bureaucracy in the government and the analytical community outside, and it is united by a consensus or near consensus of views on key international questions.[5] This set of views includes everything from united positions on large questions, such as opposition to NATO enlargement or support for Russian-led integration on the territory of the former U.S.S.R., to common positions on many lesser issues. Its formation is in itself a phenomenon that deserves closer study, for it has no parallel in the West and may be a response of a community under stress to the institutional and material weakness of the Russian state itself.

Although Russian foreign policy in practice has been less consistent and coherent than the rhetoric would suggest, the prevailing views remain an important guide to the perceptions of Russia's leaders and key analysts as they approach the problems of the Western borderlands and fashion policies to respond to them. It is also important as an influence for understanding the overlapping and conflicting interests in the region in geopolitical terms.

This consensus is more suspicious of the West than was common in the sentiments of the Russian foreign policy community in 1991–92. It is self-consciously focused on Russian national interests. It opposes NATO enlargement in any form, while recognizing that Russia cannot stop the first wave of new members. Indeed, NATO enlargement is said by some to be the cause of this consensus in the first place, although key elements of it long predate any serious discussion in the West of NATO enlargement. It finds unacceptable "a unipolar world under the leadership of the US" and sees signs of such a world all around Russia. Russia must therefore be "a great power now"[6] and a pillar of a multipolar international system. Expanding ties to China and Iran are seen within this ideological perspective. But the consensus sees the key to the restoration of Russia's status beginning with reasserting its preeminence on the territory of the former Soviet Union, particularly by promoting an integrated community there. But for all the attention such discussions of foreign policy receive both in Russia and abroad, it does not receive—indeed, does not even address—some dilemmas posed by the states of the Western borderlands and the trends shaping them.

At the core, the consensus is hollow. It puts the blame for current failures on outside actors, not on internal conditions. It encourages Russia to see itself as a humiliated and injured party, not a power in transition. It hides from Russia the changing realities around it that must be addressed, not wished away. And it puts Russian foreign policy on a collision course with the Western-oriented logic of its own economic and political reforms. The monotony of views on external challenges obscures the link between means and ends in foreign policy. Russia's limited capabilities are said not to be a bar to an active world role, because Russian policy is being carried out "by no means on the basis of current circumstances but on the basis of [Russia's] colossal potential."[7] Yet a policy conducted on the basis of potential or hopes for understanding from foreign powers is really no policy at all.

This consensus also hides the diversity of opinion that exists in Russia and is likely to grow in the years ahead. It does real harm to Russia in the outside world, regularly providing nervous neighbors and skeptical Western analysts with proof that Russian foreign policy is unreformed. At a time when the major problems Russia poses to the international system arise from Moscow's incapacity and weakness, a determined group of Russian commentators speak of nothing but the nation-state's ambitions and strength. Whatever happens in the long term, the near-term ambitions that characterize the Russian foreign policy consensus are in profound contradiction with existing capabilities. This fact cannot but help to aggravate frustration, when Russian interests cannot be defended or when its opinions are ignored.

Russia has made enormous strides since 1991. It no longer poses an ideological or military challenge to the West. In part, it is simply too weak and/or chaotic to do so. However, forces of change within the country and political, economic, and social forces outside it are changing the nation-state itself and its relations with the outside world. These forces are by no means irresistible. They take time. The Russia described earlier cannot be a serious strategic rival of the United States or the West in the near future; however, its fragile condition and scattered foreign policy priorities preclude it from being a steady partner. There will continue to be issues on which Russia is unreliable or unable to make a serious contribution. There will continue to be times when the government simply does not follow through on agreements or when individual ministries pursue policies at odds with those agreements. Russia for the next decade and probably beyond thus will be an awkward fit in the new Europe.

THE SHAPE OF THE BORDERLANDS

Russia has no single, consistent set of policies toward the western borderlands, although senior Russian political figures and leading analysts regularly describe a fairly consistent set of interests at stake in these states, singly or as a region. These lands traditionally have fallen securely within Russia's sphere of influence. Until 1991 they were, for most of the past 200 years and in some cases longer, part of the Russian empire and Soviet Union.[8] Thus Russia sees these states not only as part of a zone of vital interest but as areas still deeply interconnected to it by history, culture, and ethnic ties.

Russia sees these states as part of its extended security zone. Moscow's reluctant acquiescence to NATO enlargement in May 1997 came with a renewed statement of its opposition to NATO membership for the Baltic states and any other state of the former U.S.S.R. Ukraine's increasing tilt toward the West, especially its growing strategic partnership with the United States, also has caused Moscow increasing anxiety, evinced by Russia's recent steps toward normalization of its relations with Ukraine. So are the less successful efforts to transform a strong Russian-Belarusian relationship into a fully integrated community. Ukraine and Belarus, each in different ways, is crucial to the success of Russia's hopes to lead an integrated economic, political, and security community on the territory of the former U.S.S.R. Such a community without Ukraine in particular would be widely seen in Russia as a failure.

Russia has more than security interests in the region. It is interested in securing the economic advantages of preeminence as well as ensuring access to—and influence over—the vital sea and land transportation links that run through this area. The key pipeline linking Russian gas supplies with the European market runs through Ukraine, with an additional line through Belarus still on the drawing board. Substantial numbers of ethnic Russians live in each of these countries, except Lithuania. These ethnic Russians and "Russian-speaking" minorities have been the subject of intense Russian diplomatic agitation and exaggerated claims over the past several years.[9] The fate of these people often has seemed the sole issue in Russian-Estonian and Russian-Latvian relations. A more general concern for Russian foreign policy, in this region and throughout the former U.S.S.R., is maintaining the leading status of Russian culture and language.

But what is most striking about the region itself is that, for the first time in centuries, the balance between the states of Central and Eastern Europe and outside powers has shifted in favor of the former. The states of the region have or are acquiring the capacity to shape their own destinies. Broad forces are reshaping the key outside influences that once dominated the region. German power has been transformed—linked to strong European and transatlantic institutions. Russia's transformation is less advanced, but still impressive in comparison with the historical role of Moscow in the region. Although both Russian and Western influences will continue to matter, they are no longer supreme. The states of the region still need to be connected to the world economy, but they have the power to shape internal politics and economics in a way that makes them more or less receptive to outside forces.

The five states of the region are by no means similar. They range in size from Estonia (17,413 square miles) to Ukraine (233,089 square miles). Ukraine has a population of 52.1 million. Belarus is the second most populous, with 10.4 million, while Lithuania, Latvia, and Estonia have 3.8, 2.7, and 1.6 million respectively. These states have substantial ethnic Russian minority populations, running above 30 percent in Estonia and Latvia, 22 percent in Ukraine, 13.2 percent in Belarus, and only 8.6 percent in Lithuania.[10] Two of the group—Belarus and Ukraine—are Slavic states, while the three Baltic states each possesses a unique language and culture. The three Baltic states had an interwar period of independence that was important to preserving a strong sense of distinctiveness within the Soviet Union and fueled the powerful independence movements in these states during the Gorbachev period. Belarus and Ukraine had no substantial experience of independence, although Ukraine did establish a series of regimes that sought and failed to gain independence between 1917 and 1922.

The period since independence has further differentiated these states. The three Baltic countries have advanced impressively toward strong parliamentary democracy. Even a period of left-wing rule under its reformed Communist Party did not turn back the clock on political freedom and economic modernization in Lithuania, as some commentators first feared.

Its Baltic neighbors, although they had substantial political tumult of their own, remained governed by center-right parties throughout the period. By contrast, in Ukraine political reform has progressed slowly. It has managed to fashion a new constitution, although political power remains in a small number of hands. Civil society is still weak—people are generally apathetic politically, and a culture of dynamic nongovernmental institutions has not taken root. Ukraine is threatened less by an oppressive state than by a corrupt and inefficient one. Belarus got off to a very slow start, only reluctantly accepting the reality of its independence. Since his election in 1994, Belarusian President Alexander Lukashenko has, in fact, led his country backward to an authoritarian presidential system that is antithetical not only to European political culture but to an increasingly pluralistic Russia.

A similar differentiation has taken place in economics. Estonia has gone the farthest in economic reform, embracing serious market reforms that have produced real economic growth since 1994. The government in Tallinn has adopted what the World Bank calls "one of the most liberal external trade regimes in the world."[11] All three Baltic states have concluded associate agreements with the European Union, although only Estonia chose to forgo a transitional period of adjustment to EU rules of trade and market access. In August 1997 the European Commission recommended that the full Union begin accession negotiations with Estonia (and four other states of Central Europe), a move that places Estonia on a faster track to full membership than even its Baltic neighbors. Ukraine made no substantial steps toward economic reform until October 1994, experiencing hyperinflation in 1993. The administration of President Leonid Kuchma made substantial progress in the deregulation of prices and financial stabilization, but privatization has been slow and riddled with corruption. The reforms themselves have been plagued by substantial internal opposition, divisions within the Ukrainian government, and the lack of a stable legal foundation for investment. Belarus has made no substantial efforts at economic reform at all.

In foreign affairs, the Baltic states have made membership in the European Union and NATO their foreign policy priorities. Their progress in political and economic reform distinguishes them from the other countries of the former U.S.S.R. and makes them more akin to Poland and other countries of Central Europe. Ukraine announced in April 1996 that it too seeks membership in the European Union. A NATO-Ukrainian Charter was agreed at the 1997 Madrid summit, establishing a special relationship between Ukraine and the alliance. Senior Ukrainian officials regularly hint at the eventual requirement to rethink their policy of neutrality. Some of these officials speak openly of wanting eventual membership in NATO as well, though President Kuchma has kept official Ukrainian policy focused on deepening security ties with the United States, NATO, and other Western countries without seeking alliance membership. The country at large and the Ukrainian political class are still deeply divided along regional and ethnic lines, which manifest themselves in different security orientations. Overcoming these divisions will be a long-term task, demanding skill and patience from the government. Within the Commonwealth of Independent States, Ukraine is a leading force for its redefinition, on terms that stress the sovereignty of all members over Russia's leading role. Even Belarus, in all other respects a conservative power, agitates for fundamental change in the region by seeking to create a working model of integration between the two states, the first of its kind in the CIS.

Each state in this region presents Russian foreign policy with a unique test: Belarus challenges the viability of an integrated community on the territory of the former U.S.S.R.; all three of the Baltic states challenge the traditional Russian sphere of influence by their embrace of Europe; Ukraine is perhaps the most serious challenge of all, representing the breaking apart of the Russian-led Slavic heartland.

BELARUS: A FRIEND IN NEED?

Belarus seems at first glance less a testing ground for the new Europe than uncontested ground. Belarus has presented itself as a willing partner in creating a renewed and Russian-led community on the territory of the former U.S.S.R. For many observers, Russian-Belarusian integration, perhaps even the loss of Belarusian statehood, has seemed likely. Yet as events have shown, even here Russia confronts its own limitations and disparate forces that resist attempts to unite the two states.

The attempts to create an integrated community of the two states began 1992 and accelerated after the election of Alexander Lukashenko as president in 1994. He ran on a platform that strongly advocated union with Russia, anticorruption policies, and economic recovery. Since that time he has turned Belarus into a dictatorial regime and uses his power to extract the most he can from Russia. The two sides have negotiated numerous agreements covering most aspects of political, economic, and military integration. In pursuit of economic integration, Belarus and Russia agreed to a "new kind of ruble zone" in September 1993, followed shortly thereafter by an agreement on monetary union. In May 1995 a Russian-Belarusian Customs Union was announced. The conclusion of the two spring 1996 integration agreements—a bilateral Russian-Belarusian agreement and one uniting these two countries with Kazakhstan and Kyrgyzstan—was loudly trumpeted as a sign of integration's progress and Russia's renewed leadership in the process.

In the military and security sphere, Russian-Belarusian military cooperation began with a series of agreements in July 1992 that settled basic questions on the status of strategic nuclear forces and support for the forces that remained in Belarus. In 1993 Belarus modified its policy of neutrality and joined a collective security pact, the so-called Tashkent Treaty, which includes Russia and a subset of the CIS states.[12] However, Belarus also submitted formal reservations that stated its policy of keeping its forces out of peacekeeping and other military deployments outside Belarus. A March 1994 agreement granted Russia long-term access to Belarusian military infrastructure and established joint border protection.[13] Technical agreements followed soon thereafter, permitting long-term Russian leasing of a naval communications site and an early-warning radar.[14] Belarus signed the CIS treaty on border protection between CIS and non-CIS states in July 1995.[15] In December 1995 Russia and Belarus agreed on further military cooperation, particularly measures to strengthen ties between the military-industrial enterprises of the two states, to expand joint use of Belarusian military infrastructure, particularly in air defense, and to coordinate regional planning efforts.

Most of these agreements remain on paper or have been implemented only partially. There is no currency union. The relaxing of the customs regime—a far cry from a true customs union—has made Belarus an attractive conduit for imports from Ukraine and other countries that otherwise would be subject to Russian tariffs, thus costing Russia millions in duties and other revenues. Russia has made some inroads in influencing personnel policy within the Belarusian Ministry of Defense. The current minister and other senior advisors are rumored to hold their positions at the behest of Russia. The two sides also hold regular talks on defense planning and air defense. They established joint air defense cooperation in January and held a joint air force exercise in April 1997. Russian air defense and reconnaissance units are likely to be stationed in Belarus in late 1997 or early 1998.[16] However, even as military ties have deepened between the two states, Belarus has insisted on adhering to its constitutional prohibition of deploying its soldiers outside its borders. In accordance with international agreements, Russia pulled out its nuclear forces and supporting infrastructure from Belarus, with the last warhead leaving in late 1996 and the last troops in mid-1997.[17] Russia's foreign minister also has pledged that, in the current security environment, Russia will not redeploy nuclear weapons in Belarus, thus responding to a similar NATO pledge not to deploy nuclear weapons on the territory of new member states.[18]

The real limits of Russian-Belarusian integration have been revealed in the most recent efforts in the first half of 1997 to forge a serious bilateral union. In one of his first foreign policy moves after emerging from his long convalescence after heart surgery, Boris Yeltsin wrote a letter to Belarusian President Aleksandr Lukashenko proposing a series of measures designed to restore momentum to the process of Russian-Belarusian integration. In particular, Yeltsin proposed a referendum to win public approval for the broad synchronization of both countries' economic, political, and security policies, which already had been agreed on between the two states. Lukashenko warmly supported Yeltsin's initiative, and the two sides worked to produce, by the end of a March summit, a draft treaty that would create a formal union of the two states. Although explicitly preserving the state sovereignty of both parties, the draft treaty envisioned dual national and union citizenship and the establishment of a High Council.

The High Council, made up of the presidents, prime ministers, and leaders of the parliaments of both countries, would exercise basic control over the coordination of budgetary, monetary, tax, foreign trade, and security policies. The chair of this council would serve for two years and rotate between the presidents of the two states.[19] Foreign Minister Primakov, military leaders and other foreign policy advisors to Yeltsin and communist and nationalist deputies in the Duma strongly supported the treaty. A memorandum to the president, leaked to *Nezavisimaya gazeta*, strongly supported the draft treaty, claiming that forward movement on Russian-Belarusian integration would rouse the Russian people in ways that would help sustain internal political and economic reform and rob the opposition of its most important initiative.[20]

On the eve of its signing, the treaty was substantially gutted, eliminating the High Council and all of the most ambitious provisions. An agreed memorandum between the two sides outlined ways of "discovering and heeding public opinion" and "streamlining the contents of the Russian-Belarus Charter."[21] The radical changes in the treaty came about in large measure due to the intervention of Anatoliy Chubais and other senior reform-oriented officials in the economics and finance ministries, who argued that integration with a politically backward and economically depressed Belarus would entail huge costs for Russia. More significantly, according to a Russian participant in the negotiations and a supporter of the agreement, the opponents attacked the equal treatment accorded the two states. Russia, as the largest of the two, the wealthiest and most powerful, deserved a special status.[22] At the signing ceremony for the truncated agreement, Lukashenko complained that "preparations for the document unfortunately did not take place without bitter opposition."[23]

This opposition is not the only cause of the failure to secure the real and effective integration of the two states. In the first place, the two states are badly out of sync economically and politically. Belarus has done little to promote economic reform. Economic integration would impose an enormous burden on Russia to provide subsidies and the social safety net for Belarusian economic transformation. Indeed, much of Lukashenko's political base—and Lukashenko himself—looks for assistance from Moscow. This aspect of integration has become so controversial in Russia, particularly among those charged with managing the economy, that Lukashenko felt compelled to deny that Belarus would be an economic burden before the Russian Duma in November 1996. He dismissed "the prejudice that Belarus is allegedly sponging on Russia and wants to live at Russia's expense,"[24] and went on to remind his audience of Belarus's role in the Soviet Union as a source of high technology. However, he has also regularly admitted, as he did in a March 1997 interview, that the new union should not only sustain "good and close relations with fraternal Russia . . . [but] extricate the economy from crisis."[25]

But the period since the Russian presidential election in 1996 also has revealed deep political incompatibilities. Whatever the problems with Russian democracy—and they are many—Belarusian internal politics are out of step with Russia's. Lukashenko has moved steadily in the direction of authoritarianism. In 1996 he engineered a wholesale change of the constitution, increasing the powers of the president and stacking the legislature with his personal supporters. He has responded to street demonstrations and other signs of opposition with arrests and other repressive measures. In such an environment, Russia's relatively pluralistic political system and open media represent a subversive force in Belarus, and the regime has regularly complained of biased Russian television coverage. Russian journalists have been arrested in Belarus. The much-publicized intervention of Prime Minister Viktor Chernomyrdin into the dispute between Lukashenko and the parliament in November 1996 ended with the Belarusian president ignoring the deal that had been brokered. Lukashenko wants Russian support for himself, not adjudication of political squabbles between him and his opponents.

The latest attempt to foster interdependence also brought Belarusian leadership face to face with the reality of what they have to lose in a one-on-one arrangement with a more powerful state. For Minsk, sovereignty has made many who were or would have been relatively minor local officials in the former U.S.S.R. rich and powerful in their new state. The various groups within Belarus that control key state industries, import and export quotas, access to foreign exchange, or other important assets hardly wish for real and sustained competition from much more powerful Russian financial-industrial groups. Lukashenko himself may look to Russia as an expanded field for his political ambitions. He has reveled in the support he has received from the nationalist and communist opposition in Russia and his high name recognition in Russian polls. His colleagues and subordinates, however, are unlikely to view their own futures quite so expansively.

More than likely they are justified in their apprehension. The Russian opponents of the 1997 draft treaty attacked the equal treatment of Russia and Belarus openly; but Russian supporters are, for the most part, not overly concerned with the rights of small states. Once a deal is consummated, there are a thousand ways for the larger state to constrain the smaller. Some of the most ardent supporters of Russian-Belarusian integration mock the independence of the new states openly, and few in Moscow actually have any idea of what Belarus might want or need from such an arrangement. The supporters have from the first focused almost exclusively on Russia's geopolitical interests in securing its ties with Belarus, not on the costs. They argue that successful Russian-Belarusian integration would add momentum to a flagging Commonwealth of Independent States and provide a platform and a buffer against an expanding West. Yet there are few signs that Belarus is preparing to follow the example of Ukraine or the Baltic states. It would appear that close Russian-Belarusian ties could be maintained for a much smaller price than union or near union. In the next few years, the gap between the intended policy of integration of the two states and the reality of continued separation likely will widen.

THE BALTICS TURN WEST

Russia's relations with the Baltic states should not be judged by the harshness of the rhetoric or the tough negotiations that have characterized attempts to resolve bilateral disputes. Deep disagreements over the status of the large Russian minority in Latvia and Estonia and the desire of all three Baltic states to join NATO will continue to bedevil Russian-Baltic relations, but the foundation for these relations is stronger than many in Russia, the West, and the Baltics themselves realize. Russian-Lithuanian relations have been relatively stable for some time. Primakov even has referred to the citizenship issue in Latvia as "an unresolved dispute" in a pattern of "more or less normal, even good, relations."[26] The most serious problems are between Russia and Estonia. Ties between the two states have strained patience and public opinion on both sides. Estonia, in fact, topped the list in a 1996 Moscow survey of Russia's main enemies, with an Estonian official responding when asked to comment on the news that such a distinction was "a very great honor" for so small a country.[27] Yet in Russia's relations with the Baltic states, even in Russian-Estonian relations, there are factors at work that keep disagreements within acceptable bounds.

The first and most obvious is the size and vulnerability of the Baltic states. Without a serious ally, they pose no credible security threat to Russia. Even a constrained Russia has overwhelming and permanent advantages over these states in wealth and power. The vulnerability of these small states to their larger neighbor also introduces an important element of real long-term friction in the relationship, most notably over Baltic membership in NATO.

A second stabilizing factor is that Russia sees the Baltic states as a special case outside its integrationist framework for the rest of the former U.S.S.R. This status already emerged in the late Soviet period, as Boris Yeltsin sought issues on which he could differentiate himself from Gorbachev. In January 1991 Yeltsin and other leading Russian reformers denounced the Soviet crackdown in the Baltic states. At this same time, the Russian Foreign Ministry transferred responsibility for the Baltic states to its Northern European Department and concluded Treaties of Friendship with all three states. After the August coup, Russia recognized the independence of the Baltic states. Although this early honeymoon quickly deteriorated, the special status for the Baltic states in Russian foreign policy remains. They are a special case, separate from the CIS and other states of the former U.S.S.R.

A third factor is the demilitarization of Russian-Baltic relations. Negotiations, supported by the United States and by Nordic and other Western powers, brought about Russian troop withdrawals from all three Baltic states. Other key security questions are regulated by international agreement. Although Russian commentators—particularly those with links to the military—frequently have threatened the Baltic states in the event of their entrance into NATO, the facts on the ground speak for themselves: Save for the ballistic missile warning radar at Skrunda in Latvia, all Russian forces are out of the Baltics. Russia retains enormous military advantages in the relationship, of course, but its forces are no longer present as a potential actor inside the Baltic states or a potential target of local anger. The continued presence of a small number of Russian military and civilian personnel at Skrunda is subject to the terms of an international treaty. The pensions and other privileges of military personnel who retired in the Baltic region also have been guaranteed by agreements. The negotiations to obtain these agreements were acrimonious, punctuated by regular threats from Russian senior officials, including Yeltsin, to suspend talks and ongoing troop withdrawals or to link the issue to the problems of Russians in Estonia and Latvia. However, the results are unique in the former Soviet Union. No state in the CIS can claim to have its military relationship with Russia so regulated.[28]

Demilitarization of the relationship is an enormous advantage to both the Baltic states and Russia. For the Baltic states, the current demilitarization raises the costs to Russia, should it contemplate the threat or use of force. It is the Russians who will have to upset the existing status quo, in the face of local and international opposition. Moreover, the logistical and operational problems are compounded by having to reintroduce forces or conduct threatening field exercises in nearby Russian or perhaps Belarusian territory. For Russia, its forces are no longer at the center of potential conflict and controversy. Military power in neighboring Russian regions still influences the relationship, but Russian forces are no longer directly present. The removal of Russian stationed forces ensures that the serious and divisive issues that remain on the bilateral agenda can be settled politically. Military and security questions also have been the quickest to unite the three Baltic states and to attract the attention of the outside world. On other issues, the three Baltic states differ markedly from one another. They are economic competitors and have their own border questions to resolve. A smart Russian strategy would be to try to avoid highlighting the very issues that drive the Baltic states together and into the arms of the West.

A final stabilizing factor is growing Russian-Baltic trade relations. Both sides enjoy tangible benefit from trade. Although a substantial reorientation of trade has occurred away from the former Russia and the rest of the former U.S.S.R., from 1993 to 1995 Russian-Estonian trade has grown steadily, despite the deterioration of political relations. In 1995 Russia was Estonia's second largest export market, exceeded only by Finland. Russia is Lithuania's largest trading partner.[29] The Baltic states are reliable customers, paying cash and carrying very little debt. Russia supplies them with nearly all of their energy (93 percent), nonferrous metals (90 percent), and raw materials for the chemical industry (80 percent).[30] Russia depends heavily on Estonian and Latvian ports for much of its trade with Europe, while "at least a tenth of Estonia's economy depends on Russian transit trade."[31] Russia represents an important present and future market for Baltic agriculture, particularly given the barriers erected by the European Union to protect its own farmers.

Yet despite these stabilizing influences and quite real benefits for both sides in placing relations on a pragmatic and cooperative basis, serious irritants remain. A February 1997 Russian presidential statement on Baltic policy illustrates the continued problems, particularly the combination of past ill-will and concern over unresolved problems. The most serious of these are regional security arrangements, especially NATO enlargement, the unresolved border disputes between Russia and Estonia and Latvia, and the treatment of ethnic Russians and Russian speakers in these same two countries. The statement also complained of a "lack of balance" in trade relations, focusing especially on the problems of Baltic reexport of Russian commodities, primarily energy and nonferrous metals, and "criminal threats to Russia from Baltic territories."[32] However, as one Russian commentator noted, "the bulk of the economic problems Russia encounters in the Baltics have Russian roots"; he dismissed criminal threats from the Baltics as "equaled by corresponding threats that arise from Russian territory."[33]

The question of borders is moving toward a resolution. A Russian-Lithuanian border agreement was signed on October 24, 1997. Russian-Estonian and Russian-Latvian negotiators are on the verge of settling what have been more difficult issues. The September 1997 Vilnius meeting of presidents and prime ministers from the countries of the Baltic and Black Sea region produced side discussions that led all three parties, Russian, Estonian, and Latvian, to suggest that border agreements might be forthcoming soon.[34] The origins of the dispute are not serious Estonian and Latvian territorial pretensions, but rather are based on their desire to settle the historic balance sheet by getting Russia to recognize treaties that antedate the forcible incorporation of the Baltic states into the U.S.S.R. These two treaties reached between Russia and Estonia and Latvia—the 1920 Treaties of Tartu and Riga—contain Soviet recognition of the boundaries of the two states and set the legal basis for bilateral relations. Under these treaties, Russia recognized as Estonian about 2,300 square kilometers of land that is now part of Pskov and Leningrad oblasts and as Latvian around 1,600 square kilometers of land now in Pskov oblast. Russian territorial integrity was never threatened by Baltic irredentism, but the two republics' stubborn insistence on restoring a long-past status quo ante did seem to set up Baltic claims on Russian territory and seriously strained relations with Russia. Both insisted that broader talks must be based on these treaties, leading Yeltsin to declare a unilateral demarcation of the Russian border with Estonia in June 1994.

While one can sympathize with the desire of the Baltic states to seek to restore the status quo ante, there can be little sympathy for attempts to question the legitimacy of existing borders in the former U.S.S.R. Quite a number of historical injustices underlie these and indeed most of the post-Soviet borders, but attempts to set them right can bring only serious tension and even conflict, not just in the Baltic region but elsewhere in the former U.S.S.R. Estonia's and Latvia's desire to restore the validity of these treaties has another practical purpose: to sustain the legitimacy of their approach to citizenship, which is based on extending automatic citizenship only to the citizens of the interwar republics and their descendants. In late 1995 Estonia dropped its territorial claims, insisting only on the validity of the Treaty of Tartu in other matters. In November 1996 it abandoned even this insistence. In the wake of Estonian concessions, Latvia also agreed to similar concessions. Now that the two Baltic states have dropped their territorial claims, the obstacle to a final settlement may well be Russia's reluctance to let the territorial issue be resolved and thereby eliminate a potential obstacle to the two states' entrance into NATO.

The status of ethnic Russians is a more difficult issue to resolve. Russia has no complaint against Lithuania, which provided passports to all residents in 1991. Estonia and Latvia pursued a different approach, reflecting greater anxiety about the effect of a large Russian minority on the restoration not only of political, but of national and cultural, independence. Both adopted provisional measures, followed by citizenship laws, that restricted automatic citizenship to citizens of the interwar Estonian and Latvian republics and their descendants. The ethnic Russians, comprising more than half of Latvia's population and almost a third of Estonia's, were effectively placed outside the political process of the two states, although Estonia subsequently gave resident aliens the right to vote in local elections only. The process of naturalization for noncitizens included waiting periods, language competency tests, and loyalty oaths. The Estonian legislation—a citizenship law passed in 1992 and a law on resident foreigners passed in July 1993—placed resident aliens under significant disadvantages, particularly in the area of property rights at a time of Estonia's comprehensive market reforms.

Senior Russian officials, nearly the whole of the Russian foreign policy community, and even, at times, a significant segment of Russian public opinion have seen Estonian and Latvian legislation and administrative practices as systematic human rights abuses. Some Russians have accused Estonia in particular of fostering an "apartheid" system. Foreign Minister Primakov accused Estonia of "discriminatory practices" in August 1996 although the rhetoric has been substantially cooler since.[35] Despite

Russian appeals, key international organizations, including the United Nations, the Organization for Cooperation and Security in Europe (OSCE), and the Council of Europe, have found no pattern of discrimination. In particular, the Council of Europe reviewed both Estonia's and Latvia's citizenship laws during their admission process and found them consistent with European standards. Although Russia has been stymied in its attempt to get international support for its view that Estonian and Latvian practices violate human rights standards, it has continued to press both countries for citizenship and other ameliorative measures for the ethnic Russian population.

There is, however, little prospect for moving beyond the current standoff anytime soon. Estonia and Latvia seek to further their own internal consolidation. They believe five years has been far too little time to reverse the demographic, political, and cultural consequences of incorporation into the U.S.S.R. Yet the Russian populations themselves must be dealt with in ways that eventually will extend beyond the current citizenship rules, if only to avoid ethnic Russians becoming a serious internal opposition to state policies or even to the state itself. Although international organizations have stated that existing citizenship legislation passes muster, they also have noted, in the words of a 1992 U.N. report, "the fear of marginalization" in the Russian population. The improved economic climate in Latvia and especially Estonia has reconciled many ethnic Russians to the current regimes. However, not all ethnic Russians are happy with their status. A July 1993 referendum on autonomy sponsored by local officials in Narva, a city in Estonia with a large concentration of ethnic Russians, garnered 97 percent approval (on the basis of a 54 percent voter turnout). More serious for Estonian authorities, the trickle of Russian residents who sought Russian citizenship has grown to a steady stream, over 10,000 a month in 1996. "If we continue at this rate," stated one official, "we will end up with 300,000 or 400,000 Russian citizens" in Estonia, out of a population of 1.5 million.[36] These fears are almost certainly exaggerated, but the atmosphere of suspicion and tension that exists on both sides often overwhelms appreciation for both the complexity of the problem and what in fact has been accomplished thus far.[37] It also distracts both sides from the steps necessary to create a long-term stable solution, namely full integration of all of the ethnic Russian population that desires it into the political, social, and economic life of Latvia and Estonia.

The most difficult issue to resolve pits all three of the Baltic states against Russia on the question of NATO membership. All three have made plain their desire to join the Atlantic Alliance. The communiqué from the NATO summit in Madrid in fact takes note of "the progress achieved towards greater stability and cooperation by the states in the Baltic region which are also aspiring members," language widely interpreted in Russia and not only in Russia as signaling NATO's long-term intentions to satisfy Baltic aspirations.[38] Regardless of what the words mean, the question of NATO will be at the center of current and all future regional security efforts. Russia has consistently and categorically opposed NATO membership for the Baltic states. On the eve of agreement on the NATO-Russian Founding Act, Yeltsin warned that Russia would have to "revise" its approach to NATO if the alliance "starts admitting" states of the former U.S.S.R., such as the Baltic states.[39] Russian analysts, particularly those with ties to the military, have been more blunt: "If a genuine attempt is made to make [the] Baltic states members of NATO, we will move our troops into [these] states. . . ."[40] Prime Minister Chernomyrdin, at a September 1997 summit of Central and East European leaders in Vilnius, offered the Baltic states a package of security guarantees and confidence-building measures, but only if they stay outside NATO. The package he proposed includes enhanced communication and transparency measures for large-scale exercises and military activities in Kaliningrad.[41] In the past, Yeltsin has offered joint Russian-Western security guarantees as an alternative to NATO membership.

The conflict over NATO complicates the search for interim measures that would help to secure the current low levels of military confrontation. The Baltic states do not want to pursue measures that might look to the Western powers like an acceptable alternative to NATO. Russia does not want to pursue these measures if they will inevitably give way to NATO enlargement anyway. Moreover, a Russian strategy to withhold meaningful security cooperation with the Baltics or to link any further steps forward to a renunciation of Baltic interest in NATO membership only increases the conviction of those states of their inability to manage normal relations with Moscow outside of a secure base within the core Western economic and security institutions. The prominence of the NATO issue also creates a disincentive for Russian understanding of—and participation in—Western-Baltic security cooperation in joint exercises, enhanced Partnership for Peace programs, and U.S.-Baltic cooperation that should not exclude or be aimed against Russia.

Yet there are important security issues that could and should be addressed now. Russia and the Baltic states have other options for further demilitarizing Russian-Baltic relations and defusing Baltic security concerns. These options include steps to reduce military forces in Kaliningrad, Pskov, or Leningrad oblasts, expand on existing OSCE confidence-building and transparency measures, and place constraints upon military activities in the region. The Baltic states, which are currently outside the Treaty on Conventional Forces in Europe (CFE), must decide whether to take part in its further adaptation.

In addition, two outstanding military issues remain. The first is Russian presence at Skrunda, an early warning radar, which is regulated by an agreement that runs until the end of August 1998. However, this facility—deemed critical not only by Russia but by U.S. and other Western countries for its role in strategic stability—was to have been replaced by a new early-warning radar complex in Belarus. It appears doubtful that the Belarus facility will be ready before the August 1998 deadline to shut down the Skrunda facility. Russia thus may be tempted to try to extend its stay at the Latvian site, although it has not yet officially indicated its interest in so doing. If this should become Russia's official position, it will be loudly supported by a Russian foreign policy community seeking to demonstrate its resolve in the face of NATO enlargement. The second issue is military transit through Lithuanian ground and air space between the Russian mainland and Kaliningrad. Lithuania refused to complete a formal agreement on military transit in 1993, preferring temporary arrangements. This issue also remains to be negotiated. It too is a good candidate to be at the center of Russia's concrete response to present or future NATO enlargement.

The question of NATO enlargement will continue to be an irritant and potential wild card in Russian-Baltic relations.[42] The current creative ambiguity in the West's open-door policy fuels Russia's suspicions, without giving concrete assurances to the Baltic states. This irritant is likely to create problems at every important juncture, making Russia reluctant to participate in the full range of regional security arrangements now or likely to be available. The Baltic states too might find a prickly Russia useful in their efforts to persuade NATO of the necessity of enlarging the alliance still further. Yet it would be a mistake for the West to let the issue of enlargement erode the foundations for further improvements in Russian-Baltic relations. The Baltic states and Russia need to understand that it will take time for the first round of new members to be taken in and for the effect of enlargement to be understood both inside and outside the alliance. NATO's key European members are not looking for a quick second round of enlargement, at least not one beyond Romania and Slovenia. Thus there will be time before any decision is taken about Baltic membership in NATO that all sides should use to expand multilateral security cooperation, transparency, and basic rules of the road.

The current Russian policy of linking ambitious steps forward in addressing Baltic security concerns to a demand that the three states renounce any ambitions for NATO membership leads Russia and the region as a whole to a dead end. The Baltic states are no longer simply and inalterably within Russia's sphere. Their ambitions for NATO cannot be modified—indeed they are heightened—by policies that appear to dictate their security choices. Russia's effort to withhold normal security relations threatens the foundation for normal relations between it and the three Baltic states already in place. It ignores the crying need all parties have to fashion rules of the road that will make security relations in the Baltic region more transparent, cooperative, and predictable.

However, the most serious challenges to Russian policy are not the eventual arrival of NATO but responding to the deepening pattern of Baltic integration with the West that already is evident. The European Commission has recommended that Estonia be in the first group of countries to begin accession talks with the European Union. Denmark, Sweden, and Finland have worked hard to draw the Baltic states into special political and security arrangements of their own. Finland has a serious, if still modest, security cooperation program with Estonia. Sweden took the lead in organizing the multilateral effort to arrange the withdrawal of Russian troops. Poland and Lithuania have deepened their bilateral relationship. The United States is likewise contemplating new initiatives that will demonstrate its abiding interest in Baltic independence. These growing ties between the Baltic states and the West are irreversible, but they do not have to be fostered at the expense of Russia. In particular, serious regional cooperation, such as the meetings of the heads of state and government of the states of the Baltic Sea littoral and key outside parties, is still in its infancy but in Russia's vital interest.

UKRAINE AND RUSSIA AT A TURNING POINT

Russia's relations with Ukraine constitute one of the most significant bilateral relationships in Europe. Normal and stable relations between these states would be a substantial contribution to European stability. Conflict between them would have an immediate and chilling effect on Europe as a whole and inevitably would involve the great powers of Europe. But Russia's relations with Ukraine also say much about Russia itself, particularly whether it is reconciled to its current borders and to the stability and independence of its neighbors. Russia plays a similarly large role in Ukraine's own process of consolidation as a nation. Independence cannot be said to be truly and fairly won if Ukraine believes itself within Russia's shadow.

The past history of Ukrainian subordination to Russia, nationalist rhetoric on both sides, and the example of Bosnia led many observers to predict that the bilateral relationship would collapse swiftly, due to Ukraine's internal weakness or Russian hostility. In fact, the two sides defied the gloomy predictions. In May 1997, in the shadow of the NATO enlargement decision, the two sides completed an agreement on the status of the Black Sea Fleet and a Russian-Ukrainian Friendship Treaty. Both agreements had been under negotiation since 1992 and the subject of deep disagreements and much rancor on both sides. Their signing by Yeltsin during a much-postponed summit in Kiev may in fact signal an important turning point in the relationship, one that finally could move bilateral ties to a secure and normal state-to-state footing.

The Black Sea Fleet agreement provides Russia with a 20-year lease to key port facilities in Crimea; however, in return, the treaty is a clear Russian acknowledgment that Crimea and its chief port city, Sevastopol, are Ukrainian. The treaty also provides Ukraine with rent for the facilities in the form of debt relief and access to port facilities in Sevastopol, a provision the Russian side long resisted. Already in 1992 the two sides agreed in principle on an equal division of the ships and other assets; in 1993 they agreed on specifics, with Ukraine consenting to sell back a substantial portion of its half to reduce its energy debt. These provisions also are included in the agreement. It remains to be seen whether this agreement can overcome both parliamentary skepticism in both countries and, more important, the resistance and friction that have plagued effective implementation of Russian-Ukrainian bilateral agreements in the past. The Friendship Treaty includes a legally binding recognition of existing borders, eliminating the ambiguity created by previous agreements, in which Russian recognition of Ukrainian borders was conditional, dependent on Ukraine remaining "within the framework of the CIS."[43]

Even before this latest round of agreements, the two sides have shown a high degree of moderation and pragmatism, when it has counted. These qualities coexist with real disagreements as well as symbolic gestures and harsh rhetoric that periodically suggest the relationship is on the verge of collapse. Hence the pattern so common to Russian-Ukrainian relations of periodic crises and high-level agreements, usually followed by neglect until the next crisis. Before the May agreements, this pattern surfaced half a dozen times in negotiations over the division and basing of the Black Sea Fleet. It defined Russian-Ukraine talks on the return of Soviet nuclear weapons. The cycle of breakthroughs and breakdowns is also present in Ukrainian-Russian discussions on integration, both within and outside the CIS. In January 1997 Ukrainian President Kuchma warned of "a systematic deterioration" in ties between the two countries as a result of Russia's imposition in late 1996 of a 20 percent value-added tax (VAT) and the subsequent failure of both sides to resolve the issue. The VAT imposition arose out of Russian complaints that Ukrainian sugar and other agricultural products were flooding the Russian market. It imposed a serious burden on the bilateral relationship, yet this deterioration led in turn to the May summit. Thus the situation was no more serious than at any time in the past six years.[44]

The experience of those six years reveals that both sides have understood the importance of maintaining a stable relationship, even in the midst of serious disagreements. Much of the initial pessimism regarding the inherent instability of the relationship and hostility of the two sides was simply wrong. The pragmatism of the relationship also has been sustained by the exhaustion and preoccupations of both sides. Russia is simply too burdened by its own internal problems, and its basic institutions are too chaotic and fragmented to carry through on a sustained assertive policy. For Ukrainian politicians as well, getting through the crisis of the moment represents a job well done. Nationalists on both sides have been frustrated, but the cause of stability has been well served.

Despite the May agreements, the relationship continually has resorted to muddling through, not resolving key questions or placing relations on an enduring basis. The question raised by those agreements is whether, with a little help, both sides can conceive of something more ambitious. But muddling through is not to be sneezed at. No one expected an easy transition to normal state-to-state relations for the two countries. Both governments operate under serious internal constraints. Boris Yeltsin's illness and prolonged convalescence added an additional burden on Russian policymaking.

The two states also have had help at crucial moments. The successful denuclearization of Ukraine required U.S. political and financial support. Without the trilateral process and U.S. leadership, it is likely that the weapons would still be the subject of difficult bilateral talks. The International Monetary Fund (IMF) played a similar role in Russian-Ukrainian negotiations on bilateral debt relief. Even the latest bilateral successes in May were influenced in no small measure by Russia's desire to resolve outstanding differences with Ukraine before NATO enlargement. The agreements by and large favor stated Ukrainian positions, which Moscow long resisted. However, it is clear that the Russian leadership did not want to carry deep divisions with Ukraine into the post-NATO enlargement period. The role of outside involvement is likely to be equally crucial in sustaining these agreements and the momentum they may provide for resolving items on what still remains a complex and difficult bilateral agenda.

The two countries have been at loggerheads for most of their existence on basic security questions. Some of these, such as the initial division of the ground and air forces of the Soviet Union or the status of nuclear weapons on Ukrainian soil, have been resolved. The Black Sea Fleet also has been put on legal footing, although obstacles to parliamentary approval and subsequent implementation of the May agreement remain. Indeed, the settlement envisions Russian forces stationed on Ukrainian soil for two decades, creating the potential for future troubles in Crimea, where profound ethnic and social tensions, economic collapse, and the presence of a declining fleet provide a potentially combustible mixture.

CIS integration also deeply divides the two nations. Russia has made integration the centerpiece of its foreign policy. Ukraine has been wary of Russian-sponsored integration from the very beginning. However, it has transformed its CIS policy from one that saw the CIS as a means for arranging a "civilized divorce" into a full-fledged alternative to Russian policy, an alternative vision of cooperation among the states of the former U.S.S.R. that focuses on the primacy of sovereignty and practical economic cooperation. Ukraine refuses to participate in CIS security mechanisms, except for the common air defense initiative. Ukraine's more independent security policy and Russia's own limitations led, in mid-1997, to an agreement to bring Ukraine into the settlement and implementation of the Transdniestrian problem in Moldova. Ukraine now acts as a coguarantor of Moldovan-Transdniestrian accords and is preparing to send peacekeeping units to the breakaway province.

Russia and Ukraine also pursued radically different polices toward NATO enlargement. Ukraine from the first harbored fears that enlargement could leave it in a gray zone, complicating both its internal situation and the external security environment. Yet Ukraine chose to deal with its concern by supporting enlargement and seeking a specific Ukrainian-NATO partnership agreement. During his 1996 visit to Warsaw, Kuchma even described NATO as "the only real guarantor of security on the continent"[45] and expressed his support for Poland's desire to join NATO. Ukrainian officials, unlike Russian ones, also have an interest in supporting the notion that "each state has the right to decide itself on participation in any international organization or bloc.[46] Ukraine also proposed constraints on NATO military, particularly nuclear, forces in the new member states, hoping that such restraint will be met by a similar response from Russia. In the past two years, Ukraine has vastly expanded its ties with NATO, the European Union, and other key Western states and institutions. This leaning to the West has passed well beyond the point where it can be seen simply as a prop for Kiev's Russian policy. Ukrainian leaders have set their long-term sights on participation in Europe, although Kuchma has regularly dampened expressions of interest in NATO membership arising from other foreign policy leaders.

Another crucial issue again was Russia's October 1996 imposition of the VAT and strict quotas on Ukrainian sugar, which brought both parties to the brink of a trade war. Each is the other's largest trading partner. Ukraine is the most vulnerable, with Russia providing more than 37 percent of total imports in the first half of 1996.[47] Ukraine also remains nearly totally dependent on Russian oil and natural gas. The Russian side claims its actions are a legal response to Ukrainian dumping. There is little doubt that Ukrainian products, particularly vodka, are cheaper than Russian equivalents and have won a substantial share of the Russian market. Ukraine sees Russian policies as part of a pattern of economic intimidation that is likely to grow as other, more direct forms of intimidation prove to be ineffective. Given the current atmosphere of the bilateral relationship and the substantial domestic interests at stake, the two sides are unlikely to resolve this question on their own.

This list covers only the current sticking points. It does not exhaust the potential trouble spots on the Russian-Ukrainian agenda. A friendship treaty has been signed, but Russian-Ukrainian border demarcation, especially in the Azov Sea, is stalled. Ukraine probably will need to renegotiate its 1995 debt resettlement package with Russia in 1998, when it must begin to make payments on the principal. In these talks, as it has often in the past, Russia will doubtless return to its proposal to swap Ukrainian debt for Russian ownership in key Ukrainian assets, such as the gas pipeline and oil refinery facilities.

But beyond the specific disagreements, Kiev and Moscow still have very different views of the future of their relationship. Thus the pragmatism at the core of the relationship is strained in part by different visions of the outcome. Russia hopes that, over time, the two countries will return to what one former Yeltsin advisor called "a fraternal Slavic compromise," that is, an integrated relationship far closer than normal state-to-state ties.[48] Yeltsin himself has long tried to convince reluctant Ukrainian leaders that "the integration of Russia and Ukraine means the salvation of both states from the problems confronting us today."[49] Russia has not wanted to thwart this outcome by a settlement of outstanding issues that would normalize the relationship and thus make integrated ties less likely. Ukraine wants an unambiguous state-to-state relationship and increasingly sees its proper horizon in expanding ties with Central Europe and Europe as a whole. The strategic partnership with the United States is another sign of Ukraine's pursuit of foreign policy goals well beyond stability with Russia and a place with the CIS. But Ukraine is too weak and internally divided to impose a normalized relationship on Russia. As both sides come face to face with their fundamental differences, there is a danger of drift in the relationship, with both countries putting off resolving the differences that divide them.

Although muddling through—with timely intervention from the top—has kept relations on course so far, it is not certain that this pattern can be sustained indefinitely. Even the May 1997 agreements themselves are subject to serious obstacles and opposition. Russian consolidation of its political and economic system over time will increase its capacity to conduct a more ambitious Ukrainian policy. The key will be not Russia's size or strength but the size of the gap between it and Ukraine. Ukraine currently is experiencing a serious loss of momentum in its political and economic reforms, which leave it both weak and less of a candidate for Western support, should a crisis come. Neither Russia nor Ukraine has moved away from the old patterns of psychology, history, and Soviet inheritance that shape mutual perceptions and guarantee misunderstanding. For both sides, but especially in Russia, relations with the other is more habit than strategy. Neither state fully has understood the benefits of normal cooperation or the necessity of placing their bilateral relationship on a broader and more internationally accepted basis. Neither side currently has the policy coherence or the resources to sustain the current positive trends without help. Providing the political support and economic incentives for the continued normalization of Russian-Ukrainian relations is a task that corresponds to a basic Western interest in stable relations between the two largest post-Soviet states. Without doubt, in the coming years both sides will need some incentives, encouragement, and perhaps goading to keep them on track. This crucial bilateral relationship is simply too important to be left to develop on its own. The precedents of outside involvement in nuclear disarmament and debt relief need to be broadened to include efforts to keep the Black Sea Fleet issue, Crimea, energy supply and debt, the VAT, or other sources of conflict within the bounds of normal state-to-state disputes. Some may see Western involvement in these issues as unnecessary or costly, but the West certainly will be involved in a much more serious way should Russian-Ukrainian relations deteriorate.

THE WEST: INTRUDER, PARTNER, OR REVOLUTIONARY?

The Russian foreign policy community increasingly sees the West, especially NATO, as an intruder and competitor in its western borderlands. The West sees itself both as a partner and also a revolutionary, coming to overturn the geopolitically based international order in this part of Europe by exporting the system that has tamed old rivalries, domesticated German power, and created a high level of political stability and economic prosperity. Neither party is entirely right or wrong. Already frictions and clashes of interest have arisen from the growth of new states, the contraction and redefinition of Russian power, and the increasing activity of the West in lands once effectively sealed from contact with the outside world. The West's leading instrument of advancing to the edge of this territory is in fact the NATO alliance, which the Russian foreign policy community passionately—and the Russian people less enthusiastically—regards with suspicion.

President Clinton describes NATO enlargement as a revolutionary act, aimed not at Russia or at occupying better ground for some future military challenge but at transforming the old order. The administration and some of its supporters hope this transformation will go further, perhaps even to a future in which Russia will be part of the alliance itself, or at least where the distinction between a NATO member and a cooperating nonmember will be a trivial one. However, NATO is still a military alliance that provides a crucial hedge against the reversal of the current environment, facts that unite another important group of NATO enlargement supporters. The states that seek NATO membership also want that hedge, just as they too want a transformation of their regional environment that would make the hedge unnecessary. The current military environment in Central and Eastern Europe is an unthreatening one. NATO has wisely taken steps to ensure it will not be the cause of the reintroduction of nuclear or serious conventional power projection capabilities into the region. However, the only sure test of its success is time. Russia cannot be expected to become a convert overnight to NATO enlargement or to the institutions of NATO-Russian cooperation that were created by the NATO-Russian Founding Act. Nor will it be clear immediately whether Russia has accepted these institutions as a way to improve consultation and cooperation with the alliance.

These contradictions will take time to resolve, and they will cause problems along the way. In addition, as NATO moves east, the importance of Poland and the lands beyond its eastern boundaries will grow.

Their successes or failures will have an immediate impact on NATO's new front line. The internal and external situation in these border lands will be a key factor in determining NATO's posture in Poland and the costs eventually associated with enlargement. NATO cannot help sooner or later being influenced by the security problems of its front-line state. Poland may not have Germany's weight or influence within the alliance, but it will occupy a security position analogous to Germany's in the old Cold War alliance. This corresponds to the deepest Polish national interests, once Poland finds itself securely anchored in the West, to urge its allies on to a constructive involvement in the east, to head off problems before they become a challenge to Polish security and stability. However, Poland's efforts at an eastern policy still do not match the importance of the goal of reaching out to Russia and the five states between. In the future, however, rising Polish economic interests will provide an additional motivation for reaching to the east, with the prospects of enhanced trade with Russia, Ukraine, and the former U.S.S.R.

But Poland's concerns are not automatically those of NATO's, particularly at a time when the central organizing threat to NATO has disappeared and a regionalization of security concerns is under way both throughout Europe and even within the NATO Alliance. The NATO-Russian Founding Act is an important accomplishment, yet several factors at work in the West will make it difficult—but not impossible—to sustain momentum on Russian-NATO cooperation. However important such cooperation is, it no longer has the center stage. NATO has done its work in designing a framework for security cooperation, but for many in Europe the old urgency has passed. The apocalyptic clash of NATO and Warsaw Pact forces is no more. Measures designed to ensure that NATO enlargement does not revive old-style military confrontation are in place. Russia is in no position to revive that competition in the next decade, even if its generals or a new set of political leaders wanted to do so.

The security agenda itself has been transformed in ways that raise questions about Russia's immediate relevance, especially given its current problems. In part, that agenda has been regionalized, creating even among close allies markedly different threat perceptions and policy priorities. The Danes want the Baltic states in NATO. Turkey demands attention to what it sees as a much more threatening regional environment. Other Mediterranean members of NATO see North Africa, not the old Central Front, as NATO's strategic front line. In future crises, states such as France may wish to draw Russia in. In its current condition, Russia has little to offer in conflicts far from home. except its presence as an indication of the concert of Europe. In other ways, the security agenda has turned to global issues. It is crucial that Russia participate in efforts to address the proliferation of nuclear weapons and other weapons of mass destruction, narcotics trafficking, and terrorism, but its weakened condition and strained resources make it unlikely that it will contribute much—at least initially—on these issues. On proliferation, Russia must be present because it is a main source of potential problems. It is quite likely then that the West's interests and abilities to carry out sustained policies in the former U.S.S.R., particularly the western borderlands, will far exceed Russia's ability to reciprocate in other areas of the world. The West itself will be far from united on how to deal with this diverse region and will be more active there than Russia can be in Europe.

If the West is to make good on its intentions to revolutionize the international system itself, NATO cannot remain the cutting edge of policy toward the region. The European Union also has to go through a parallel process of expanding its core membership and extending its vision well beyond the boundaries of its member states. While currently it is seen in Russia as the preferred leading edge of Western involvement in the former U.S.S.R., the European Union brings problems of its own, particularly with regard to market access, agricultural policy, and trade between members and outsiders. There also will have to be a wider U.S.-European consensus on the strategic stakes in the western borderlands, one that leads to a broad-based strategy of engagement that can prosper over the long term.

Strong precedents already exist that the United States and its European allies can follow to include Russia, as both a key object of Western policy initiatives and as a partner in Western initiatives toward other states of the region. The negotiations of Russian troop withdrawals from the Baltics, Ukrainian denuclearization, and Ukrainian debt rescheduling provide models for structures that give all parties with interests at stake a place at the table. These structures do not ensure harmony of views. They are designed to regulate competition, not eliminate it. Still, they have done far more than currently credited in creating a soft landing for the region. Even if successful, on the eastern half of Europe such structures will be far less robust than their Western equivalents for some time to come. They remain hostage to deterioration of U.S.-Russian and Russian-NATO relations.

But the most important element of a Western strategic consensus on both Russia and its western borderlands is a deep respect for the profound changes in the geopolitical situation in Europe. The events of the past decade have brought the West inherent advantages and time. Despite the ups and downs in Russia, particularly the growth of increasing suspicion and irritants in the relationship between it and the West, the geopolitical context in which problems will be addressed remains favorable. The profound East-West clashes of perspective and interest, backed up by large numbers of opposing conventional and nuclear arms, no longer define European security. Even a prickly and resentful Russia is a far more cooperative—and far less dangerous—interlocutor than the Soviet Union ever was. Russia is still in the midst of an internal and external process that will define it as a power in Europe. There is no reason to believe that this process is over or that the outcome is foreordained.

CONCLUSION

These crucial borderland states of Belarus, Estonia, Latvia, Lithuania and Ukraine will remain an important testing ground for the new order in Europe. At best, this region will face a long and uneven transition, leaving some states imperfectly within or even outside the basic institutions and interactions of Europe. At worst, some or all of the region could become a burden or challenge to this emerging Europe due to internal instability, economic backwardness, or frictions with Russia. Between these alternatives lie a number of intermediate scenarios. What is certain is that this region will not stand still. It will remain a central preoccupation of Russian foreign policy and an increasing field of Western activity. The states here increasingly will bring their own preferences to the fore and thus define the terms for this encounter. Therefore, there are plenty of sources for future friction, misunderstanding, and even potential conflict.

However, a solid underpinning of military restraint and growing economic interdependence also exists that, if well managed, could over time transform international politics in this part of Europe. Russia is in no position to rekindle the strategic rivalry that the Soviet Union could not manage. The position of the West, even with deepening disagreements between allies over economic and security questions, is a strong one, particularly if it intends to change the shape of international politics in the region, not contain Russia. However, the failure to manage change in this region almost certainly will put the benefits of the current environment at risk and turn the region into a serious source of concern along NATO's (and eventually the European Union's) new front line. The West, particularly after the enlargement of NATO, cannot put the development and management of policy toward this region on the back burner.

Regional events also will force the Russian leadership to find a sustainable balance between ambitions and capabilities. The West has every interest in encouraging Russia to do so, for those capabilities will expand, as economic growth and governmental coherence returns. Russian foreign policy by and large has performed better than the debate on it in the West would suggest, establishing some of the building blocks necessary for truly postimperial and sustainable ties to the states of the region. However, it has not yet embraced such ties as a strategic goal and built a foreign policy mechanism to pursue it. Until it does, a crucial uncertainty limits the progress of states in the region toward building Eastern economic, political and security institutions that in any way resemble those of Western and Central Europe.

The work of bringing Russia into the new European order always has been a matter of decades, not years. It is neither destined to succeed nor doomed to fail. Russia could well play the role of a disgruntled state on the periphery of Europe and its core institutions. Such a Russia would not represent the return of the Soviet threat, but it would complicate the security picture enormously and make more likely frictions and even potential conflicts on the edge of Europe and in the former U.S.S.R. It would lay the groundwork for the return of even greater strategic rivalry in the future and narrow the chances for wider Western-Russian cooperation on important global issues. It would bring a halt to the expansion of Europe. The first and most persistent signs of this negative outcome will occur in the region between Russia and Central Europe. Indeed, the problem of Russia's full entrance into the new European order is inextricably linked to these lands also having the same chance, of their not remaining outside of the emerging European order.

Such an outcome depends on harmonizing Russian, Western, and local policies in this crossroads of Europe, which means that there must be a broad-based Western understanding of the stakes, not simply for these new states or for Russia but for Europe as a whole. Such an understanding will not come easily to Western states and institutions distracted by internal challenges or foreign policy problems elsewhere on the globe. The trends that have brought the end of the U.S.S.R.—low levels of military force and the absence of strategic rivalry in this part of Europe—must be nurtured. The contradictions and synergies of the polices aimed at encouraging Russia's transformation—the enlargement of the West's core institutions and the reform and stability of the states in between—have to be managed. The work here is only half finished. It is on this broad stretch of plain between Russia and Poland that what was so hopefully sown in 1989 and 1991 will eventually be harvested. But, as the people of this region know so well, the quality of the harvest depends on what is done now, between the sowing and the reaping.

Notes

1. Although the enlargement of both institutions is still under debate and serious parliamentary examination of the 1997 NATO summit invitation to the Czech Republic, Hungary, and Poland has only begun, this chapter assumes that both NATO and European Union (EU) enlargement, at least to the states of Central Europe, will be a part of the basic regional framework to which Russia must respond. I make this assumption not only because I believe both institutions will, in fact, enlarge at least as far as the states of Central Europe but also because key Russian decision-makers and analysts have made the same conclusions and are basing their analysis on this assumption.

2. "Situation in the Army Fraught with National Catastrophe," Statement by the Foreign and Defense Policy Council, *Nezavisimaya Gazeta,* February 14, 1997.

3. This document fully entitled "Founding Act on Mutual Relations, Cooperation and Security between NATO and the Russian Federation " was signed May 27 in Madrid. The act lays the foundations of a cooperative Russia-NATO partnership in which the two parties consult regularly and strive to coordinate efforts to bring stability and security to Europe. It describes the relationship's many dimensions, but most notably, the act established a NATO-Russia Permanent Joint Council for dialogue. The arrangement provides no veto for Russia.

4. "Ezhegodnoe poslanie prizidenta Rossii Borisa El'tsina Federal'nomu Sobraniyu RF" (the annual letter of the president of Russia Boris Yeltsin to the Federal Assembly of the Russian Federation), March 6, 1997, text distributed by Natsional'naya sluzhba novostey.

5. For a recent overview of this consensus, see Aleksey Arbatov, "Vneshne-politicheskiy konsensus v Rossii" (the foreign policy consensus in Russia), *Nezavisimaya gazeta,* March 14, 1997.

6. See, for example, the interviews with Foreign Minister Yevgeniy Primakov in *Trud,* June 25, 1996, and *Krasnaya zvezda,* April 2, 1996, as well as his article on the coming multipolar world. Yevgeniy Primakov, "Multipolar World on Horizon," *Nezavisimaya gazeta,* October 22, 1996.

7. Primakov in *Trud* and *Krasnaya zvezda.*

8. The sole exceptions are portions of western Ukraine, which remained Polish or Habsburg territory until 1939, and Estonia, Latvia, and Lithuania, which enjoyed a period of interwar independence. Most of Ukraine was annexed by Russia in the seventeenth century as a result of its wars with Poland. Peter the Great acquired large tracts of what is now Estonia and Latvia in his Great Northern War with Sweden; these areas achieved independence after World War I. The Grand Duchy of Lithuania was part of Poland until it passed under Russian control after the third and final partition of Poland in 1795.

9. Both the pre-Soviet Russian empire and the Soviet Union implemented full-scale Russification and Sovietization policies. The purpose was to impose the imperial center's language and culture on peoples of the periphery. As a result, many people in the western borderlands and in the rest of the former U.S.S.R. speak Russian, are fully assimilated culturally, and yet are not ethnically Russian. They tend to identify closely with Russia.

10. *New States, New Politics,* edited by Ian Bremmer and Ray Taras (Cambridge: Cambridge University Press, 1997), contains excellent essays on each of the five countries of Russia's western borderlands, providing historical background and an overview of key political developments from the Gorbachev period to 1996. It also includes tables of population data and ethnic breakdown for each state, which I have used in this chapter (pp. 706–7, 712–14).

11. "Estonia: Country Overview," The World Bank: http://www.worldbank.org.

12. In addition to Russia and Belarus, Armenia, Kazakhstan, Kyrgyzstan, Tajikistan, and Uzbekistan are member states of the treaty. The text of the treaty was published in *Rossiyskaya gazeta,* May 23, 1992, p. 2.

13. *ITAR-TASS,* March 11, 1994.

14. *Krasnaya zvezda,* May 24, 1994, p. 3.

15. The treaty was published in *Rossiiskaya gazeta,* July 7, 1995, p. 4. The text of a parallel bilateral undertaking is contained in the May 1995 Treaty on Friendship. *Rossiiskaya gazeta,* May 5, 1995, p. 10.

16. See the interview with Belarusian Minister of Defense Alyaksandr Chumakow, circulated by *Belapan,* February 19, 1997, quoted in *FBIS Daily Report: Central Eurasia,* February 19, 1997.

17. "All Strategic Nuclear Warheads Reported Out of Belarus," *Interfax,* November 25, 1996, quoted in *FBIS Daily Report: Central Eurasia,* November 25, 1996.

18. "Primakov Says No Nukes on Belarusian Territory in Peacetime," *RFE/RL Reports,* May 26, 1997.

19. An abridged version of the draft treaty was published in *Nezavisimaya gazeta,* March 29, 1997.

20. "Vazhenyshiy proekt utochnyaetsya na khodu" (A most important draft is clarified on the run), *Nezavisimaya gazeta,* April 1, 1997.

21. Both the approved treaty and an agreed memorandum on how to proceed with the elaboration of a detailed charter and consultation with publics were published in *Rossiyskaya gazeta,* April 3, 1997.

22. Author's interviews in Moscow, June 1–4, 1997.

23. Alessandra Stanley, "Russia Dilutes a Treaty with Belarus, Then Signs," *New York Times,* April 3, 1997, p. 9.

24. "Speech by the President of Belarus Alexander Lukashenka at the State Duma Session (November 13, 1996)," *Federal News Service Transcripts,* November 13, 1996.

25. "President on Integration, Foreign Policy," *FBIS Daily Report: Central Eurasia,* March 14, 1997.

26. *The Economist,* August 17, 1996, p. 67.

27. *The Economist,* May 4, 1996, p. 46.

28. Russian deployments in the Baltics also became less tenable in the face of the collapse of the defense budget and conscription system. Russian withdrawals continued even during the most difficult periods of bilateral talks. The Estonian example is instructive. At the end of 1991 the Russians claimed to have 35,000 forces in Estonia, although some estimates place the number at closer to 50,000. By the end of 1992 fewer than 10,000 remained. A year later less than 3,000. The Russian-Estonian troop withdrawal agreement was signed on July 26, 1994. The last Russian military forces left the submarine

training base at Paldiski in September 1995. This pattern was repeated, with some variations, in Latvia and Lithuania. On declining Russian troop levels in each of the Baltic states, see Ben Lombardi, *Russian Troop Withdrawal from the Baltic Region* (Ottawa: Department of National Defence, April 1994), esp. p. 41.

29. *Statistical Handbook 1996: States of the Former USSR* (Washington, DC: World Bank, 1996), pp. 141–42, 324–25.

30. "External Sector: Merchandise Trade," Economist Intelligence Unit Country Reports, September 22, 1997.

31. *The Economist,* May 4, 1996, p. 47, and August 17, 1996, p. 69.

32. "Soobshchenie press-sluzhby prezidenta Rossiyskoy Federatsii: 1997-02-11-005" (Announcement of the press source of the president of the Russian Federation: . . .), author's copy from the Kremlin Press Center. *FBIS* (February 18, 1997) translated a text of the statement from *Rossiyskaya gazeta,* February 13, 1997, p. 7.

33. Dmitri Trenin, "Baltiyskaya kontseptsiya Rossii" (Russia's Baltic policy), *Nezavisimaya gazeta,* March 11, 1997, p. 4.

34. See reports of progress at the Vilnius meeting in *Interfax,* September 3, 1997, and *ETA,* September 10, 1997.

35. Ibid, *Interfax.*

36. *The Economist,* August 17, 1996, p. 67.

37. A Russian observer of the Baltics reported in an interview with the author in October 1997 that small improvements do seem to be emerging in Estonia, where a greater percentage of ethnic Russians now pass the Estonian language examination than ever before. He did not know, however, whether this trend occurred as a result of a deliberate Estonian policy to relax standards or simply from time-honored methods of cash for high scores. In any event, he doubted whether more ethnic Russians actually were learning Estonian.

38. *Madrid Declaration on Euro-Atlantic Security,* NATO Press Office, July 8, 1997.

39. *Interfax,* May 19, 1997.

40. "Interview with Anatoliy Surikov," *Postimees,* April 27, 1996. Reprinted in *FBIS Daily Report: Central Eurasia,* April 30, 1996.

41. "Russia Offers Guarantees to Baltic States," *Jane's Defense Weekly,* September 10, 1997, vol. 28, no. 10, p. 4.

42. An issue often neglected in the debate over NATO enlargement is that posed by the economic decisions of the European Union on market access and expansion to the Baltic states. The European Commission has placed Estonia among the five states it recommends for accession negotiations. All three Baltic states continue their march toward EU membership, with Estonia in the lead. This march even has Primakov's endorsement: "Russia's attitude to the Baltic countries' possible membership in the European Union," Primakov stated in Denmark, "is positive . . ." *ITAR-TASS,* February 27, 1997. Russia's obsession with NATO obscures the implications of Baltic membership in the European Union, which will have profound consequences for Russia, accelerating the reorientation of trade away from Russia and potentially erecting new economic barriers between it and the Baltics. Although the larger question of Russian market access to the EU overshadows the enlargement issue,

EU rules and policies cannot help but affect Russian access to Baltic markets and ports. There are also security implications from such membership, both within the terms of the European Union itself and via the direct links between the core members of the Union and NATO. This security linkage is precisely why leading exponents of NATO enlargement see EU membership for the Baltics as an important part of a Western postenlargement strategy for the region. See, for example, Ronald D. Asmus and Robert C. Nurick, "NATO Enlargement and the Baltic States," *Survival* 38 (Summer 1996), pp. 121–42.

43. Sherman Garnett, *Keystone in the Arch: Ukraine in the Emerging Security Environment of Central and Eastern Europe* (Washington, DC: Carnegie Endowment for International Peace, 1997), p. 57. See "Russia, Ukraine: Treaty on Ukraine, RF Cooperation," *Kiev Uryadovyy Kuryer*, June 3, 1997, reprinted in *FBIS Daily Report, Central Eurasia,* June 3, 1997, and "Russia, Ukraine: Agreement on Russian Black Sea Fleet," *Moscow Rossiyskaya Gazeta,* June 7, 1997, reprinted in *FBIS Daily Report, Central Eurasia,* June 7, 1997.

44. Reuters, January 17, 1997.

45. *Zycie Warszawy,* June 24, 1996, pp. 1 and 6.

46. *ITAR-TASS,* October 4, 1995.

47. *The Financial Times,* September 10, 1996.

48. *Kievskie vedomosti,* April 28, 1995, p. 4.

49. Boris Yeltsin, "Press Conference Regarding the Results of the CIS Summit in Moscow," January 19, 1996, *Federal News Service Transcript.*

CHAPTER THREE

After Empire: Russia and the Southern "Near Abroad"

Rajan Menon

With the unexpected fall of the Soviet Union came both a new strategic reality and a new terminology to describe it. The sham federation called the Union of Soviet Socialist Republics (U.S.S.R.) was replaced by 15 new states referred to as the the Newly Independent States (NIS) or the former Soviet Union (FSU). In Russian political discourse, the label of choice for the other 14 erstwhile Soviet republics became the Near Abroad (*blizhnee zarubezh'e*). The context of its use suggests that this curious term is also a loaded one. It implies that Russia has special interests in the other ex-Soviet republics based on the historical background of these states (they were part of the tsarist and Soviet empires), their proximity, and the presence in them of a multimillion Russian diaspora. The claim to special privileges follows naturally.[1] In sum, Near Abroad emits a pro-prietorial aura.

This perspective is not mere aspiration and rhetoric; it is under-written by the propinquity and preponderance of Russian power. The Near Abroad adjoins Russia; it is still governed in the main by Russified, Soviet-era elites; and it depends overwhelmingly on Russia for needs rang-ing from trade and energy to arms, military training, and protection against rebellions. In the tsarist and Soviet eras, the outside world dealt with the south Caucasus and Central Asia on Moscow's terms: Access was calibrated or denied by the center. In the post-Soviet period, the United States, Iran, Turkey, Japan, China, Israel, Saudi Arabia, the United Nations, the Organization for Cooperation and Security in Europe (OSCE), and the North Atlantic Treaty Organization (NATO) have increased their presence in the south Caucasus and Central Asia. Over time, the states of the southern Near Abroad will, as a result, have a wider range of political and economic choices. That said, for the foreseeable future no other state has the combination of interests, power, and ease of access to serve as a counterweight to Russia there, as the region's leaders and academic experts on foreign affairs realize all too well.[2] In the jargon of international relations theory, the Near Abroad is a unipolar region (Russian preponderance is overwhelming) characterized by asymmetric interdependence (Russia is dependent on the other 14, but they are far more dependent on it), and the dominant strategy of regional states toward Russia will be "bandwagoning" (accommodation), not "balancing" (resistance). By this I do not mean that the leaders of the southern Near Abroad do not (and will not) have their own agendas or that their foreign policies will be choreographed in Moscow. My point is that even their decisions to diversify economic and political transactions so as to decrease dependence on Russia will be made with a keen awareness that Russia is nearby and powerful and that they inhabit a zone that it considers vital for its national security.

True, power ratios alone do not account for the way states deal with one another. Russia's foreign policy will be shaped not just by its capacity vis-à-vis other countries but also by the kinds of political forces that control the Russian state. The differences among, say, a Yeltsin, a Zhirinovsky, a Lebed, and a Zyuganov are hardly trivial in determining Russian conduct beyond its borders. The fate of democracy in Russia, the nature of Russian nationalism, whether economic recovery and political stability emerge and endure—these questions also will shape Russia's dealings with the rest of the world, particularly the ex-Soviet republics fated to be in its shadow. Yet it is also a mistake to let the analysis of Russian policy in the Near Abroad rest on alluring and popular dichotomies such as "liberal versus conservative," "civilian doves versus military hawks," "communists versus democrats," "Atlanticists versus Eurasianists." The popularity of these labels is understandable given the interest scholars and policymakers have in the domestic sources of Russian foreign policy. These paired opposites also have a heuristic value. They help differentiate the divergences of perception and preference among Russian elites on questions of statecraft. And yet they obscure the extent to which a consensus toward the Near Abroad unifies them.[3]

Individuals in each category of these binary opposites would accept the following propositions: First, for historical and geopolitical reasons, the Near Abroad has a significance for Russian security that it does not have for other great powers. Second, as a consequence Russia can rightfully claim overriding interests there. Third, Russian leaders should thwart hostile alliances or coalitions and counter instabilities that could erode Russia's position in the region.[4] Fourth, the status of ethnic Russians in the Near Abroad is not purely an internal affair of regional governments but a legitimate concern of the Russian state for reasons both symbolic and tangible. Fifth, while these new states have sovereign status and juridical boundaries, the perimeter of the former Soviet Union constitutes Russia's geostrategic, as opposed to legal, boundary. Sixth, the West is using Russia's weakness to undermine its position in vital areas such as the post-Soviet space.[5] As Alexei Arbatov, a leading strategic analyst and member of the Russian Duma, observes, from late 1992, "a major realignment" occurred in Russia's foreign policy debate. The liberals who championed integration with the West, and who generally stood for disengagement from the other ex-Soviet republics, were displaced. The "presently dominant centrist and moderate conservative group . . . sees Russia as being entitled to a special role because of its size, historic preponderance and other advantages over the smaller republics on the territory of the former Soviet Union. . . . Preserving and, wherever needed, reinstating its dominant role . . . is the principal goal in their version of Russian foreign policy."[6]

In pointing to this consensus and adopting an analytical approach that emphasizes the importance of state interests that endure over time and transcend shifting divisions among institutions and groups, I do not wish to minimize the debate over foreign policy among influential Russians.[7] There has never been a state in which divisions on matters of statecraft among ruling elites have been absent. With the emergence of democracy in Russia, one can now study these divisions and observe and read about policy debates in a way that was never possible when analyzing the Soviet Union. There is an understandable fascination with the internal sources of Russian foreign policy. But the result should not be a perspective that reduces the Russian state to an epiphenomenon—a mere arena for battle among elites and institutions. A wealth of recent scholarship has demonstrated that the state is more than the sum of its parts or a reflection of rivalrous social and institutional forces and that, although its capacity to do so waxes and wanes, it can articulate a transcending and abiding interest rooted in durable historical and geostrategic conditions.[8]

None of this is meant to imply that Russia is a lurking predator out to resurrect empire. To the contrary, my view is that the support for imperial regathering is thin among Russian citizens—who are in any event preoccupied with more mundane matters of survival—and that it is confined to a fringe even within the elite. As Russians contend with the

Darwinism of a market economy, adjust psychologically to the loss of superpower status, and live amid pervasive crime and disorder, there is nostalgia for the U.S.S.R. among certain segments of society. But there is no groundswell of support for risking war or spending large sums of money to re-create the Soviet Union. What I do wish to stress is that the historical legacy—dating from nineteenth century—of Russia's colonial control over the south Caucasus and Central Asia, the overwhelming superiority of its power, and the circumstances of geography together create enduring conditions. And they impose a logic of their own on Russia's relations with the Near Abroad—the logic of Thucydides' Melian dialogue.[9] Any Russian government will seek to assert and maintain its preeminence in that region, just as other great powers (the United States in Central and South America, France in its former African colonies) have done in areas they deem vital. This will occur despite Russia's numerous problems and diminished power; it should surprise no one. The quest for hegemony—a state of affairs wherein what the states of Central Asia and the south Caucasus do at home and abroad is shaped strongly by an assessment of Russia's likely reaction—will prove burdensome and entangling. It may even fail: Russia may be unable to occupy a hegemonic position, or it may become mired in debilitating conflicts in the region. But this will not necessarily prevent Moscow from trying. Governments frequently miscalculate. They do not conduct foreign policy based on cost-benefit analyses in which the pluses and minuses of alternative courses of action are quantified and compared precisely: Clausewitz wrote of the "fog of war," but there is also the fog of diplomacy: the unknown, the unknowable, the unexpected, the accidental.

The preceding assumptions, which I will refine and illustrate, guide my analysis in this chapter. It focuses on Russian policy in the southern Near Abroad,[10] which is defined as the states of the southern Caucasus (Armenia, Azerbaijan, and Georgia) and Central Asia (Kazakhstan, Kyrgyzstan, Tajikistan, Turkmenistan, and Uzbekistan). It is not a blow-by-blow account of Russia's relations with these eight countries since December 1991, the month that the Soviet Union formally disappeared. Accounts of the richness and variety of specific developments and inter-governmental transactions—summits, communiqués, agreements—are plentiful.[11] My aims are to illuminate how Russia and the states of the Near Abroad regard each other, to show how power differentials among states and developments within them combine to influence the inter-relationship between Russia and the southern Near Abroad, to demon-strate the varieties and limits of Russian power and influence, and to present probable scenarios for the future and their implications.

THE IMBALANCE OF POWER

The convention in academic and journalistic writing on Russia now is to emphasize its plethora of problems and its predicament as a former great power in virtual free fall.[12] If the refrain in the Soviet era was that "the Russians are coming," in the post-Soviet era it is that the Russians are crumbling. There is undoubtedly truth to the depiction of Russia as a reeling giant. A mass of evidence can be adduced to show that it is mired in seemingly intractable problems. Indeed, its position as a great power seems more a matter of self-assertion, ritualistic incantation by other states, or outright tokenism[13] than of reality. The contraction of its gross national product (GNP), the fall in the life expectancy of its male population, the contrast between the scandalous wealth of a nouveau riche minority and penurious majority, and the metamorphosis of its once-proud and powerful military into an ill-fed, ill-equipped, demoralized mass are but some of signs of decline. But the widespread tendency to argue from this foundation that Russia is a strategic paper tiger with little if any capacity to exert leverage in foreign policy is mistaken. The reason is that power is dynamic and relational.

Because power is dynamic—changing quantitatively, qualitatively, absolutely, and relatively, and consisting of diverse elements that are not fungible—extrapolations based on Russia's current circumstances are likely to be shortsighted. As signs of Russia's recovery emerge, its present constraints are a weak foundation on which to base future expectations about its foreign policy. Russia's recovery undoubtedly will be protracted and uneven, but it is almost certainly likely to be more rapid than that of the states in the southern Near Abroad. This implies that the imbalance of power between them and Russia will persist and, indeed, for reasons that will become clear as the difficulties of these states are examined, increase. Moreover, the sharp diminution in Russia's might does not change a basic point: Power in world politics is meaningful principally as a comparative concept. And so one must ask "Power against whom, to do what, in what context?" Once the question is posed in this way, it is apparent that there has been no across-the-board decline in Russian power. Against the West, China, Japan, Eastern Europe, and even Ukraine, the most powerful state in the Near Abroad, the case for diminished Russian power can be made convincingly. Some of these states are able—individually or collectively—to amass more power than Russia. For others, their distant location or the availability of buffer states or putative strategic partners enables them to complicate the projection of Russian force, thus raising to an unacceptable level the costs of a policy based on the threat or use of violence.

I would even argue that the small and proximate Baltic states have improved their position with respect to Russia because of their relatively good economic performance, expanding ties with the West, and, above all, their success in building stable democratic polities and cohesive societies.

But the balance of power and the record of Russian policy look rather different if one turns to the states of the southern Near Abroad. This region has experienced a decline in power far steeper than Russia's. The data in Table 3–1 provide the basis for comparison, using some standard measures for gauging national power. Admittedly these are crude comparisons. But they do underscore the contrast between Russia and the southern Near Abroad in mobilizable power. While its resource mobilization base has diminished significantly since 1991, the data show that Russia still has almost 26 times the GNP, four times as many soldiers, and a defense budget almost 40 times larger than the other eight states *combined.*

The same gross imbalance emerges if one compares the stock of specific items of major military equipment. The eight states of the southern Near Abroad together have 16 percent of the tanks, 18 percent of the armored personnel carriers, 17 percent of the artillery, 19 percent of the combat aircraft, and 8 percent of the helicopters that Russia does.[14]

Table 3–1. Russia and the Southern Near Abroad: Power Indices

	Population (millions)	GNP ($billions)	Armed Forces (thousands)	Defense Spending ($millions)
Russia	148	1,100	1,240	32,000
Armenia	3.3	1.4	60	92
Azerbaijan	7.1	1.4	66	120
Georgia	5.5	3.3	33	60
Kazakhstan	16.7	18.0	35	211
Kyrgyzstan	4.4	2.1	12	13
Tajikistan	5.3	1.1	9	70
Turkmenistan	3.6	4.9	18	140
Uzbekistan	20.3	11.0	70	113

SOURCE: International Institute for Strategic Studies (IISS), *The Military Balance, 1997–98* (London: Brassey's, 1997), pp. 74–75, 84–85, 108, 157, 162, 163. Data on GNP, size of armed forces, and defense spending; figures are for 1997. Population (for 1990) figures from *The First Book of Demographics for the Republics of the Former Soviet Union 1951–1990* (Shady Side, MD: New World Demographics, 1992), p. A 3 (Table A-1).

The Russian army has suffered a drastic decline in morale, readiness, training, and the quality and quantity of conscripts. But these problems are even more severe in the case of the states of the southern Near Abroad that, moreover, also virtually lack the capacity to generate their own military power. Azerbaijan and Uzbekistan have reached agreements for training and arms supplies with countries such as Turkey, but they remain overwhelmingly dependent on Russia for training and equipment and for spare parts for a force structure that is overwhelmingly of Soviet vintage. While some Central Asian states, such as Uzbekistan, have made progress in developing an indigenous officer corps, ethnic Russians generally account for an overwhelming majority. Turkmenistan's armed forces are under joint Russian-Turkmen command, and Kazakhstan agreed in 1996 to an integrated military structure with Russia. Absent anything that could really be called a professional army in Tajikistan, Russia's 201st Motor Rifle Division and border security forces in essence are the Tajik military force. Russian border troops patrol Kazakhstan's and Kyrgyzstan's border with China and Turkmenistan's border with Iran. Russian forces were not withdrawn from Armenia after the Soviet collapse, and they have been reintroduced into Georgia. Because their titular nationalities had a higher representation in the Soviet officer corps relative to Central Asians, Armenia, Azerbaijan, and Georgia (particularly the first of the troika) are in a better position when it comes to indigenous military leadership. But they too have inherited Soviet-era force structures. And this necessitates dependence on Russia for training, modernization, replacement, and spare parts. Once Azerbaijan's oil starts flowing to hard currency markets in large quantities, it will be able to reduce its military dependence on Russia over time by buying arms from the West. (Russia's ability to prevent this will be a good test of its influence.) Georgia and Armenia are far less fortunate and will have to rely on Russia for their military hardware for a much longer time.

Russia's wars in Afghanistan and Chechnya and the American war in Vietnam demonstrate that power differentials do not translate automatically into successful policy. Russia's advantages in power should, therefore, be seen alongside other realities in the southern Near Abroad that make the skewed balance of power between center and periphery meaningful. One of these realities is the ethnic conflicts and civil wars that have raged in the southern Near Abroad.[15] Armenia and Azerbaijan have been embroiled in war over Nagorno-Karabakh since 1992 and in hostility verging on war since 1988. The war, which stopped in 1994 due to the tenuous cease-fire arranged by Russia, has sapped their strength; it has contributed to a severe economic crisis that has eroded the legitimacy of both governments; it has created an internal setting favorable to coups and revolts (as evidenced by the fall of Ayaz Mutalibov and Abulfaz Elcibey and the rebellion of Surat Husseinov in Azerbaijan). In Tajikistan, a government that presides over a deep economic crisis while barely controlling its territory is wholly dependent on Russian military support and economic largesse for survival. The net result, as I shall show, has been to increase Russia's influence in these three countries by making Moscow's support decisive in determining who will win and who will lose and whether brittle cease-fires hold. The second reality is that the states of the southern Near Abroad are still heavily—although unevenly—dependent on Russia economically, as I shall show in discussing trade patterns and energy pipeline routes. The third reality is that, when it comes to internal insurgencies or external threats, the ruling elites of these states, while they desire to reduce their reliance on Russia, see it as the ultimate guarantor of their survival in the meantime. The bottom line: In the southern Near Abroad, a region with several poor, weak, fragmented states, Russia's influence is far greater than one would suspect from the steady output of books and articles depicting Russia's crises and from the tendency of Russians themselves to bemoan their country's plummeting power and prestige.

THE PULL OF PERIPHERAL INSTABILITY

I have argued that, its numerous problems notwithstanding, Russia retains considerable capacity to influence the policies of states in the southern Near Abroad. The corollary is not that the Russian elites who have been responsible for foreign and security policy since December 1991 are committed to, let alone cavalier about, using force to establish Russian paramountcy in the region. Nor does it follow that efforts to do so will not land Russia in quagmires and subject it to debilitating overcommitment.[16] While Russia's leaders do believe that their country should at a minimum be *primus inter pares* in the post-Soviet space, they understand that public support for spending blood and treasure to this end is extremely weak, especially in the wake of the Chechen war. They realize as well that assuming the responsibilities of a regional fire brigade–cum–gendarme could have pernicious consequences. Among these would be deflecting Russia from the path of economic reform, distorting budgetary priorities, and increasing the influence of nationalist and communist counterelites who would thrive as jingoism and a siege mentality gained ground.

But these restraints face some powerful countervailing pressures. There are many reasons to expect that the southern Near Abroad will experience considerable instability in the years ahead. One is the process of far-reaching economic change under way as Soviet-style economies gradually are transformed. The power of markets and the pace of economic reform, while uneven, will gain ground with time. Both are essential for creating efficiency but may be at odds with short-term stability. Markets determine prices and allocate goods and services better than any alternative. But they also create economic disparities and unemployment, especially in a post-Soviet world littered with inefficient enterprises that are awash in red ink. In multiethnic societies, which exist throughout the southern Near Abroad to varying degrees, they also can unleash internecine struggles over relative gains and losses from privatization. The reason is that the Soviet polity suppressed nationalism that was secessionist or hostile to the official ideology but, by establishing an ethnically demarcated federal structure and promoting non-Russian languages (albeit for its own purposes), it also reinforced ethnicity as a source of separate identities.[17] Not surprisingly, with the disintegration of the USSR, the ideological-political void has been filled by ethnonationalism. It is by no means the sole mode for identity, organization, mobilization, and competition in politics, but it is the dominant one. This is true not just for titular nationalities but also for small ethnic minorities. Often in reaction to the nationalism of the majority, Abkhaz, Ossetians, Lezgins, Talysh, Tats, Karakalpaks, Kurds, and others have embraced ethnicity as the basis for orientation and solidarity and for evaluating gains and losses.[18]

The countries that emerged from the detritus of the Soviet Union are not just creating new economies; they are simultaneously fashioning new national identities. In ethnically diverse societies, this can produce struggles over a host of issues: the privileging of indigenous languages over Russian (a contentious matter, particularly in Kazakhstan and Kyrgyzstan, where Russians account for 35 percent and 25 percent of the population respectively); the status of minority languages and cultures (an explosive topic in Georgia), and the role of ethnic criteria in determining access to political power and socioeconomic benefits (a sensitive issue in Kazakhstan). Because these matters have to do with rights, belonging, and authenticity, disputes over them have the potential to become heated—even bloody.

The mismatch between state and national boundaries—a legacy of Soviet state formation in the region during the 1920s and 1930s—is another feature of the southern Near Abroad.[19] State borders divide Russians, Tajiks, Uzbeks, Azeris, Armenians, Ossetians, Lezgins, and others and are viewed as pernicious demarcations that allow minorities to be oppressed by majorities. The classic preconditions for irredentist and separatist conflict are thus plentiful. The bloodshed between Abkhaz and Georgians, Ossetians and Georgians, and Azeris and Armenians in the south Caucasus shows that this is not just a theoretical possibility but the grim reality. In Central Asia, such conflicts have so far been absent; the civil war in Tajikistan is not driven by ethnic animosities. But there are sizable minorities that could mobilize and press their demands with violence: Uzbeks in Kyrgyzstan, Russians in Kazakhstan and Kyrgyzstan, and Tajiks in Uzbekistan. The fate of Kazakhstan's Russians will concern Russia directly: Northern Kazakhstan has a 3,000-mile border with Russia, and the majority of the population in most northern provinces is Russian. It is difficult to imagine Russia turning a blind eye should violence erupt between Kazakhs and Russians. Other potential ethnic flashpoints are less important for Russia. The percentage of Russians in the total population in the rest of the southern Near Abroad—except in Kyrgyzstan, a quarter of whose population is Russian—is small, ranging from a low of 1.6 percent in Armenia to 9 percent in Turkmenistan.

But instability in a contiguous periphery that is deemed vital for Russian national security would make it difficult for Moscow to desist even when the safety of ethnic Russians is not a major issue. Formless anxiety about upheaval in sensitive areas, fears about contagion, and suspicions that rival powers will take advantage are among the considerations that historically have led to imperial involvement.[20] And involvement has proven easier to begin than end. There are always reasons to stay: the fear of even worse consequences or the desire to extract concessions. Russia's role in the wars in the south Caucasus and Tajikistan shows that it is not immune from the pull of the periphery. Neither public opinion nor the fear of mounting costs and strategic quicksand were strong enough keep Russia out; nor have they been able to force Russia out.

The southern Near Abroad has other characteristics that could produce instability and draw Russia into the fray as peacekeeper or partisan. The regimes of the region tend to be overpersonalized and underinstitutionalized. By this I mean that there are no robust executive, legislative, and judicial institutions to serve as mechanisms for establishing ground rules. Instead, they are dominated by powerful leaders. Civil society and organized political opposition are virtually absent (Tajikistan, Turkmenistan, and Uzbekistan), weak or vulnerable (Azerbaijan and Georgia), or losing strength after a promising start (Armenia, Kazakhstan, Kyrgyzstan).[21] In the absence of institutions permitting real political participation, pentup grievances can erupt in violence (as in Georgia and Tajikistan). These countries have strong leaders (hence my reference to overpersonalization) capable of keeping the lid on and mediating regional and ethnic differences. Haidar Aliev in Azerbaijan, Eduard Shevardnadze in Georgia, Islam Karimov in Uzbekistan, Nursultan Nazarbaev in Kazakhstan, Askar Akaev in Kyrgzystan, and Saparmurad Niazov in Turkmenistan exemplify the phenomenon of overpersonalized polities, albeit in distinctive ways. The danger is that charisma and strength are not transferrable and that suppressed tensions will surface after the departure of a strongman, such as Aliev, Karimov, and Niazov, or that the successors of Akaev, Nazarbaev, and Shevardnadze will not command the confidence of national minorities or possess the adroitness to bridge ethnic differences. Another danger is that, absent legitimate institutional mechanisms for transferring power upon the death or retirement of a leader, successions could become occasions for infighting.

Another condition prevalent in the southern Near Abroad is the high rate of population growth. The tempo is generally significantly higher among the Turkic-Persian peoples than in Russia, Ukraine, or the Baltic states, and their populations tend to be young: 70 percent of all Central Asians, for example, are under 30 years of age.[22] This has several implications. Population growth rates will continue to be high because of the youthful demographic structure of these societies. Leaders will struggle to generate rates of economic growth sufficient to absorb the rapidly increasing pool of those who need jobs, especially if ethnic wars or other forms of instability scare off foreign investors. Rural unemployment will push more and more people into the cities, leading to overcrowding and the creation of an anomic, discontented, mobilizable mass—a familiar phenomenon in the developing world. The current cohort of Soviet-trained, Russified leaders (exemplified by men like Shevardnadze, Nazarbaev, Akaev, Aliev, Karimov, and Niazov) will be replaced by a new generation unconnected to, or only lightly touched by, Soviet-Russian mores. Russia then will have to translate its advantages (superior power and easy reach) into hegemony under new and more challenging conditions.

A comparison between the south Caucasus and Central Asia demonstrates that the orientation of ruling elites has been important to Russia. In the latter region, nationalist movements (such as *Birlik* in Uzbekistan, *Azat* and *Alash* in Kazakhstan, or *Agzybirlik* in Turkmenistan) whose objectives include breaking with what they perceive as Russian/Soviet colonial dependence did emerge. But they were marginalized by intricate regulations governing elections and the registration of political organizations or simply repressed by regimes headed by the Soviet-era communist officials who became the leaders of the independent Central Asian states. Despite the tensions that have existed between Russia and their countries, these leaders have pointedly avoided mobilizing anti-Russian sentiment. Georgia under Gamsakhurdia and Azerbaijan under Elcibey represent a glaring contrast.[23] Neither leader was from the Soviet ruling class. To the contrary, both were nationalist dissidents in the Soviet years and were determined to foster indigenous nationalism and reduce dependence on Russia. Gamsakhurdia refused to join the Russian-led Commonwealth of Independent States (CIS), championed a Caucasian league of states—encompassing Russia's volatile north Caucasus—that would have gravitated away from Russia, and continually warned of Russian imperial conspiracies. This outlook led him to make common cause with the secessionist Dzhokar Dudayev in Chechnya. Elcibey, who likewise spurned the CIS, promoted Turkic nationalism and strengthened Azerbaijan's ties with Turkey—both out of a sense of cultural affinity and as a means to detach his country from Russia's orbit. Moscow welcomed the replacement of Gamsakhurdia by Shevardnadze and Elcibey by Aliev, and there has been much debate about whether it engineered their falls. Russia's role in their downfall is unclear (both leaders certainly did much to bring about their political demise), but Russian satisfaction was obvious. Shevardnadze and Aliev were much more in the mold of Central Asia's leaders in the sense that both had been part of the Soviet ruling structure at both the republican and central level. I do not mean to imply that either man is therefore an instrument of Russia. As I make clear later, both have sought to build ties with the West as part of an explicit strategy of reducing their dependence on Russia. But, because of their backgrounds and experience, they understand Russia and have a clear-eyed recognition of the limits imposed by power, geography, and the legacy of the past. Both have sought to take account of Russia's sensibilities even as they have worked to whittle away its leverage. They have not stoked anti-Russian nationalism and, in different ways, have made the necessary compromises: Shevardnadze agreed to permit Russian bases in Georgia, joined the CIS, and reluctantly acceded to Russia's predominant diplomatic role in the conflicts in Abkhazia and South Ossetia; Aliev too joined the CIS and has sought to co-opt Russia by encouraging its companies to invest in Azerbaijan's oil ventures. A prudence that nationalist critics condemn (quietly in Aliev's case) has been the watchword of both leaders in dealing with Moscow.

I have identified several conditions that mark the southern Near Abroad: the tension between markets and stability, ethnonationalism and irredentism, overpersonalized polities, and high rates of population growth. They are structural in that they can be expected to last for the long term and synergistic in that their political effect must be understood in combination, not isolation. Consequently, they virtually guarantee that instability will prevail in the area for the foreseeable future. It is theoretically possible for Moscow to adopt either a neoisolationist, Russia-first attitude in response. It could refuse to assume the burden of being the provider par excellence or the 911 number that besieged leaders call when coups, secessionist movements, or civil strife erupt. It could focus on building democracy and markets and on forging economic ties with the West and Asia-Pacific on the grounds that economic success is paramount and the pursuit of peripheral dominance a wasteful endeavor at odds with it. Such a Russia would eschew hegemonic policies and limit its involvement even in peacekeeping operations, viewing them as distracting, wasteful, and debilitating. But I do not believe that either scenario is likely. Neoisolationism, advocated by those such as Aleksandr Solzhenitsyn, would be a fundamental break with the legacy of tsarist, Soviet, and post-Soviet policy. There is no evidence that forces advocating such an approach are, or are likely to be, powerful in Russian politics. To the contrary, although they differ radically on what the goals and instruments of Russian foreign policy should be, democratic reformers, Eurasianists,[24] Communists, and nationalists share the vision of Russia as a great power engaged in the big issues of world affairs. While democratic reformers may want to reduce the priority given the southern Near Abroad, Eurasianists, communists, and nationalists do not, albeit for radically different reasons. The (admittedly brief) history of post-Soviet Russia proves that the political influence of the last three groups is strong enough to ensure that the government accommodates their views by adjusting its proclamations and policy. That Boris Yeltsin has systematically co-opted many of their foreign policy slogans since late 1992 proves this. Until then he and Foreign Minister Andrei Kozyrev had focused on ties with the West and had regarded entanglement in the southern Near Abroad warily. But he subsequently adopted a more assertive posture in the region.[25] The involvement in the wars in Georgia, Tajikistan, and Nagorno-Karabakh deepened; states in the Near Abroad were warned about the treatment of ethnic Russians; Russian officials began to lobby for dual citizenship for the Russian diaspora and for official status for the Russian language; Moscow began to demand changes in the "flank limits" of the Conventional Forces in Europe (CFE) treaty that set armaments and manpower ceilings for the North Caucasus military district;[26] and Russian officials began to emphasize that Russia was determined not to allow its preponderance in the post-Soviet space eroded by forces from beyond. The personnel change that symbolized this shift in orientation was Yeltsin's decision to jettison Kozyrev in 1995 and to replace him with Yevgeni Primakov, a man far more in tune with the emerging strategic consensus.

Geographic contiguity and the imperial legacy also rules out Russian indifference or abdication in the southern Near Abroad. The United States was able to extricate itself from Vietnam after a disastrous war. Britain withdrew from its colonies remarkably smoothly (in terms of consequences to itself, not necessarily to its former colonial subjects). France fought bloody wars in Algeria and Indochina before throwing in the towel. In each case one—not the only—facilitating condition was that the locales of conflict or the colonial domains were distant. Once they had decided to leave, American, British, and French leaders could claim credibly that vital national security interests were not involved, that space offered a buffer. Russian leaders will not have this luxury in the case of the southern Near Abroad precisely because it is "near."

Events in the southern Near Abroad will affect Russia itself, in such regions as southern Russia, the north Caucasus, Tatarstan and Bashkortostan. The tsarist-Soviet imperial legacy, transborder religious and cultural affinities, and the realities of geography guarantee that Russian leaders, of whatever political coloration, will never see happenings in this region as "foreign" policy. The specter of falling dominoes, the ripple effects of turbulence in the periphery on the homeland (fleeing refugees, the inflow of drugs, Islamist and separatist ideologies), and endangered Russian kin will evoke strong emotions precisely because of geographical circumstances. Leaders who look on passively will be accused of jeopardizing national security in a neighboring area Russia traditionally has dominated. The fear of strategic setbacks and the power of domestic coalitions harping on their danger account for the interventionist role the United States has played in Central and Latin America for 100 years now, regardless of which party governs in Washington. Although the parallel to American policy in Central and South America is not an exact one, Russia will not be able to stand aloof from crises in its southern periphery for these very reasons.

How quickly Russia responds to peripheral crises, how it responds, the nature of the legitimating rhetoric, and whether Western reactions are taken into account will depend on both its power and the composition of its ruling elites. As a broad generalization, I would suggest that the more nationalistic and undemocratic the regime in Russia and the greater the degree of peripheral instability, the greater the danger of intemperate Russian intervention.[27] But the nature of Russia's government alone will not necessarily make the difference between intervention and nonintervention. The belief that the triumph of democracy in Russia in itself will guarantee a benevolent policy toward the southern Near Abroad is an instance of the wish fathering the thought.[28] Preponderant power (and the desire to preserve it) will supplement the pull of the turbulent periphery. So will the synergistic pressures of domestic coalitions whose members

may have distinctive versions of why the national interest requires assertive action in the periphery but who nevertheless act in tactical concert for
increased efficacy. There is no reason to assume that democracy will
immunize Russia from such pressures; it has not done so when other great
powers have faced instability in strategically vital regions. These were the
very conditions (superior power, pressure from domestic lobbies, peripheral upheaval) that led the democratic government of Boris Yeltsin to
get involved in the Azerbaijan-Armenia conflict and in the civil wars in
Georgia and Tajikistan. Russian leaders committed to democracy and
economic reform thus confront a difficult balancing act. They must defend
Russia's interest in the southern periphery for external-strategic and
domestic-political reasons. They must count on considerable volatility in
that region and realize that Russian involvement may not always be a
matter of choice but of necessity and that entry may prove easier than
exit. They must ensure that the pressure of parochial domestic groups (the
energy lobby, military leaders, tub-thumping ultranationalists) and their
own hubris (a product of superior power and atavistic colonial attitudes)
do not land Russia in the predicament of Gulliver or Sisyphus.

TRADE AND MONEY: RUSSIA CONTESTED

Seventy years of a centrally planned economy based on a specialization in
production among the 15 union republics of the U.S.S.R. made for intricate patterns of interdependence that continue to be a powerful constraint
for the ex-Soviet republics today. Most still depend overwhelmingly on
Russia for markets and supplies. True, the southern Near Abroad has
opened up in the post-Soviet era to trade and investment from the United
States, Western Europe, Japan, South Korea, China, Israel, and the Arab
world. But the economic salience of Russia is still impressive. This
is demonstrated by the trade data in Table 3–2. Column A represents
exports to Russia as a percentage of the country's total exports and column B imports from Russia as percentage of its total imports. (The data
pertain to 1994, the most recent year for which statistics complete enough
to calculate degrees of trade dependence are available.)[29] While there are
variations (the relatively low levels of dependence in the case of oil-rich
Azerbaijan and Turkmenistan is noteworthy), overall the extent of dependence on Russia for trade is strong even four years after the collapse of
the Soviet Union and holds even for those countries that are large and
have sought to diversify their trade (Kazakhstan and Uzbekistan) and
that have pretensions of countering Russian influence in their regions
(Uzbekistan). And as the table shows, the trade dependence is unequal.

Table 3–2. The Southern Near Abroad and Trade with Russia, 1994

	A	B
Azerbaijan	22.1	15.2
Armenia	52.7	48.8
Georgia	58.0	14.9
Kyrgyzstan	83.6	99.0
Kazakhstan	67.6	59.4
Tajikistan	26.4	57.5
Turkmenistan	10.1	16.1
Uzbekistan	45.7	47.5

SOURCE: International Monetary Fund, *Direction of Trade Statistics: 1995 Year Book* (Washington, DC: IMF, 1995), pp. 105, 112, 210, 274, 266, 368, 409, 426, 441.

The dependence of the southern Near Abroad on Russia may well change with time. In particular, the natural resource abundance of Kazakhstan, Uzbekistan, Turkmenistan, and Azerbaijan may enable them to break or reduce sharply their economic dependence on Russia. There is also no doubt that the exclusive economic relationship that tsarist Russia and the Soviet Union had with the Central Asia and the south Caucasus is over for good: Independent states eager to forge trade and investment links with the outside world now have emerged in these two regions, and Russia, on account of its economic difficulties, will be poorly placed to compete with the United States, Western Europe, Turkey, Japan, and China. Yet the erosion of Russia's economic position in Central Asia and the south Caucasus should not be exaggerated. This point will be apparent when energy development in the Caspian Sea is discussed in the next section.

To reiterate an earlier point, the dependence is asymmetric: Russia has far more scope for using trade as a means of political leverage than do governments of the southern Near Abroad. Table 3–3 depicts the asymmetry for the year 1995. It shows the importance to Russia of these countries by presenting their share both of Russia's total trade and of its trade with the members of the CIS. Column A represents exports to the given country as a percentage of all Russia exports; column B, imports from the given country as a percentage of all Russian imports; column C, exports to the given country as a percentage of Russian exports to the CIS states; and column D, imports from the individual country as a percentage of Russia's imports from the CIS.

Table 3–3. Russia's Trade Dependence on the Southern Near Abroad

	A	B	C	D
Azerbaijan	.1	.3	.6	.3
Armenia	.2	.2	.4	.6
Georgia	.1	.2	.3	.4
Kazakhstan	4.0	8.2	19.0	20.0
Kyrgyzstan	.2	.2	.7	.8
Tajikistan	.3	.4	1.3	1.2
Turkmenistan	.1	.2	.6	.8
Uzbekistan	1.2	1.9	6.0	7.0

SOURCE: Goskomstat Rossii, *Rossiia v tsifrakh: ofitsial'noe izdanie* (Russia in figures: official publication) (Moscow: Finansy i Statistiki, 1996), Table 5.2.3, pp. 142–44. Percentages have been rounded and were calculated from data rendered in billions of current rubles.

Although Russia remains an important trade partner, China, Japan, Turkey, Iran, and Western countries have eroded its position as a customer and supplier for the states of the southern Near Abroad. The dependence of Azerbaijan and Uzbekistan on Russia for trade has diminished markedly since 1992.[30] And Georgia's economy also is progressively turning away from Russia. Should Russia's economic problems worsen, and if companies from the West, East Asia, and Turkey continue to be active in the south Caucasus and Central Asia, Russia's role in regional trade will diminish further. While this also could occur as a consequence of regional economic integration schemes that exclude Russia, their achievements so far have been minimal.[31] War within and among states does not make for a setting conducive to economic cooperation in the south Caucasus. In Central Asia there have been five attempts at regional economic cooperation, the latest being the Central Asian Economic Union (CAEU) of January 1994. But they have been long on aspirations and proclamations, short on tangible results. The other Central Asian states worry that regional cooperation will prove to be a Trojan horse for Uzbek domination. Kazakhstan has been ambivalent about arrangements that exclude Russia; it has joined them but prefers actual or potential integration involving Russia, be it the CIS or the Eurasian Union proposal floated by Kazakh President Nursultan Nazarbaev. The gap between declarations and achievements also characterizes the Economic Cooperation Organization (ECO) that was revived in 1992 and enlarged by Turkey, Pakistan, and Iran (the original members) to include Azerbaijan, the five Central Asian states, and Afghanistan.

The combination of asymmetric economic interdependence and Russia's superior power also has enabled Russia to exert significant influence over economic decisions in the southern Near Abroad when it comes to monetary policy. An example is the negotiations over the extended ruble zone. When Kyrgyzstan left the ruble zone and set up its own currency, the *som,* in May 1993, the other Central Asian states criticized it. But by the end of the year all of them except Tajikistan, which remained in the ruble zone but replaced the Russian ruble with the Tajik ruble in May 1995 and said that it would introduce the *somon,* its own currency, sometime in the future, had left the ruble zone and established separate currencies; so had the states of the south Caucasus, except for Azerbaijan, which introduced its own currency on the first day of 1993.[32] The reasons were that Russia imposed a stiff price for admission, including the sole right to issue rubles and to control the foreign exchange and gold reserves of these countries. These were terms that even the most fervent proponents of integration with Russia, such as Nazarbaev, could not accept. To be sure, Russia's demands could be justified by the need to prevent the monetary policies of other states from deciding the success or failure of its fight against inflation. Yet the conditions that Russia set essentially would have abrogated the economic independence of the Central Asian states.

At the same time, the stringency of Moscow's terms and its decision to rebuff attempts by Georgia and Armenia to stay in the ruble zone suggest a divergence between Russian strategic and economic policy, which are defined by institutions and elites with very different perspectives and priorities. Military and national security elites in Russia may want to draw the ex-Soviet republics closer and create a coalition dominated by Russia. But their economic counterparts are not prepared to spend a great deal of money to this end or to allow strategic aims, such as binding the Near Abroad to Russia, to hijack economic reform. When combined with the expansion of Western, Middle Eastern, and East Asian economic activity in the southern Near Abroad, the exit of the region's economies from the ruble zone will accelerate the decline of Russian economic influence. But to say that Russia's economic role in what used to be its imperial periphery will never be what it used to be is to state the obvious. The real question is whether Russia will retain an appreciable level of economic power in Central Asia and the south Caucasus despite the growing economic role of other states. That remains uncertain because it is tied to the complex question of the pace and extent of Russia's economic recovery. What is certain is that extrapolations made at a time of acute Russian economic weakness should be treated skeptically.

THE CASPIAN CONUNDRUM

Both the extent and limits of Russia's influence in the southern Near Abroad also are demonstrated by the controversy over the legal status of the Caspian Sea and the implications of current and prospective pipeline routes for transporting Caspian hydrocarbon wealth. On the former issue, Russia (together with Iran) opposes a division of the Caspian Sea into exclusive national jurisdictions. The legal basis for its preference is the contention that the Caspian is an inland sea to which legal principles governing maritime resources do not apply and that its status is governed by the 1921 and 1940 treaties between the Soviet Union and Iran. The practical motivation for its condominium model, under which decisions on Caspian oil and gas development would be taken jointly by the littoral states with the export revenues being shared among them, is the desire to have what in effect could be a veto on the origin of foreign investment, its extent, and the conditions under which it operates. In the Russian view, proceeds from the extraction of Caspian energy resources should be shared among littoral states and decisions about awarding foreign companies prospecting and drilling contracts be taken in common, not by individual states laying exclusive claim to sectors of the Caspian. This in turn is connected to Russia's desire to maintain its predominance in Central Asia and the southern Caucasus at a time when that position is being challenged as never before.

Of the states on the Caspian littoral, Azerbaijan has been the most outspoken in challenging the Russian model. It has rejected the idea of joint management, insisted on the legal validity of dividing the Caspian Sea into national jurisdictions, and proceeded to form a number of consortia with foreign oil companies to develop offshore fields that lie in what it considers to be its sector. But it also has encouraged the participation of Russian oil companies. Its message to Russia is essentially that the legal dispute over the Caspian will not prevent it from seeking foreign investment based on the view that the Caspian consists of national sectors and that Russia can either join the investment parade or stand and watch. Azeri leaders are well aware that the large, politically influential Russian oil companies such as LUKoil and key Russian officials (foremost among them Prime Minister Viktor Chernomyrdin and First Deputy Prime Minister Boris Nemtsov) feel that nonparticipation would be foolish for at least two reasons. First, while absent the legal dispute over the Caspian it may be that there would have been an even larger amount of foreign investment (there is no way to ascertain the validity of such counterfactual propositions), what is truly remarkable is how much has occurred in spite of it. Russia's legal argument has not had much effect. Second, a Russian boycott would amount to Moscow cutting off its nose to spite its face. Western, Turkish, Japanese, and Chinese investment in Caspian oil and gas ventures would proceed apace, and Russia simply would have accelerated the erosion of its economic position in a strategically vital, contiguous area. Azerbaijan's calculation that Moscow would understand both points and allow its firms to participate in oil deals has proven correct.

Kazakhstan supports the Azerbaijani position. It too has welcomed foreign investment in offshore sites. But it has been careful not to be a confrontational and defiant spear-carrier in the Caspian fracas. The difference in style is attributable to Kazakhstan's greater dependence on Russia and its consequent vulnerability. Kazakhstan has a 3,000-mile border with Russia. Unlike the other Caspian states, it is directly exposed to Russian power along a wide front. (Azerbaijan's border with Russia is about 100 miles long, and Turkmenistan does not share a border with Russia.) Russians constitute 35 percent or so (emigration makes for uncertainty on the exact proportion) of its population and between 45 percent and 64 percent, depending on the area in question, in the northern and northeastern provinces of Aqmola, East Kazakhstan, North Kazakhstan, Qaraghandy, Qostanay, and Pavlodar.[33] Kazakhstan's trade dependence on Russia, as I have already shown, is very high. In addition, despite its energy wealth, because of the absence of a well-developed internal distribution network Kazakhstan's oil refineries at Chimkent and Pavlodar, which supply its high-demand eastern and southern regions, depend on Russian crude oil from Siberia. Pavlodar relies totally on Russian crude; Chimkent, for about 70 percent of its needs.[34] In addition, the natural gas and condensate from Kazakhstan's vast Karachaganak field is processed at Russia's Orenburg, Salavat, and Novo-Ufimskii refineries.[35] The dependence on Russia exists in the realm of security as well. Kazakhstan's officer corps consists overwhelmingly of ethnic Russians, and it relies almost completely on Russian military training, equipment, and spare parts.[36]

Turkmenistan's position is somewhat more complex, even curious. Soon after the fall of the Soviet Union, it favored the concept of exclusive sectors in the Caspian. But it has changed course since 1995, and Russian pressure was not irrelevant in bringing this about. According to a senior official in the Turkmenistan Foreign Ministry, Russia told Turkmen officials that Russian military officers and border troops—who play a critical role given Turkmenistan's lack of military expertise and a sizable local officer corps—would be removed from their country if they backed Azerbaijan's position on the Caspian and that, in addition, Turkmenistan's commercial vessels would be denied access to the Volga.[37] The Turkmen position is now that all littoral states should avoid unilateral actions until a negotiated settlement on the Caspian's status is reached.[38] At the same time, it has disputed Azerbaijan's claim to the Kyapaz offshore field (which Turkmenistan calls Serdar) on the ground that it lies within Turkmenistan's sector of the Caspian and also has announced plans to elicit tenders for its offshore energy sites—actions that imply an acceptance of national jurisdictions and a willingness to act unilaterally.

The movement of foreign capital into the Caspian Sea zone and Azerbaijan's defiant attitude show that Russia has not been able to enforce the condominium model under which the Caspian would be jointly managed by coastal states rather than being divided into exclusive national sectors. Indeed, since the appointment of Yevgeni Primakov as foreign minister, Russia has moderated its position. In November 1996 it proposed that 45-mile national jurisdictions be established for oil and gas (with the added provision that currently known energy sites beyond that limit also could be exploited unilaterally) and 10-mile boundaries for fishing, with joint ownership as the principle governing elsewhere.[39] But it would be wrong to conclude from this that Russian policy in the Caspian has failed. Russia's predominant strategic position is precisely why Azerbaijan has sought the participation of Russian oil companies. It realizes that Russia needs to be co-opted so as to moderate its position on the Caspian. Senior Western oil executives in Azerbaijan concede that LUKoil and other Russian firms have been invited into energy consortia because the Russian state has lobbied aggressively for them and because Western companies and littoral states see the political value of having Russia on board—not because of what these firms contribute technologically and financially.[40] Russia may be well aware that its preferred model for the Caspian cannot be implemented now. But it has not disavowed it and may calculate that the concept of a condominium can be revived and pursued from a stronger position in the future.[41] In the meantime, by acting as a potential spoiler and challenging the legal validity of national zones in the Caspian Sea, it has acquired leverage. The states that support the division of the Caspian, and the foreign oil companies that operate within them, have sought to co-opt Russia by bringing Russian companies into the energy and pipeline consortia being formed.[42] From Moscow's perspective, this ensures that Russia remains a major participant in Caspian Sea energy development.

Russia initially may have believed that its proposed regime for Caspian Sea management could be implemented. And it may well prefer that solution to any other. But it understands that it is not currently achievable. Why, then, has it not closed the book on the legal dispute? The reason is that keeping it open and advocating—even if ritualistically—a regime of joint management for the Caspian provides Moscow some leverage. States that favor the division of the Caspian, and foreign companies that operate in them, hope that a growing economic stake will decrease the chances that Russia will be obstreperous. From Moscow's perspective, this ensures that Russian firms are sought as partners in energy ventures and that the West (along with Turkey, Japan, and China) does not rule the Caspian roost. Moreover, if the condominium model is the ideal solution from Russia's standpoint, why not hold it in reserve for a time when Russia's bargaining position might be stronger? If this argument is valid, the commonplace view—one that so nicely complements the reigning Russia-in-decline-and-disarray paradigm—of the Russian approach to Caspian energy matters is wrong. That view is that the balkanized Russian state has no coherent policy because it is pulled in different directions by competing interests: oil companies and officials for whom economic interests are paramount on the one hand, and national security elites and institutions for whom Russian strategic predominance is the overriding imperative on the other. The former want to invest in Caspian energy free of restraints; the latter consider a collective regime essential. The foundation for this view, once again, is the state-as-cipher theoretical perspective so popular among analysts of Russian politics.

Russia's leverage is also apparent when it comes to transporting Caspian hydrocarbons to global markets. Azerbaijan, Kazakhstan, and Turkmenistan, for understandable reasons, do not want to rely for their energy exports on Soviet-era pipelines that run through Russia and are thus directly or indirectly subject to its control. Ideas for new oil pipelines abound, and some are moving ahead.[43] But this will not necessarily erode the Russian position. The three principal pipeline routes for Caspian oil are Tengiz-Atyrau-Astrakhan-Novorossiisk, Baku-Novorossiisk, and Baku-Supsa. None will render Russia irrelevant. The first, the result of the Caspian Pipeline Consortium (CPC), will build on the existing pipeline that runs from Tengiz and Atyrau in Kazakhstan to Astrakhan (just southwest of the Russian-Kazakh border) to Komsomol'sk. From Komsomol'sk, a new line will run west to Tikhoretsk (in Russia's Krasnodar province) and then turn southwest and end just north of Novorossiisk on the Black Sea. This route will pass entirely through Russian territory once it leaves Kazakhstan, and the Russian government and two Russian oil companies (LUKoil and Rosneft) together control 44 percent of CPC's equity.[44] This gives Russia considerable influence over Kazakh oil and gas

Existing and Potential Oil and Gas Export Routes From the Caspian Basin

exports and over Kazakh domestic and foreign policy generally. More-over, until it is finished (there have been several construction delays and completion is now expected in late 1999), oil from Tengiz will be carried by the existing pipeline that runs from Atyrau to Samara, a major junction from which oil can be exported to various markets.[45]

The second pipeline, commonly known as the northern route, is 1,500 kilometers long and runs from Baku to Grozny (Chechnya's capital) and on to Novorossiisk via Tikhoretsk. It was built in the Soviet period to bring oil to Baku for refining. The direction of flow will be reversed and repairs conducted on the Chechen segment (153 kilometers), and the security of the pipeline in turbulent Chechnya will have to be guaranteed. Its reliability will depend on the ability of Russia and Chechnya to address two problems: the durability of the September 1997 agreement on sharing transit revenue, and the far more vexing question of Chechnya's future relationship with Russia.[46] Should war resume between the two nations, any agreement on revenue sharing will be superfluous and the pipeline will be at risk. Indeed, the radical Chechen military commander Salman Raduyev has said that it will be a target unless Russia gives Chechnya its independence.[47] Even a pipeline that skirts Chechnya (an option that Russian leaders have mentioned is a 283-kilometer line from Khasavyurt in Dagestan to Terskaia in north Ossetia) is not a reliable solution. The Chechens could widen any future war with Russia to encompass the territory through which pipelines built to circumvent them run.[48] But even if all of these problems are settled, the northern route will, once it crosses the Azerbaijan-Russian border, run solely through Russian land and end at a Russian port. The hope that Russia will benefit from pipeline revenues and thus refrain from compromising its reliability is not unreasonable, but it is anchored in an assumption of friendly relations between Azerbaijan and Russia. This does not mean that it is foolhardy. But Azerbaijan's leaders certainly do not want to stake their economic plans on it.

The above scenario is one reason why the "western route" was created; it is the third export route for Caspian oil (part of which existed in Soviet times), is 700 kilometers long, and runs from Baku to the Georgian Black Sea port of Supsa. The other is Turkey's hope that the pipeline through Georgia will set the stage for yet another from Georgia to the Turkish Mediterranean port of Ceyhan that will carry long-term Azerbaijani oil production exceeding the capacity of the northern and western lines. The Ceyhan project has several attractions for Turkey: Azerbaijan's dependence on Russia will be reduced, Turkey will gain from transit revenues and various spinoff benefits, and tanker traffic through the Turkish Straits (oil sent through CPC's Tengiz-Novorossiisk pipeline and the northern and western route would head across the Black Sea and out through the Straits) will be reduced by creating an alternate route for long-term Caspian production.[49] Yet neither the western route nor the possibility of the Ceyhan conduit will marginalize Russia. As I shall show in the next section, Russia has ensconced itself in Georgia and is the decisive outside power when it comes to stability there. Russia, as I shall also demonstrate in the following section, is crucial to the continuation of peace in the dispute over Nagorno-Karabakh, and, inasmuch as the western route runs close to the Karabakh border as it crosses Yevlakh in Azerbaijan, it is vulnerable to renewed fighting between Armenians and Azeris. Furthermore, the Ceyhan route, while favored by Azerbaijan (and obviously Turkey), is not without problems that could prevent it from being built. It will require construction through mountainous zones, and its backers will have to prove that it is more cost-effective than other choices, one of which is another pipeline through Russia supplementing the northern route. There are security problems as well. The most economical way of building the Ceyhan line is to link it at Midyat with the existing Iraq-Turkey pipeline. But it will then have to traverse Kurdish populated areas in which the Turkish armed forces have been waging a protracted war against the Kurdistan Workers' Party (PKK).[50] Circumventing these areas (by, say, constructing a new pipeline from Tbilisi to Ceyhan via Sivas and Kayseri and not using the Turkey-Iraq line) would make an already expensive undertaking even more so.[51]

Turkmenistan, which has the world's third largest reserves of natural gas, is even more dependent on Russia for export channels. Gazprom, the Russian gas company that is 40 percent state-owned, controls the pipelines that Turkmenistan needs to export gas, and Turkmenistan relies on Gazprom specialists for the upkeep of its natural gas infrastructure. Gazprom essentially has relegated Turkmenistan to be a supplier to the former Soviet republics—which are financially strapped and have run up large debts—while limiting the amount of gas Turkmenistan exports to hard-currency markets. In 1995, to retain access to Gazprom's expertise and in the interests of a stable export arrangement, Turkmenistan formed a joint company with it called Turkmenrosgaz. When it terminated the venture in 1997, the head of Gazprom declared that he was ready to "give up entirely" on Turkmenistan—a potentially serious development considering the extent of its dependence on the company's pipelines and technical expertise.[52]

Like Azerbaijan and Kazakhstan, Turkmenistan has been trying to develop pipeline routes that would ease its predicament, but a mix of political and financial factors make the outlook uncertain.[53] One possibility is a gas pipeline from Turkmenistan through Afghanistan to Pakistan and on to India. In October 1997 Unocal, Delta (of Saudi Arabia), the Turkmen government, and various companies from Japan, Pakistan, and South Korea formed a consortium led by Unocal and called Central Asia Gas Pipeline Limited that Russia's Gazprom was expected to join. Construction was to begin in December 1998 and to end in 2001 with a 1,271-kilometer pipeline to Multan in Pakistan. An extension to India was also envisaged.[54] But so long as Afghanistan remains convulsed by civil war, as it has since 1978,[55] this pipeline may prove to be a pipedream. Turkmen leaders also have spoken about a gas pipeline through Uzbekistan, Kyrgyzstan, and China to Japan. But this would be an 8,000-mile project and, given the much higher costs of transporting gas relative to oil, it is unlikely to be cost-effective; at best it is a very long-term solution to an immediate problem. Yet another possible export route—and apparently the most promising—is through Iran and on to Turkey, and it has been moving forward ever since the agreement signed among Iran, Turkey, and Turkmenistan in April 1995. Iran agreed to fund a 287-kilometer pipeline from the Korpedzhe fields in western Turkmenistan to Kord-Kuy in northern Iran and to link it with the existing 1,000-kilometer line running west across northern Iran to the Turkish border. From there a second new pipeline is to take the gas into Turkey. In April 1997, under another trilateral agreement, Turkey agreed to purchase 28 billion cubic meters of Turkmen gas a year via the Iranian pipeline.[56] But, for financial and political reasons, experts are skeptical that a pipeline from Turkey that sends Turkmen gas on to western Europe will materialize.[57]

The conclusion is that Russia will remain an important player when it comes to the question of getting Caspian oil and gas to market no matter what the route. This does not mean that it has its hand on the economic jugular of regional energy producers. Nor does it means that the Russian government is implementing some grand strategy. The terms that Russia demands for the use of its pipelines may indeed partly reflect the parochial and pecuniary interests of bureaucratic cliques within the Russian state and not a policy of pressure conceived, orchestrated, and executed from Moscow. One astute analyst who rejects the idea of a Russian master plan argues that, while Kazakhstan has been allowed to export only half the full capacity (220,00 barrels a day) of Russia's Atyrau-Samara pipeline to customers outside the CIS, Russian oil-producing companies from Siberia have faced even more severe restrictions at the hands of venal bureaucrats.[58] Yet what matters to Kazakh leaders (and to their Azeri and Turkmen counterparts) is surely not the etiology of Russian restrictions but their existence—and the likelihood that they will continue to be an actual or potential problem until non-Russian export channels emerge.

REGIONAL CONFLICTS: OPPORTUNITY OR QUICKSAND?

There is no doubt that the increasing activity of non-Russian economic forces offers the states of the southern Near Abroad leverage against Russia. Paradoxically, another source of leverage is the very weakness and instability of these states. This creates a context for possible Russian domination, but it also makes for bargaining power over Moscow, because

Russian elites regard the area as a critical defense perimeter that should be kept free of upheaval. As a result, they have developed vested interests in existing regimes, which can, therefore, turn to Russia to cope with domestic or foreign threats or when economic problems that could create unrest arise. Assistance from Russia increases dependence and often is resented because it requires concessions of one sort or another. But it is solicited nevertheless because, as George Bernard Shaw quipped when asked how it felt to be eighty years old, the alternative is worse.

For Russia, the pursuit of influence in the Near Abroad inevitably will be accompanied by expenditures and quite possibly overextension (economic burdens) and entrapment (burdens without relief in sight). The historical record of weak states parlaying their weakness into an asset by manipulating great powers' fear of instability to drag them into internal conflicts is a long and rich one, and Russia has not been able to escape its logic. It was Russia's fear of upheaval in Tajikistan, manipulated adeptly by Uzbekistan, that got Moscow involved in Tajikistan's civil war in late 1992. Russia stayed on—nominally as peacekeeper but in truth as bodyguard and bouncer for the government of Emomali Rakhmonov (a communist holdover with his base of support in the southern region of Kulob) and as its principal financial benefactor. And reluctant involvement often begets entanglement. By providing troops to keep the tenuous peace among Georgia's ethnic groups, Russia has won strategic concessions; but this has not been without risks. The dangers are equally apparent when one considers Russia's importance to the Nagorno-Karabakh conflict.

The larger the strategic stake—bases, military facilities, security treaties, dependent ruling elites—Russia acquires, the greater the likelihood that it will become committed to the particular regimes with which that relationship was established. And the more difficult it will be—for external-strategic and domestic-political reasons—to stay clear when these regimes are threatened by economic crises or insurgencies led by counter-elites who are either hostile to Russia or whose orientation is uncertain. Nothing about this is unique to Russia. Great powers have time and again found that the danger of deepening involvement and increasing costs is part of the quest for predominance in regions they deem vital. They nevertheless persist—not because they are unfamiliar with Santayana's celebrated dictum, but because that is what powerful states do. Burdens and risks make for uncertainty; but the combined effect of the allure of influence, internal pressures to act forcefully, and a dread of the consequences of inaction generally prove overriding. And often, despite the risks, the gains made are inconsiderable. I shall illustrate these general observations by considering Russia's role in conflicts in the southern Near Abroad. My conclusion amplifies the point made previously that Russia's economic and military decline has not rendered it ineffectual in the area and that no regional or extraregional state or coalition has or is likely to displace it. If what Russia has achieved in the southern Near Abroad is measured in relation to what other great powers (such as the United States in Vietnam, Somalia, and Haiti; or France in various African locales) have accomplished when they have intervened in civil conflicts, the record is hardly one of abject failure.[59]

THE KARABAKH CONFLICT

The war over Nagorno-Karabakh is the oldest of the still-unresolved conflicts in the former Soviet Union. It is a civil war: The Armenian majority of the Nagorno-Karabakh enclave within Azerbaijan wanted to secede, and Karabakh fighters were prepared to resort to war to achieve that outcome. It is also an interstate war: Despite repeated denials, there is overwhelming evidence that the Armenian government has provided—and continues to extend—financial and material aid to the Karabakh forces and that the long-range goal of the leaders of Armenia and the leaders of Nagorno-Karabakh is a merger of the two to create a greater Armenia. Although Russia has been far more than a mere disinterested party, impartial mediator, or declining power caught in crossfire, this is not a conflict that Moscow started.

Its roots are diverse.[60] The Soviet pattern of state formation turned on ethnicity: Union republics, and autonomous republics and regions within them, were based on ethnic criteria. This approach nevertheless sowed the seeds for future conflicts by dividing people who felt as one. In this case Nagorno-Karabakh, overwhelmingly Armenian, was part of the union republic of Azerbaijan. This incongruity between national and state boundaries—a classic recipe for conflict—created a setting suited to hypernationalism as imperial decay led to imperial collapse (1988–91). Nationalities divided by state borders yearned to be united; minorities within countries wanted their own state based on ethnic criteria. The erosion and ultimate end of Soviet power made irredentism and ethno-nationalism—suppressed under the Soviet system—a powerful force for political mobilization in Nagorno-Karabakh, Armenia, and Azerbaijan.[61] A political void emerged once Soviet-era institutions atrophied and could no longer control what people did, what they saw and heard, and how, when, and for what they organized. The conflict over Nagorno-Karabakh underwent transformations that increased the danger of mass violence. What began as the collection of petitions in 1987 led to a declaration of secession in July 1989 by the provincial legislature in Nagorno-Karabakh and to declaration by the Armenian Supreme Soviet that Nagorno-Karabakh would from that point on be considered part of Armenia. Moscow handled the escalating crisis in a manner that ultimately angered both sides. Armenians felt that they were being denied the right to self-determination; Azeris believed that the Soviet authorities did not see the situation for what it really was: a secessionist movement launched by the Karabakh Armenians strengthened by Armenia's determination to effect a creeping annexation. Azeris' sense of outrage and injustice was brought to a fever pitch by what they regarded as an insidious partnership between the irredentism of Armenia and the separatism of the Armenians of Nagorno-Karabakh. Stereotypical, worst-case thinking and white-hot animosity triumphed on both sides with the pogroms against Armenians in the Azerbaijani cities of Sumgait, Ganca, and Baku (1988–90) and the exodus of Azeri refugees from Armenia and the flight of Armenians from Azerbaijan.[62] Psychological battle lines were being drawn even before war began. In January 1990 Soviet forces launched an attack in Baku—ostensibly to restore calm amid expanding ethnic violence, but in fact to decapitate the nationalist Popular Front movement that was becoming steadily more powerful and putting the position of the local Communist party in doubt—and killed over a hundred civilians and wounded many more.[63] Compromise became increasingly difficult. Passion ruled on both sides, and moderation was equated with cowardice—or worse, treachery. In September 1991, Azerbaijan's Supreme Soviet nullified the autonomous status of Nagorno-Karabakh, and the Armenian leadership of Karabakh responded with a declaration of independence. As the Soviet Union hovered on the brink of collapse, all possibility of avoiding open war between Karabakh fighters (assisted by Armenian troops) and Azeri forces vanished. The imperatives of ethnic solidarity with the Karabakh Armenians in Armenia's politics, and national integrity in Azerbaijan's, became simply overwhelming.

The fall of the governments led by the communist leader Ayaz Mutalibov in March 1992 and the nationalist Abulfaz Elcibey of the Popular Front in June 1993 showed that the staying power of political leaders and governments depended on strong rhetoric and the willingness to back it up with commensurate and successful action against Armenia. The disintegration of the U.S.S.R. and the withdrawal of Russian forces from Nagorno-Karabakh in March 1992 ensured that the war would escalate and turn nasty. The disarray in the Soviet armed forces led soldiers from units in the south Caucasus (the 7th Army in Yerevan, the 366th Motor Rifle Regiment in Nagorno-Karabakh, the 104th Airborne

Division in Ganca in Azerbaijan, and the 147th Motor Rifle Division in Akhalkalaki just north of the Georgia-Armenia border) to sell arms to the warring parties and to join the fighting on both sides—out of conviction or as mercenaries. The divvying up of Soviet army weapon stocks under the May 1992 Tashkent treaty among the former Soviet republics strengthened the ability of Armenia and Azerbaijan to wage war.

The chaos of imperial collapse explains what has happened in the Karabakh war better than Kremlin machinations. There is no irrefutable proof of a Russian military role orchestrated from Moscow on behalf of some well-crafted plan; chaos and improvisation reigned supreme. But the circumstantial evidence that Russian units were involved, whether as a result of the breakdown of discipline and command structures, the initiatives of local commanders, or sporadic orders from Moscow, is compelling. Karabakh fighters who took the predominantly Azeri town of Khojali, north of Stepanakert, Nagorno-Karabakh's capital, in February 1992—evicting the Azeri minority and killing numerous civilians in the process—appear to have been aided by troops from the 366th Motor Rifle Regiment.[64] Russian soldiers from the 147th Motor Rifle Division played a role in the fall of Shusha, the principal Azeri-populated town in Nagorno-Karabakh, located south of Stepanakert, in April 1992. Troops from this unit also appear to have helped overrun Lachin, an Azeri town southwest of Nagorno-Karabakh less than ten miles from the Armenian border, thus setting the stage for the creation of the so-called Lachin corridor that connected Armenia and Nagorno-Karabakh for the first time—and still does so. During the (short-lived) Azeri counteroffensive in December 1993, Russian Defense Ministry officials reportedly ascertained the military needs of the Karabakh fighters, and Russian weapons were sent in through the Lachin corridor.[65] The Armenian counteroffensive appears to have been strengthened by the delivery, through Armenia, of Russian military equipment, including air defense missiles.[66] Some of the Armenian advances of 1993 occurred at a time when Azerbaijan was governed by the Popular Front led by Abulfaz Elcibey, a nationalist intent on building ties with Turkey. Elcibey fell because of a combination of factors: his own political ineptness, the military fiasco, and a mutiny led by Surat Husseinov, a self-styled colonel with close and long-standing ties to Soviet, and subsequently Russian, military officers. Was Moscow aware of, or did it tacitly approve, the freewheeling activities of its local commanders and troops on behalf of the Karabakh fighters? Was it involved even more directly? These questions cannot be answered conclusively. What seems much clearer is that Russia had little reason to assist Azerbaijan or restrain the Armenians so long as Elcibey was in power.

Whatever the pattern of past Russian involvement, the current reality is that Karabakh is no longer under Azerbaijan's control. Azerbaijan also has lost seven districts that adjoin Nagorno-Karabakh: Lachin, Kelbajar, Fizuli, Agdam, Jebrail, Qubadly, and Zangelan, which form corridors linking Nagorno-Karabakh to Armenia. All told, Azerbaijan's losses account for roughly 15 percent of its prewar territory. Some 750,000 refugees lead a precarious economic existence in Azerbaijan: 233,000 of them are Azeris from Armenia proper, the rest those who fled the fighting from Nagorno-Karabakh.[67] Azerbaijan remains determined to retake the lost territories—by diplomacy or by war if necessary.[68] The result is a simmering conflict contained by an uneasy cease-fire that breaks down intermittently. The roots of the conflict remain deep and robust. The Karabakh Armenians, supported by Armenia proper, are determined not to rejoin Azerbaijan. Yet no Azeri leader can possibly concede the loss of Nagorno-Karabakh; the most that can be—and has been—offered is far-reaching autonomy. But this is incompatible with the desire of the Karabakh Armenians for independence as a means to join Armenia one day.

Owing to the conflict with Azerbaijan, Armenia has become dependent on Russia for its security—a historically familiar circumstance reinforced by religion and geography. It is an enthusiastic (indeed founding) member of the CIS and supports Russia's desire to dominate mediation and peacekeeping in the Nagorno-Karabakh dispute. Russian troops were withdrawn from Azerbaijan in June 1993. But they remained in Armenia, and in 1995 Russian and Armenia signed an agreement formalizing Russia's deployments and basing rights at Gyumri and Yerevan. The number of troops stationed in Armenia across the borders from Turkey and Iran is estimated at 12,000 to 15,000.[69] In August 1997 Russia and Armenia signed a comprehensive security treaty that supersedes the previous one signed in December 1991. The new document contains a number of provisions creating the closer alignment sought by Russia.[70] Indeed, by providing for "mutual assistance" if either is attacked, the coordination of defense production and foreign policy, the standardization of military hardware, and a pledge not to join treaties or alliances injurious to the other party, it creates a security relationship between Armenia and Russia closer than that which Russia has with any other state.[71] Armenian President Levon Ter-Petrossian hailed the treaty as "a qualitatively new stage" in relations with Russia and the basis for a "strategic partnership" stronger than that created by the Russia-Belarus treaty of union.[72] Azeri leaders, not surprisingly, criticized it as a hostile act.[73] Other signs of the close relationship include joint military maneuvers, continuing Russian economic aid, an agreement between Gazprom and Armenia for a gas pipeline through Armenia to Turkey, an agreement rescheduling Armenian debt to Russia based partly on exchanging Armenian debt for Russian equity in Armenian industries, and a signature campaign mounted by pro-Russian Armenian groups to mobilize support for joining the union between Russia and Belarus—a step that, in a unanimous May 1997 resolution, the Russia Duma invited Armenia to take.[74] None of this means that Armenia feels that Russian support is rock solid. It is particularly apprehensive that Azerbaijan's oil wealth could lead to a shift in Russian policy. Armenia's decision to retain the forces allotted to it under the CFE treaty instead of ceding part of its quota to Russia betrays its anxiety. And the Armenian Foreign Ministry's decision to advise the parliament (in the summer of 1997) to delay ratification of the basing agreement with Russia may have been intended as a signal to Moscow not to take Armenia for granted.[75] Yet from Moscow's perspective, Armenia's strategic dependence, the bilateral security treaty, and basing rights all strengthen Russia's position in the south Caucasus.

Azerbaijan for its part has realized that Russia is not a spent force but the dominant one in the region. Under Elcibey's successor, Haidar Aliev, Azerbaijan joined the CIS in September 1993 and became a member of its collective security coalition. The Azeris have maintained their position on the Caspian Sea and have rejected Russian requests for the right to station troops in Azerbaijan territory and border guards along its frontier with Iran.[76] According to Aliev, Moscow has offered to help regain lost Azerbaijani territory in exchange for basing rights—a claim Russian officials deny.[77] Burgeoning foreign investment, an oil boom, and pipelines that skirt Russia may alter the Azeri-Armenian balance of power, negate Azerbaijan's dependence on Russia, perhaps even induce a tilt in Russian policy toward Azerbaijan. Russia has been careful not to burn its bridges with Azerbaijan. It is one of the three cochairs, along with the United States and France, of the OSCE "Minsk Group" (which is seeking to settle the Nagorno-Karabakh dispute), and has never endorsed the idea that Nagorno-Karabakh's secession is final or that it should be allowed to join Armenia. Russia has condemned the elections that have taken place in Karabakh as illegal and appears to have embraced the Azeri position that calls for a solution based on generous autonomy for Nagorno-Karabakh within Azerbaijan. In July 1997 Russia and Azerbaijan signed a Treaty of Friendship, Cooperation, and Mutual Security. While it is fundamentally different from the Russian-Armenian treaty—it does not provide for mutual assistance in the event of war, coordinated defense policies, or Russian arms supplies—it does show that Russia is aware of Azerbaijan's rising strategic and economic significance and that it wants to keep its options open. The treaty notes pointedly the importance of territorial integrity and condemns the use of force to change established borders as well as all forms of separatism.[78] In March 1997, Russia met a long-standing Azeri demand that Surat Husseinov, who mounted the 1993 coup that culminated in Elcibey's fall and paved the way for Aliev's advent, and who later was charged with plots against Aliev himself, be extradited from Russia.[79] Russia also decided in the summer of 1996 to reopen its border with Azerbaijan, which was closed in response to the flow of arms and supplies across it to the Chechen resistance. The closure had severe consequences for farms in northern Azerbaijan that depended on the Russian market. It is obvious that Moscow neither wants Armenia to take its support as a given nor to accelerate Azerbaijan's already concerted effort to balance what it sees as a Russian-Armenian entente by cultivating economic, political, and security links with Turkey and the West.

Russia's diplomatic role in the Nagorno-Karabakh conflict has been an essential part of its effort to preserve its position in the south Caucasus. It was because of Russian mediation that a cease-fire was negotiated among the leaders of Armenia, Nagorno-Karabakh, and Azerbaijan in May 1994.[80] The cease-fire has held and saved an untold number of lives. Yet neither the Karabakh nor the Armenian leadership has a compelling reason to be receptive to Azerbaijan's contention that Nagorno-Karabakh's status can be discussed only after Azeri territory beyond it is evacuated. Despite the economic blockade that Azerbaijan instituted against Nagorno-Karabakh and Armenia in late 1992, the Armenians' negotiating position is strong—both because they prevailed in battle and on account of the military assistance that Russia has provided after the 1994 cease-fire. Evidence for this assistance comes from Aman Tuleev (who served as Russia's minister for CIS Affairs until he was appointed by Yeltsin as the governor of the Siberian province of Kemervo in July 1997), from former Defense Minister Igor Rodionov, and from a detailed account provided by the chairman of the Russian Duma's Defense Committee, retired General Lev Rokhlin. Their accounts show that, from August 1992 to late 1996, $720 million worth of Russian arms, including T-72 tanks, BMP infantry fighting vehicles, multiple rocket launchers, surface-to-air missiles, howitzers, heavy artillery, and antitank guided missiles were provided to Armenia—apparently without payments to Russia.[81] The logistical operation to ferry the weapons was large and complex, and could hardly have been a scheme devised and implemented by a handful of rogue commanders. It involved 139 flights by AN-12, AN-124, and IL-76 transport aircraft from various Russian bases in

Russia, Armenia (Gyumri), and Georgia (Vaziani and Batumi) as well as vessels that docked at Novorossiisk and unloaded shipments for transportation overland. The supply of so vast an arsenal to Armenia is important in at least two respects. First, it could affect the prospects for a settlement of the Nagorno-Karabakh dispute—or the tide of battle should the cease-fire crumble. Second, the timing suggests that it may be linked to Russian goals regarding energy and security in the south Caucasus. During this period Russia was pressing Azerbaijan to give Russian companies a share in the Azerbaijan International Operating Company (AIOC, the multinational consortium developing oil off the coast of Azerbaijan) and to alter its position on the Caspian Sea. It was also seeking military base rights in Azerbaijan. The arms sent to Armenia may have been a reminder to Azerbaijan of the compelling reasons to accommodate Russia, although it is unclear whether the initiative reflected Russian policy or was undertaken by senior military leaders—about whose involvement there is no doubt—without authorization. Armenia has both downplayed the extent of Russian weapons deliveries and suggested that Azerbaijan received even more. Yet senior Armenian leaders have simultaneously conceded (without necessarily intending to) that Russian arms supplies have been significant. Thus Defense Minister Vazgen Sarkisian said in April 1997 that Armenia had been able to double its military power over the past two years free of charge.[82]

As one of 11 members and cochair since January 1995 of the OSCE Minsk Group involved in mediating the Nagorno-Karabakh dispute, Russia's diplomatic role is central. Moscow wants to retain a role in OSCE efforts so that decisions taken by the organization do not harm Russian interests in the south Caucasus. But what it really wants is to limit the role of international organizations so that Russia is the fountainhead of diplomatic agreements.[83] Thus Russia has both participated in and circumvented (particularly in the early years of the Minsk Group) OSCE efforts.[84] Despite its membership in the Minsk Group, Russia embarked on independent diplomacy on Nagorno-Karabakh from September 1991 with little or no coordination with the OSCE.[85] For example, despite objections from Azerbaijan, the talks organized by Russia that produced the May 1994 cease-fire excluded the OSCE.

Russia has not always prevailed. Moscow wanted Russian (or CIS) troops to be the sole members of the peacekeeping force in Nagorno-Karabakh. But Azerbaijan objected staunchly in the negotiations that preceded the 1994 cease-fire, and the United States and Turkey supported its insistence on a multinational force.[86] The December 1994 OSCE decision to assemble a peacekeeping force stipulated that no more than 30 percent of the soldiers would come from any member of the OSCE. Yet Russia's attempts to dominate diplomacy and peacekeeping in Nagorno-Karabakh is itself significant. It attests to Moscow's belief that it has special interests and rights in the Near Abroad and that peacekeeping there should be conducted by Russian-led CIS contingents blessed by the OSCE or the United Nations. Should that prove impossible, its second preference is for multinational peacekeeping within parameters set by Russia—primarily by ensuring a substantial role for its military units. The OSCE decision on peacekeeping suggests that Russia will have to settle for its fall-back position. But the failure of the multinational force to materialize means that Moscow's first preference may yet be realized. A Russia-only peace-keeping operation in Nagorno-Karabakh will show that Moscow has been able to shunt aside Azeri misgivings and to overcome Western opposition.

In contrast to its earlier conduct, Russia has been working in concert with its Minsk Group comembers. The Minsk Group set forth a plan in the summer of 1997 that included Armenian troop withdrawals from the seven occupied Azeri districts, monitoring by OSCE peacekeepers, the return of Azeri refugees, reductions in the size of the Karabakh Armenian forces, and a step-by-step schedule of negotiations leading to autonomy for Nagorno-Karabakh within Azerbaijan. But the Karabakh Armenians have rejected this approach. While the Armenian government (whose prime minister and defense minister previously held positions in the Nagorno-Karabakh government) has been somewhat more receptive, no Armenian leader could survive politically if he were widely perceived as breaking ranks and selling out the Karabakh Armenians. (The February 1998 resignation of Armenian President Ter-Petrossian is further proof of this argument's validity.) As periodic outbreaks of fighting demonstrate, the cease-fire is frail.[87] If it collapses and Russia meanwhile has filled the peacekeeping void because no other state will do so, its troops could be caught in deadly crossfire. Renewed war between Armenia and Azerbaijan cannot be ruled out, especially if a settlement proves elusive, oil-rich Azerbaijan builds its military strength, and Armenia feels increasingly vulnerable. History is replete with examples of just how dangerous such power transitions can be.

GEORGIA'S CIVIL WARS

If the Nagorno-Karabakh war has enabled Russia to entrench itself in the south Caucasus, so has the civil war in Georgia. Developments in the two countries are strikingly similar, as are the motives and tactics of Russian policy. The ethnic tensions that led to war flared in both Azerbaijan and Georgia within the context of an imperial collapse. Ethnic animosities deepened as hypernationalism filled the vacuum created by the political and ideological crisis of the Soviet polity and the declining power of Moscow.[88] Radical nationalist leaders—Gamsakhurdia in Georgia, Elcibey in Azerbaijan—emerged in both countries. Both leaders (the former much more so than the latter) promoted ethnic nationalism to terminate what they regarded as a colonial dependence on Russia, alienating Russia and national minorities in the process. Minority nationalities ultimately took up arms for separatist (the Abkhaz in Georgia) or irredentist (the Ossetians in Georgia and the Armenians in Karabakh) ends. Elites from the titular nationality were determined to stop impending national dismemberment. The result was full-scale war.

Gamsakhurdia and Elcibey were replaced by Aliev and Shevardnadze, leaders more to Moscow's liking: Russified individuals who had for long held leading positions in the Soviet power structure. Neither is a creature of Moscow; both understand that anti-Russian nationalism is a powerful force at home; but they also realize that a confrontational policy toward Russia is doomed. Their decision to join the CIS despite the unpopularity of the decision among their citizens exemplifies this. Both leaders have realized that a lasting settlement of the ethnic conflicts that have ravaged their countries requires Russian cooperation. Moscow has sought military bases in both countries to bind them closer to Russia. This was policy motivated by geostrategic considerations: Azerbaijan is adjacent to the energy-rich Caspian Sea, shares a border with Iran, and—by virtue of faith and ethnicity—can influence the stability of the sensitive north Caucasus region; Georgia occupies over 200 miles of the Black Sea coast, borders Turkey, and—particularly because of the divided status of the Ossetian people and the kinship between the Abkhaz and the peoples on the other side of the Caucasus—also can disturb the delicate equilibrium of southern Russia; Azerbaijan and Georgia—along with Armenia— served as the forward edge of a tsarist/Soviet empire for nearly two centuries, and post-Soviet Russia is not prepared to concede dominance or even equal status in the south Caucasus to what it regard as parvenu powers.

Yet the war in Georgia and Russia's objectives and achievements there also have specific features. Georgian nationalism became a powerful force after 1988: the killing of civilians by Soviet troops in Tbilisi in April 1989 was a decisive event. The antagonism between the Georgian majority and national minorities, who constitute 30 percent of the population, grew apace. The consequences were especially serious in Abkhazia and South Ossetia.[89] In both regions, nationalist movements took up arms against the central government in reaction to the intensification of Georgian nationalism, which grew stronger as the Soviet political order weakened. As the wobble of the Soviet edifice became pronounced, Georgian nationalists' calls for promoting Georgian language and culture grew into demands for autonomy within the U.S.S.R. (the precedence of republican laws over central laws was declared in the fall of 1989) and finally into demands for secession, until independence was proclaimed in April 1991. The fears of the Ossetians and Abkhaz for their own language, culture, and political autonomy—the former had an autonomous *oblast'*, the latter an autonomous republic—became progressively more acute as Georgian nationalism dominated political discourse.[90]

Georgian ultranationalists' portrayal of the Abkhaz and Ossetians as interlopers, settlers, and fifth columnists that an imperial Russia had used to create and preserve its domain in the south Caucasus hardly reassured the two peoples. This demonization of the other is typical of radical nationalism. But it also grew out of Georgia's colonial relationship with Russia. The strategic importance of Abkhazia and South Ossetia for Russia only heightened Georgian anxieties about Russian motives, especially when suspicions arose that Russia was aiding both secessionist movements. That Russia had both opportunity and motive to do so made the role imputed to it plausible. Abkhazia has a coastline on the Black Sea, rich soil, coal reserves, and vacation resorts. The M-27 military highway and the railway (which, because of the war, does not operate now beyond Gagra) through Abkhazia are important logistical pathways to supply Russian forces south of the Caucasus, whether in Georgia itself or in Armenia. Abkhazia also gives Russia access to western Transcaucasia— the Surami Mountains divide Georgia into eastern and western segments— and thence to Turkey through Ajaria. South Ossetia fulfills the same function as a corridor into the central south Caucasus inasmuch as the Georgian Military Highway connecting Russia and Georgia runs through it. Both regions have ties to the peoples of the north Caucasus, and detachments from there crossed the border between Russia and Georgia to help the Abkhaz fight Georgian forces. Thus what happens in Abkhazia and South Ossetia affects the stability of Russia's volatile north Caucasus region.

The tensions between Georgians on the one hand and Ossetian and Abkhaz on the other have a long history.[91] But the policies of the nationalist Zviad Gamsakhurdia (Gamsakhurdia's party won the October 1990 parliamentary elections; he was elected president in May 1991 and served until his ouster in January 1992) added fuel to the fire.[92] Gamsakhurdia considered the Abkhaz and Ossetians to be foreign elements and sneered at the concept of minority rights. Steps such as the decision to abolish the South Ossetian Autonomous *Oblast'* in December 1990 and the initiation of a multifaceted cultural policy of Georgianization showed that he meant business.

Georgia's civil wars are not, of course, simply the product of personal pathologies. Ethnic strife not only continued after the return of Eduard Shevardnadze, it became worse. In March 1992 Shevardnadze was invited back from Moscow by the groups that had deposed Gamsakhurdia; he was elected speaker of the parliament—in effect head of state—in October. But he was unable to bring Georgia's ultranationalist paramilitary groups and their powerful political leaders, such as Tengiz Kitovani and Jaba Ioseliani, to heel quickly.[93] Doing so would take time. Meanwhile, his reputation in the West as statesman and democrat notwithstanding, Shevardnadze too began to wave the nationalist banner to strengthen his political base and to dispel fears that he was a tool of Russia.[94]

Freebooting Georgian nationalist forces, particularly Kitovani's National Guard and Jaba Ioseliani's *Mekhdrioni* (The Horsemen), worsened the simmering ethnic tensions. The first, nominally Georgia's state defense force, was in reality Kitovani's instrument; the second, a private army. Neither was effectively controlled by Shevardnadze; both made it impossible for him to offer significant compromises to the Ossetians and the Abkhaz. Georgia's radical nationalists, such as Kitovani and Ioseliani, considered the Ossetians and Abkhaz participants in a Russian plot to dismember Georgia. In equally charged language, their Abkhaz and Ossetian counterparts portrayed Georgian policies as a reincarnation of the very chauvinism ethnic minorities endured during Georgia's earlier phase of independence (1918–21). A pattern all too common in ultranationalist conflicts set in. Myths, legends, and stereotypes hardened conflicting attitudes; extremists defined political discourse; compromise became an indication of tepidity toward the sacred cause.

In this Manichaean atmosphere differences began to be aired through violence, and negotiation became well-nigh impossible. Ultranationalist paramilitary groups formed in both breakaway regions. Georgian military units and irregulars moved against them. The South Ossetians sought unity with the North Ossetian Autonomous Republics located within the Russian Federation. Abkhaz nationalists, while less clear about their aims, seemed to see independence as a prelude to a possible union with the anti-Russian Confederation of Mountain Peoples that had been formed in the north Caucasus in 1989. Sometimes Georgian nationalists took matters into their hands with disastrous consequences. Ioseliani unleashed the *Mekhdrioni* against Mingrelian rebels (Mingrelia in western Georgia was the stronghold of Gamsakhurdia and his loyalists) in a campaign of pillaging and brutality. Kitovani led his detachments into Abkhazia in August 1992, and disaster followed. A full-scale war against the Abkhaz that lasted 13 months resulted in the Georgians being routed. Although outnumbered, Abkhaz fighters took Sukhumi, the regional capital. They proceeded to evict Georgia's armed forces[95] and forced 250,000 Georgian civilian refugees, who have become a hard-line constituency in Georgian politics, to flee.

Within a year of the Soviet collapse, then, Georgia was trapped in a cycle of violence with no end in sight. Its government did not control South Ossetia and Abkhazia; paramilitary bands were laws unto themselves; revolts continued in the western region of Mingrelia, located just south of Abkhazia; the capital, Tbilisi, was engulfed by crime, lawlessness, and political assassinations. As in Azerbaijan, peripheral instability featuring ethnic conflict and rickety governments set the stage for Russia to enter the fray in pursuit of its own aims. Three were particularly important. The first was to ensure that instability from the south Caucasus did not seep north of the mountain range and exacerbate the tense situation already created by Chechen separatism.[96] The second was to prevent other countries, particularly Turkey or Iran, from becoming the dominant outside powers in the south Caucasus now that Russian (which is to say former Soviet) military formations had been withdrawn from all the countries of the region except Armenia. The third was to guarantee that the south Caucasus continued, as it had been since being wrested from Iran and Turkey in the nineteenth century, as a Russian strategic bulwark across from these two countries.

Georgia's predicament was not created by Moscow. The principal causes were virulent nationalism, the lack of sensitivity toward minority nationalities, and the tendency to interpret the desire for autonomy as treason. Once the fighting began, an unprofessional and incompetent military waged the war in Abkhazia without a clear-cut strategy. There was little if any coordination, and there was an utter failure to establish a secure staging ground in war-torn Mingrelia. An arrogant and cruel policy toward non-Georgians drove them toward the Abkhaz.[97] But, as in Azerbaijan, the evidence suggests that Russia did play a role in Georgia's civil wars, using them to pursue its three objectives.[98] Russian troops stationed in Abkhazia provided Abkhaz fighters with weapons and allowed airfields and bases under their control (Bombora and Gudauta) to be used for operations against Georgian troops. Although it is unclear whether they acted on orders from Moscow, Russian pilots appear to have flown missions using SU-25s and SU-27s. In March 1993 an SU-27 crashed in Abkhazia and the dead pilot was identified as a Russian officer.[99] The precise nature of Russia's role may never be known, but the available evidence points to the initiative of local troops, corruption, and the sale of weapons to both sides rather than a Machiavellian plot originating in Moscow. Both in Moscow and in Abkhazia, there was just too much chaos for such foresight and planning. The fighters from the north Caucasus also appear to have acted independently in aiding the Abkhaz. But the men and their weapons had to cross a border controlled by Russia to reach Abkhazia—a border that Russia has been able to seal since the 1994 cease-fire in Abkhazia to prevent military support from reaching Chechnya.[100] In the war against Gamsakhurdia's forces in western Georgia, Russia at first withheld support but began providing it once Georgia decided to join the CIS in October 8, 1993, thus enabling the rebellion to be defeated.

Whatever its contribution to the outcome of war in Abkhazia, as in Azerbaijan Russia sought its strategic objectives in Georgia by becoming indispensable to peace. In July 1993 Russian mediation produced a cease-fire between the Abkhaz and Georgians that ended the war begun in August 1992. It fell apart barely a month later, and by the end of September the Abkhaz controlled the entire region. Shevardnadze's efforts to obtain an international peacekeeping force to avoid conceding Russia a dominant role failed. And in May 1994 Georgia had no recourse but to sign an agreement under which, in June, a CIS—essentially Russian—force with an authorized strength of 3,000 (but now numbering only 1,500) was stationed in Abkhazia. The CIS contingent now enforces a separation-of-forces arrangement encompassing a swath of territory on either side of the Inguri River, which divides Georgia from Abkhazia. There are two zones on either side of the Inguri. In the first, which is 12 kilometers wide, rival army units are forbidden but police with small arms can operate; in the second, which spans 15 kilometers, army units are allowed but without tanks, armored personnel carriers, or guns with a caliber larger than 81 millimeters. This CIS force has been keeping the peace. The best that could be achieved by way of a non-Russian role was the creation of a U.N. monitoring group, the United Nations Observer Mission in Georgia (UNOMIG). UNOMIG was conceived as a 136-person group, but it now has 106 personnel whose mobility is restricted by the hazards posed by mines and whose effectiveness is undermined by a skewed force-to-space ratio and their unarmed status in what is a very dangerous place.[101] There is also a commission with representatives from

Georgia, Abkhazia, Russia, and the United Nations to negotiate the return of Georgia refugees. But there is little doubt that Russia, not the United Nation, plays the dominant role in Abkhazia—both in keeping the peace and in mediating a final settlement. Russia's continuing efforts to nudge the Georgian and the Abkhaz toward a settlement based on mutual compromise may not succeed because leaders on both sides have little room to maneuver. But there is no better diplomatic alternative in sight.

This also true in South Ossetia, where a Georgian-Russian agreement in June 1992 provided for the withdrawal of forces by both sides and the deployment of a multinational peacekeeping contingent of Georgian, Russian, and Ossetian soldiers. While Russia's peacekeeping role does not loom as large as in Abkhazia, Russian soldiers still make up 47 percent of the 1,489-person force, they are the best equipped, and the overall operation is under the command of a Russian officer. On the diplomatic front, although the OSCE is involved in the negotiations on a solution (along with Russia and the principals) Russia is the dominant party by virtue of this military presence.

In exchange for policing the peace in Abkhazia and South Ossetia, Russia has extracted concessions that exceed those gained in Azerbaijan. Shevardnadze was unenthusiastic about a Russian peacekeeping operation in Abkhazia. He and other Georgian leaders accused the Russians of having aided the Abkhaz fighters and of seeking to undermine the Georgian government and attempting to penetrate the Georgian military. Yet he found—and finds—himself dependent on Moscow, with few reliable counterbalances, and he has realized that appeasing Russia is the only option. Despite the fierce opposition of Georgian nationalist elites and the unpopularity of the decision among ordinary citizens, Shevardnadze took Georgia into the CIS in October 1993, and the decision was ratified by the Georgian parliament the following March, although 69 of 194 legislators voted against it. In February 1994 he signed a friendship treaty with Russia. In March 1995 Georgia and Russia reached an agreement on military cooperation that gave Russia the right to station a maximum of 25,000 troops free of charge at four military bases for 25 years: Batumi in Ajaria, Vaziani near Tbilisi, Gudauta north of Sukhumi in Abkhazia, and Akhalkalaki in the Samstkhe-Javakheti region just north of the border with Turkey and Armenia.[102] The result is that Russian troops, which were to be withdrawn fully from Georgia by 1995 under a February 1993 agreement, will remain, with Tbilisi serving as the headquarters of the Group of Russian Forces in the Transcaucasus (GRFT).

Shevardnadze's position in Georgia has improved considerably. He has prevented the fragmentation of his country by ending the war in South

Ossetia and Abkhazia and defeating the September-November 1993 insurrection of Gamsakhurdia in Mingrelia. Under OSCE auspices, peace talks with South Ossetian leaders began in May and an agreement was reached in Moscow prohibiting the resort to violence and affirming the need for a negotiated settlement. The prospects for such an outcome have improved as the South Ossetians appear to be willing to remain within Georgia in exchange for far-reaching autonomy. Shevardnadze also strengthened his authority by ousting Kitovani as defense minister in May 1993. Kitovani was jailed in October 1996 for trying to reignite the war in Abkhazia and attempting to lead forces into the region. Shevardnadze also instituted a new constitution with a strong presidency (1995) and trounced his rivals in the November 1995 presidential elections. He curbed the lawlessness in Tbilisi, arrested Ioseliani and disarmed the *Mekhdrioni* (1995), and initiated the creation of a professional Georgian military. Yet Georgia's dependence on Russia has not attenuated significantly. To the contrary, an increased reliance on Russia has been a principal means through which Shevardnadze has restored order. Russian cooperation and assistance were essential not only in stabilizing South Ossetia and Abkhazia but also in routing Gamsakhurdia's rebellion in Mingrelia.

While progress toward a settlement had been made in South Ossetia, the two sides remained far apart in Abkhazia. The ability of Abkhaz leader Vladislav Ardzinba to be flexible is limited by hard-liners within his camp. It is unlikely that he can accept the best that Georgia has offered: autonomy within a Georgian state. A sign of the Abkhaz determination to assert independence was the holding of legislative elections in November 1996 notwithstanding the opposition of Georgia and the international community. Ardzinba has gone so far as to propose a confederation with Georgia, with both sides having coequal status. Even were he inclined to do so, Shevardnadze (or, for that matter, any future Georgian leader) would run serious risks in accepting such a plan. There are many Georgian opponents of compromise: militant members of the parliament, the Abkhaz government-in-exile (headed by Georgians who were once part of Abkhazia's power structure), paramilitary formations (such as the White Legions, drawn from former members of the Abkhaz security apparatus) who regularly infiltrate Abkhazia, and Georgian refugees from Abkhazia (who are a conspicuous presence in Tbilisi). In combination they are formidable political force.[103]

The Georgian government has complained about the failure of Russian troops to protect those Georgian refugees who have been able to return to Abkhazia and has asked Russia to act more forcefully against Abkhaz fighters, hinting at a possible loss of its bases.[104] Both Shevardnadze and the Georgian parliament have at various times called for the withdrawal of CIS peacekeepers unless they implement the March 1997 CIS summit decision to expand the peacekeeping zone to cover the Gali district just north of the Inguri River and to assume police functions there. The ostensible rationale for the decision was to facilitate the return of Georgian refugees. But while the Georgian government claims that only a few refugees have returned, the Abkhaz and UNOMIG sources maintain that some 40,000 to 60,000 have returned to Gali.[105] In the eyes of the Abkhaz, the Georgian call for an expanded peacekeeping mandate was a ploy to force them to evacuate their heavily fortified defense line along the Gali canal. Georgians already heavily outnumber Abkhaz in Gali (even more than in the rest of Abkhazia), and the Abkhaz understand that it will be difficult—given that they account for only 17 percent (100,000) of Abkhazia's prewar population—to control the region once all the refugees return. They may, therefore, give up Gali and settle for a smaller but more manageable state. But this is a card that Ardzinba will play in the endgame—and for real Georgian concessions over Abkhazia's future status. Without such gains, he will not give up a critical defensive position, thereby improving Georgia's military position and increasing Abkhazia's vulnerability to attack.[106] This situation involves difficult choices for Russia. Backing Georgia and coercing Abkhazia could stir up anti-Russian feelings in Russia's north Caucasus region. Furthermore, if Russian pressure induces Abkhazia to accept autonomy rather than independence, Georgia will be far less dependent on Russia, and the strategic gains that Moscow has made there may become less secure. Controlled tension without war minimizes the risk to Russian peacekeepers while keeping Georgia and Abkhazia dependent on Russia. The danger is that such an environment is inherently unstable. War could erupt again, deepening Russia's involvement and increasing the pressure on it to take sides. And that is precisely the denouement Russia wants to avoid.

Despite Georgia's threats to pull out of the CIS and to terminate Russian bases, Russia has little reason to oblige nor much reason to fear. It can claim, as it has, that the March 1997 CIS resolution on an expanded mandate cannot be implemented unless both parties agree, and that the Abkhaz have not done. It also can claim, as it has, that the peacekeepers are in Abkhazia under a CIS mandate and can be removed only by a collective decision. It can be confident that neither side wants to increase the risk of war by seeing the peacekeepers depart—the Abkhaz because they have what is in effect a state; Georgia because its military, despite ongoing improvements, suffers from a number of problems: insufficient

weaponry and officers and deficiencies in command, control, and com-
munication that have so far limited exercises to the battalion level.[107]
Russia can be confident that, despite Georgia's efforts (manifested during
Shevardnadze's visit to the United States in the summer of 1997) to seek
NATO or U.N. peacekeeping forces to reduce the Russian role, no one
will step forward to replace the CIS troops. Finally, Russia has been the
haven for well-known opponents of Shevardnadze, such as the former
Interior Minister Igor Giorgadze, and within the Georgian cabinet there
are individuals (foremost among them is Defense Minister Vardiko
Nadabaidze) who are regarded as having close ties to Moscow. This gives
Russia the means to influence political outcomes in Georgia in more sin-
ister ways.[108] Thus although the mandate of the CIS peacekeepers came
and went, most recently at the end of July 1997, for the Georgian leadership they are the only game in town.

Russia will assuredly not take on the Abkhaz in pursuit of Georgian
aims; it does not want its demoralized troops caught in a vicious civil
war that, as the experience in Chechnya and Tajikistan proves, would
only stir controversy at home. Nor does it wish to face a tide of anti-
Russian feeling in the north Caucasus, should the fighting in Abkhazia
and South Ossetia resume with Russia perceived as Georgia's ally. What
Russia wants it has: There is a status quo under which it dominates
peacekeeping operations, the peace is fragile but holding, and Russian
diplomacy remains critical. Moscow has not been able to achieve dramatic progress on the diplomatic front, although there have been some
advances: In the summer of 1997, Russian mediation led Ardzinba and
Georgia to agree to reject a recourse to force and to work on resuming
economic and communication links.[109] While diplomatic breakthroughs
have eluded Russia, it has become indispensable to both parties in a
no-war-no-peace environment. This is a foundation, albeit an unstable
one, for the continuation of its strategic gains in Georgia. If Georgia turns
against it, Moscow has the option of becoming the principal protector of
a strategically located, dependent statelet. If Georgia's orientation proves
compatible with Russian objectives, Abkhaz self-determination can be
sacrificed. This is not a position devoid of risks (the foremost being
overextension and entrapment). But it is certainly not a quagmire.

Georgia cannot easily change this state of affairs. It can neither
evict Russia nor force it to ram through a settlement in Abkhazia and
South Ossetia—which Moscow could not do even if it so desired—
that would make its presence superfluous. The Abkhazia conflict in
particular remains intractable.[110] Georgia hard-liners have sought to
resume the war, and there is no sign that key issues—the future politi-

cal status of Abkhazia and the return of Georgian refugees—will be settled soon. Even the seemingly technical solution of refugee repatriation is complicated by the Abkhaz leadership's realization that a mass return of Georgians would enable Georgia to achieve demographically what it cannot do militarily. Georgia cannot remain whole and dispense with Russian peacekeepers unless it can offer the Abkhaz reasons to abandon independence and settle for autonomy within Georgia. For Shevardnadze—and for the leaders who will follow him—this is an unhappy, untenable situation; for Russia, considering the strategic gains it has made in Georgia, it is not.

TURMOIL IN TAJIKISTAN

In Tajikistan a contest to control the state and determine the country's future identity and economic and political direction began as the Soviet empire was on its last legs.[111] Newly mobilized political groups— democrats, Islamists, ethnic Pamiris, and nationalists— coalesced as an opposition to enter the political arena. Rakhmon Nabiev, a former head of Tajikistan's Communist Party, won the November 1990 presidential election but this did not end the struggle between the opposition and the ancien regime. In May 1993, after prolonged mass protests involving demonstrators from both camps, Nabiev was forced to include the opposition in a coalition. But the elites of the northern region of Leninabad refused to accept the compromise. Leninabad (its capital is Khujand, and its elite thus is referred to here as Khujandis) is Tajikistan's industrial center and home to 90 percent of the country's Uzbek population. The Khujandis controlled the political structure in the Soviet era and have close ties with neighboring Uzbekistan. To preserve their power, they allied with the southern region of Kulob. Matters came to a head in September when the opposition forced Nabiev to resign and in effect overturned the established political pecking order in Tajikistan. The Khujand-Kulob bloc began to arm itself and "seized or received weapons from Russian garrisons, with at least local Russian complicity."[112]

The stage was set for a bloody battle between the opposition-controlled government and the Popular Front, the Khujand-Kulob alliance's fighting force, which received extensive military and logistical support from Uzbekistan. Uzbekistan's president, Islam Karimov, feared that the demonstration effect of upheaval in Tajikistan would rock his authoritarian regime and, in particular, stir up Uzbekistan's 933,560 Tajiks, who account for 5 percent of the population.[113] Tajikistan's deeply rooted localism (*mahalgaroi*) exacerbated by competition between top-dog

(Leninabad) and underdog regions (Qurghan Teppe and Garm) added to the combustible mix and produced a civil war. The Khujand-Kulob axis regained power in November by convening the communist-dominated parliament, nullifying Nabiev's ouster, and having the Kulobi Emomali Rakhmonov appointed chairman. The opposition, which was then driven out in a brutal war in which Uzbekistan provided critical assistance to the Popular Front, has since waged war against it. Russia neither instigated the conflict nor was particularly eager to get involved. But it was drawn in for several reasons. Uzbekistan artfully elicited its intervention by playing on Moscow's fears about instability, the safety of the local Russian community, and the tide of Islamic "fundamentalism."[114] Ultra-nationalist and communist elites in Russia began to emphasize these very themes, invoking them to berate the government for failing to defend a Russian security interest in a vital zone. Yeltsin's government was eager not to be depicted as ineffectual. But the imagery of falling dominoes and power vacuums was not conjured up by Russian hard-liners alone. It became increasingly common in the statements of those, including Yeltsin, seen in the West as democratic reformers.[115]

Russia is now the key outside party in determining Tajikistan's political order.[116] Had it not been for Russia's 201st Motor Rifle Division and border guards (a total of about 15,000 troops), Rakhmonov's government would have crumbled. It controls less than a fifth of the country and has nothing that could in any precise sense be called an army.[117] Without Russia's backing, it would have had been forced to share power with the armed opposition—which has waged war from Afghanistan and within Tajikistan itself—much earlier. And it would have entered the negotiations holding a much weaker hand. Its strategy of engaging in multiple rounds of peace negotiations—Russia and Iran were the prime sponsors—aimed at a peaceful solution while refusing to share power or even to allow the opposition to participate in the 1994 parliamentary and presidential elections would have been untenable. Russian military support and economic aid—the dependence on Russia symbolized by the 1994 friendship treaty—was essential to the regime's strategy. True, Uzbekistan, Kyrgyzstan, and Kazakhstan have also provided peacekeeping troops. But their numbers are small, Uzbek units are stationed in the northern Khujand region, and the token Kazakh and Kyrgyz forces arrived only in 1994. Economic and military support for the Rakhmonov government is essentially a Russian affair despite the multilateral veneer of a CIS peacekeeping mission in Tajikistan.

Russia's record in Tajikistan has been a checkered one. On the one hand, the current Tajik regime is friendly and dependent. This would not have been the situation had the opposition retained power or regained it by defeating Rakhmonov's government. Despite the rubles spent and Russian soldiers killed since 1992, therefore, from a Russian strategic standpoint the alternative could have been worse and Moscow has averted it successfully. Moscow also has displaced Uzbekistan's traditionally dominant position in Tajikistan for two reasons. First, Russia is the principal external supporter of the Rakhmonov regime and can offer more to bolster it. Second, Rakhmonov's base of power is in Kulob; the Kulobis dominate the Tajik government, not the Khujandis, with whom Uzbekistan has long had close ties. With the accession to power of the Kulobi Rakhmonov and his victory in the 1994 presidential election against the Khujandi candidate, Abdumalik Abdullojonov, the Khujand faction no longer controlled the Tajik state. As a result, Uzbekistan's influence has fallen relative to Russia—so much so that Karimov adopted a new strategy: To reassert Uzbekistan's role in Tajikistan's political melée, he opened a dialogue with the Tajik opposition.[118] Through a concerted public relations campaign and cosmetic political changes, Karimov also has sought to convince the United States that Uzbekistan is democratizing and that it is Central Asia's foremost power and thus a partner against Russian neoimperialism.[119]

While the existence of a dependent regime in Tajikistan is a gain for Russia, the country nevertheless has been a strategic and economic burden—and there seemed to be no light at the end of the tunnel. The Tajik economy is in shambles. Always Central Asia's poorest country, Tajikistan's plight worsened because of the ravages and costs of war. To maintain its position there, Russia would have had to continue serving as primary benefactor. Nor was there any sign that the Tajik government would one day be able to survive without Russian military support. This obvious implication was that the war along the Afghan border with the opposition would have to be fought by Russian soldiers while the toll of Russians (not to mention Tajiks) killed and wounded continued to mount. To make matters worse, the Tajik government faced an internal security problem as well.[120] It was—and is—continually being shaken by fighting among paramilitary forces led by warlords and regional elites. Byzantine power struggles between Khujandis and Kulobis were a staple of political life, as were clashes between military units loyal to rival commanders. Kidnapping and a thriving drug trade complete the portrait of a country in chaos. Russia could in theory have cut its losses and walked away, perhaps after proclaiming victory in the time-honored manner. But this was judged undesirable in practice. The existing pro-Russian regime would have fallen, to be replaced by one ill-disposed toward Moscow and feared by the conservative authoritarian governments of Central Asia. With the radical Islamist *Taliban* movement gaining ground in Afghanistan and standing before Central Asia's gates, Tajikistan strategic significance increased.

As in Azerbaijan and Georgia, so too in Tajikistan, Russian strategic gains, while undeniable, have been accompanied by current costs and future dangers. Moscow understood the precarious condition of the regime it was shoring up in Tajikistan. It also was well aware that the Russian military role in Tajikistan was unpopular at home. But precisely because of the shakiness of the Tajik regime and the ramifications for stability in Central Asia—especially in light of the situation in Afghanistan—it could not cut and run. Russia, therefore, adopted a strategy of supporting the Rakhmonov regime economically and militarily while nudging it to participate in peace talks with the opposition. While other parties helped arrange these talks, which commenced in 1994, and shepherded them along, Russia and Iran (which looks askance at turmoil in Central Asia and the penetration of the region by Sunni fundamentalist forces) were the major outside players. After much effort, visible signs of progress emerged in 1996.[121] In December of that year, the Tajik government and the opposition agreed to the latest of many cease-fires. A week later peace talks in Moscow culminated in the formation of a "reconciliation council" to hammer out a settlement, a significant step even though Rakhmonov acquired the right to veto its proposals. In March 1997, talks between the government and the opposition led to an agreement on creating an integrated military force, even though opposition leaders rejected the government's position that their combatants had to disarm before being included in a unified force. These developments paved the way for the signing in Moscow of the General Agreement on Peace and National Accord by Rakhmonov and Said Abdullo Nuri, the head of the United Tajik Opposition (UTO).[122] It provided for the creation of a 26-member National Reconciliation Commission (chaired by Nuri) with equal representation from both sides, an interim power-sharing agreement under which the UTO would get 30 percent of all government posts, the integration of UTO fighters into the government's forces, amnesty, the repatriation of the 20,000 Tajik refugees in northern Afghanistan, and the holding of elections within 18 months.

Considering the mayhem that has been visited upon Tajikistan, the peace accord was no small achievement. Yet it was precarious for a number of reasons. The Tajik government has never exercised effective control over its military commanders, and there is already evidence that some of them reject the agreement with the opposition and will reserve the right to act as free agents. While the UTO has been brought into the power-sharing agreement, Abdullojonov, whose base of power is in the critical

Khujand region, has not. Given his close ties to Uzbekistan, which failed to join Russia, Iran, and other states in signing the documents guaranteeing the accords, his exclusion bodes ill. The process of handing over many important governmental positions to the UTO and incorporating its fighters into a unified military structure could, considering the legacy of hatred bequeathed by the nasty civil war, provoke conflicts between the UTO and Rakhmonov's regime and within the regime itself. But, at the end of the day, the Russian achievement in Tajikistan must be evaluated in comparison with what other major powers have accomplished when they have become entangled in complex and bloody civil wars. In this light, Russia's policy can hardly be judged a failure. It prevented the Rakhmonov government from being swept away, and the other Central Asian states (even Uzbekistan initially) looked to Moscow to stabilize Tajikistan. Despite Uzbekistan's subsequent effort to outmaneuver Russia for influence in Tajikistan, it has been unable to do so. And a peace accord was signed that, despite its potential pitfalls, constituted the best hope for peace in Tajikistan—and an achievement due in no small measure to Russian diplomacy.

THE BALANCE SHEET

Russian influence in the southern Near Abroad is not based purely on superior military power and proximity, although these are hardly unimportant. It is multifaceted. It stems from continuing economic dependence as reflected in trade patterns and debt. It arises from regional instability, including conflicts among and within states, which makes Russia's role as protector or arbiter indispensable. And it derives from the nature of the current ruling elites in the southern Near Abroad: Russified individuals whose political socialization occurred in the Soviet era. The net result is that Russian influence may be manifested overtly (for example, withholding or providing support at critical junctures) or simply as a consequence of what Carl Friedrich called the "rule of anticipated reaction,"[123] where an understanding of Russia's preferences and priorities affects what leaders in the southern Near Abroad do or do not do.

Despite the sharp decline in its power, Russia has been far more successful and far less reticent in asserting its interests in the southern Near Abroad than is generally acknowledged. The continuing heavy economic and military dependence of these countries on Russia and the instabilities that have shaken some of them, together with Russian proximity and preponderant power, account for Russia's influence. This does not presage an imperial regathering by Russia, let alone a reconstitution of the socialist empire. But it does mean that, for the foreseeable future, Russia will be the dominant power in the region.

Yet Russia has not embarked on a policy of risk-taking and confrontation. It has availed itself of opportunities but has steered clear of situations that are potentially truly dangerous. A case in point is Kazakhstan. Despite the warnings about impending Russian-Kazakh conflict within Kazakhstan, what is interesting, and needs explaining, is why such conflict has not occurred. There are several reasons. Russia been careful in handling Kazakhstan (as well as Ukraine, which also adjoins Russia and has a large Russian population) and avoided pushing disputes over joint citizenship and the status of the Russian language to a breaking point. Kazakh-Russian tensions exist, but several factors dilute them and work against confrontation. Interpretations of interethnic relations in Kazakhstan that present Kazakhs and Russians as two monolithic communities on a collision course are simplistic.[124] Kazakhs are divided by class as well as by differences among and within the three *zhus* (hordes), between north and south, town and countryside. As the market economy becomes more robust, class distinctions will emerge that mediate, perhaps even transcend, Russian-Kazakh differences. Above all, Kazakhs, leaders and average citizens alike, are well aware that ethnic war would be a calamity that would in all likelihood lead to the country's breakup. While a confrontation between Russia and Kazakhstan could indeed occur, were an ultranationalist regime in power in Russia when ethnic conflict was rife in Kazakhstan, what is notable in the post-Soviet period is the care with which the two states have handled their potentially explosive relationship.

While Russia has been careful, it is incorrect to say that its position in the region is in peril. The routine argument that Russia will be supplanted by other states is premature at best. Consider the states usually mentioned as candidates to achieve this displacement. China undoubtedly has major interests in the southern Near Abroad, especially in Central Asia. It has become an important trade partner, communications links between China and the region have expanded, and China has begun to play an important role as an investor in the Kazakh oil industry. But China's strategic ambitions are directed to its east and south. In Central Asia, it sees Russia as welcome enforcer to stamp out radical Islamist and ethnonationalist movements. Beijing is particularly worried that such movements will radiate eastward into the western Chinese province of Xinjiang and stir up the increasingly restive Muslim-Turkic Uighur population.[125] And Kazakhstan (which has a 1,000-mile border with China) and Kyrgyzstan (which has a smaller border with it) worry about potential Chinese expansion and the migration of Chinese into their countries, which has been occurring since the Soviet collapse.[126] The net effect is to increase Russia's significance for all three countries. A Chinese-Russian strategic convergence also has been under way, driven by burgeoning economic and military ties and a common uneasiness about a unipolar post–Cold War world dominated by the United States. To solidify the alignment with Russia while focusing its strategic energies eastward, China has conceded Russia's preeminent role in Central Asia.[127]

Soon after the states of the southern Near Abroad became independent, Turkey and Iran were touted as challengers of Russia's longstanding supremacy—and as rivals—in the south Caucasus and Central Asia.[128] Turkey, like China, has established a significant economic, cultural, and political presence, especially in Central Asia. It plays a key role in the Economic Cooperation Organization (ECO) and organized the Black Sea Consortium. Its quest for influence also has been helped by cultural and religious ties with Turkic peoples of the region. Yet six years after the Soviet collapse it was clear—even to Turks captivated by dreams of a zone of special influence—that Turkey's reach had exceeded its grasp. The so-called Turkish economic and political model, vague to begin with, has not taken hold. Turkey's war with the Kurds is a distraction as well as a point of vulnerability that Russia can exploit, should it choose to aid the Kurdistan Workers' Party (PKK) in its war against the Turkish army. Turkey's own economic limitations reduce the extent of its economic influence in Central Asia and the south Caucasus. Its troubled history with Armenia is one of the reasons behind that country's tendency to regard Russia as a protector. Turkey itself is exposed to Russian power by virtue of its location. Finally, its sizable economic dealings (exemplified by robust trade with Russia and the activities of Turkish firms in the Russian economy) offer compelling reasons for not spoiling its relationship with Moscow by challenging it in a region that Russians regard as vital to their national security. Thus Turkey has been careful. For instance, it did not intervene on Azerbaijan's behalf in the Karabakh war, despite widespread sympathy among Turks for the Azeri cause, and was mindful of Russian warnings to stay out.

Iran has confounded predictions that it would challenge Russia and export radical Islam in the southern Near Abroad. While it has increased its economic ties with the region and established an organization bringing together states of the Caspian Sea littoral, it has been cautious on the political front. Iran also has been careful not to take sides in the Tajik civil war and the Nagorno-Karabakh conflict. (In both it has tried to be a mediator.)[129] It recognizes that the southern Near Abroad generally is governed by secular elites, most of whom held high positions in the

Soviet system and look askance at Islamist movements. Iran realizes that promoting radicalism would erode, not strengthen, its influence. Except for Shi'a Tajikistan and Shi'a Azerbaijan—and Iran sees the latter as harboring irredentist ambitions vis-à-vis the Azeris of Iran—the Muslims of the southern Near Abroad are Sunnis. Persian Tajikistan is the only state with close cultural and linguistic ties to Iran. The Iranian model—to the extent that there is one—is limited by these conditions. Iran has important reasons to avoid policies in the region that alienate Russia. Russia is a major power, and it is nearby. A confrontational policy toward it is not only risky, it would strengthen the American policy of ostracizing Iran. A cooperative approach is thus more sensible for Tehran and has been pursued through diplomacy, trade, and the acquisition of Russian military and nuclear technology. The two countries also have compatible strategic interests.[130] Iran has an estimated 15 million Azeris (there is much disagreement on the exact number) and 1 million Turkmen. Like Russia, it is leery of radical nationalist movements because they could generate irredentist claims. As noted earlier, Russia and Iran have a common view about the appropriate legal regime for the Caspian Sea, and both regard Turkey as a rival and as a stalking horse for the United States in the southern Caucasus and Central Asia. Iran regards the Islamist Sunni *Taliban* movement in Afghanistan as a threat (both to its regional interests and to the Shi'a Hazara community in Afghanistan, with which it has close ties); so does Russia, which has a persistent fear of militant Islamist movements spreading to Central Asia and the southern Caucasus—not just because they would destabilize these strategically important regions but also because, over time, they could affect the orientation of the Muslim peoples in Russia's north Caucasus and in Tatarstan and Bashkortostan. There are signs that some non-Russian states—such as Azerbaijan, Ukraine, Moldova, and Georgia—see a common stake in reducing Russian influence. But a regional coalition from the south Caucasus and Central Asia that works like a quasi-alliance to offset Russia is a chimera. Divisions between the Persian and Turkic peoples of the southern Near Abroad and between Christians and Muslims are one reason. Armenia would not only reject any such scheme, it would help Russian undermine it. Geographic barriers also complicate an effective alliance uniting the south Caucasus and Central Asia.

A Central Asian alliance headed by Uzbekistan, which does aspire to lead the region and to reduce Russia's role,[131] is also unlikely. It is precluded by the economic and military dependence of Central Asian states (Uzbekistan included) and the simple fact—to return to Table 3–1—that Russian power would dwarf such a coalition. Moreover, Karimov's posturing should not obscure the cold reality that Russia is his ultimate guarantor against domestic and regional instabilities. This was evident during the early stage of the Tajik civil war. Despite their subsequent rivalry in Tajikistan, it is evident again as the *Taliban* movement's advances in Afghanistan have the states of Central Asia—including Uzbekistan, which has a 150-mile border with Afghanistan—looking to Russia and emphasizing its importance to their security.[132] Russia's role in training Uzbekistan's 700-man National Guard (charged with defending the top leadership) and the formal cooperation between the Russian and Uzbek intelligence agencies shows that Moscow also is relied on to bolster the Karimov regime against internal instability.[133] Finally, the other Central Asian states reject the idea of an anti-Russian alliance, particularly one led by the Uzbeks. Deeply rooted rivalry between Uzbekistan and Kazakhstan would prevent such a grouping. Kazakhstan, Central Asia's other major power, would never participate in an anti-Russian alliance even if it were not a rival of Uzbekistan. Given its demographic composition, an anti-Russian alignment would endanger the prerequisite for its (or any other state's) national security, namely, its territorial integrity. This is why Nazarbaev always has entered or proposed arrangements that increase Kazakhstan's integration with Russia: the CIS and its 1992 collective security treaty, the 1995 customs union (which also includes Belarus and Kyrgyzstan), the Eurasian Union (proposed in 1994), the 1995 agreement integrating the Russian and Kazakh armed forces, and long-term leases (finalized in 1994) for Russia on the Baikonur satellite launching and missile testing complex. The Kyrgyz and Tajiks have profound apprehensions about the possibility of a hegemonic-irredentist policy by Uzbekistan, and Turkmenistan has signed a number of bilateral security agreements with Russia and opposes the idea of a Central Asian alliance. These realities are overlooked by those who seek to present Uzbekistan as a worthy partner with which the United States should work to counter Russian hegemony in Central Asia.[134]

Nor are the United States, other Western powers, or international organizations (the United Nations, the OSCE) likely to weaken Russian dominance in the southern Near Abroad. No western country has an interest that is compelling enough to permit a leader to justify to parliament and the public the extension of concrete security guarantees to the countries of the south Caucasus and Central Asia. Bridge-building schemes such as the Partnership for Peace, contact between military officers, and even joint military exercises are one thing; full-blooded alliances are quite another. No matter what they proclaim publicly, Western leaders see the southern Near Abroad as an area in which Russia has special interests and advantages. Misleading the countries in the region about what can be expected from the West is the strategic equivalent of writing a rubber check. The United Nations and the OSCE have played important roles in the conflicts in Nagorno-Karabakh, Georgia, and Tajikistan. But their activities have not, will not, and are not designed to supplant Russia. What these organizations can do is limited by the reluctance of Western states to commit forces for peacekeeping in the Near Abroad as well as by the limits set by Russia's overriding influence and interests in the region.

It is premature, therefore, to write Russia's strategic obituary in the southern Near Abroad. But it is also a mistake to overlook the problems it will face. With time several developments will reduce the margin of Russian dominance. For reasons previously explained, demographic realities will promote generational turnover, and elites not cut from Russian-Soviet cloth will emerge. Not infrequently, Western discussions of Islam in Central Asia have been impoverished by their preoccupation with "fundamentalism." This protean term invariably confuses and conflates the religious, cultural, and political role of Islam and ignores its diversity. Alarmist pundits preoccupied with the danger of radical Islamist movements in Central Asia obscure the extent to which class, region, clan, and tribe compete with Islam for the hearts and minds of Central Asians. They also seem unaware that, for complex reasons, Islam has had made a lighter imprint on nomadic peoples of the region than it has on sedentary cultures and that, even within the latter, there are differences among regions and between town and country.[135] Nevertheless, the influence of Islam in Central Asia will increase in the post-Soviet period, particularly as the area becomes part of what Bernard Lewis has called the new Middle East. In addition, as is already apparent, Central Asians (and the people of the south Caucasus) also will search for new identities, re-evaluate local histories, revive local culture and languages, and establish post-colonial identities. The Muslim peoples of the southern Near Abroad in particular will acquire a new sense of who they are and where they want to go.[136] Russia, in the process, will become "the other." And Islam undoubtedly will play a role in these changes of identity and outlook.

Among the non-Muslim peoples, particularly Armenians, this shift in identity and attitude may be less powerful, but Georgia shows that anti-Russian nationalism is not a negligible force. In much of the south Caucasus and Central Asia, the allure of the West's culture, the wealth of its corporations and banks, its mastery of modern technology, its domination of international financial institutions will render Russia progressively less important in the economic realm (trade, investment, and even pipeline routes) in the next century.[137] This can be averted only if Russia's efforts at building democracy and capitalism succeed, enabling it to become an effective vehicle for transmitting in Central Asia and the south Caucasus the values, skills, and resources needed for economic advancement. True, Russia has established a strong position in a number of states. But they tend to have overpersonalized and underinstitutionalized polities and thus are potentially unstable; some are torn by civil war; most are caught in the economic doldrums. This is a weak foundation for lasting hegemony and possibly a blueprint for overextension and embroilment in nasty wars. Yet the southern Near Abroad is important to Russia's national security. Moscow therefore has decided that the risks are worth it and the alternatives worse. Only time will tell if this calculation is sound.

Notes

I would like to thank Stephen Blank, Alton Frye, Sherman Garnett, Anne Garrels, George Kolt, John Kunstader, Michael Mandelbaum, Peter Reddaway, Lilia Shevtsova, S. Enders Wimbush, and the other participants for their incisive comments at the May 1997 Council on Foreign Relations Pieter Fisher Symposium at which the first draft of this chapter was presented. I have also benefited from subsequent discussions with Robin Bhatty, Robert Legvold, Alexander Motyl, Alvin Z. Rubinstein, Laurent Ruseckas, Christopher Panico, Peter Rutland, Oles Smolansky, and Jack Snyder.

1. Consider the following examples. In May 1992 Yevgeni Ambartsumov—then chairman of the Russian Duma's Committee on International Affairs—observed that "Russia is something larger than the Russian Federation in its present borders. Therefore, one must see its geopolitical interests more broadly than what is currently defined by the maps. That is our starting point as we develop our conception of mutual relations with 'our own foreign countries.'" Quoted in Boris Rumer, "The Gathering Storm," *Orbis* 37, no. 1 (Winter 1993), p. 91. Andranik Migranian, a prominent political commentator and now an advisor to Yeltsin, has argued that the ex-Soviet republics are a "sphere of . . . [Russia's] vital interests" and that they should not be allowed to form alliances "either with each other or with third countries that have an anti-Russian orientation." Quoted in Alexander J. Motyl, *Dilemmas of Independence: Ukraine after Totalitarianism* (New York: Council on Foreign Relations Press, 1993), pp. 122–23. While he was foreign minister, Andrei Kozyrev asserted Russia's right to use force to protect "geopolitical positions that took centuries to conquer" in the Near Abroad. *RFE/RL News Briefs,* October 4–8, 1993, p. 7.

2. This has been a consistent theme in the wide-ranging interviews that I have conducted in Central Asia and the south Caucasus since 1995 with civilian officials, military officers, academic experts on security and foreign policy, and journalists. The contrast to the dominant tendency in the United States to highlight Russia's failures and limitations is striking.

3. For an elaboration of this argument and the relevant documentation, see Rajan Menon, "In the Shadow of the Bear: Security in Post-Soviet Central Asia," *International Security* 20, no. 1 (Summer 1995), esp. pp. 156–61.

4. As the 12 states that constitute the Commonwealth of Independent States (CIS) gathered for a summit in Moscow in the spring of 1997, Andranik Migranian accused them of "consolidating power on an anti-Russian basis," adding that "[i]f they develop alternative economic and military unions, Russia will be unable to maintain its territorial integrity, because they will serve as an example to Russia's regions." *OMRI Daily Digest,* March 28, 1977, p. 5.

5. This last attitude is gaining ground with the widespread opposition in Russia to NATO expansion and the end of the period of romanticism toward the West.

6. Alexei Arbatov, "Russian Foreign Policy Thinking in Transition," in Vladimir Baranovsky, ed., *Russia and Europe: The Emerging Security Agenda* (New York: Oxford University Press for the Stockholm International Peace Research Institute, 1997), pp. 142, 146.

7. On group and institutional differences in Russian policy toward the Near Abroad, see, for example, Amin Saikal, "Russia and Central Asia," in Saikal and William Maley, eds., *Russia in Search of Its Future* (Cambridge: Cambridge University Press, 1995), pp. 142–46; Irina Zviagelskaia, *Russian Policy Debates on Central Asia* (London: Royal Institute of International Affairs, 1995).

8. See, for example, Stephen D. Krasner, *Defending the National Interest* (Princeton, NJ: Princeton University Press, 1978); Kenneth N. Waltz, *Theory of International Relations* (Reading, MA: McGraw-Hill, 1979); Peter B. Evans, Dietrich Rueschemeyer, and Theda Skocpol, eds., *Bringing the State Back In* (Cambridge: Cambridge University Press, 1985), esp. pp. 4–37; and Joseph M. Grieco, "Realist International Theory and the Study of World Politics," in Michael W. Doyle and G. John Ikenberry, eds., *New Thinking in International Relations Theory* (Boulder, CO: Westview Press, 1997), pp. 168–69 and p. 193, n. 24–26, where Grieco cites the relevant literature that stresses state autonomy.

9. In urging them to submit or be destroyed, the Athenians told the leaders of Melos: "[Y]ou know as well as we do that . . . the standard of justice depends on the equality of power to compel and that in fact the strong do what they have the power to do and the weak accept what they have to accept." Thucydides, *History of the Peloponnesian War,* trans. Rex Warner (Harmondsworth: Penguin, 1986), p. 402.

10. Needless to say, I use the term "southern Near Abroad" for convenience, not to endorse the policy prescriptions that flow from the way in which it often is used in Russian foreign policy discourse.

11. See, for example, Ahmed Rashid, *The Resurgence of Central Asia* (London: Zed Books, 1994); Ali Banuazizi and Myron Weiner, eds., *The New Geopolitics of Central Asia and Its Borderlands* (Bloomington: Indiana University Press, 1994); and the relevant chapters in Ian Bremmer and Ray Taras, eds., *New States, New Politics: Building the Post-Soviet Nations* (Cambridge: Cambridge University Press, 1997).

12. See, for example, the vivid portrait in David Remnick, *Resurrection: The Struggle for A New Russia* (New York: Random House, 1997). Remnick ends by criticizing the doomsayers on Russia, but the wealth of evidence that he provides on its problems leaves one wondering about the relationship between the substance of the book and its upbeat conclusion.

13. The likely mutation of the Group of Seven (G-7) into the G-8 is an example inasmuch as the inclusion of Russia in a group of countries distinguished by their global economic influence is, to put it charitably, symbolism.

14. Calculated from data in Institute for National Strategic Studies, National Defense University, *Strategic Assessment 1995* (Washington, DC: USGPO, 1995), p. 65.

15. On the human and material toll of the wars in the southern Near Abroad, see Vladimir Mukomel', "Vooruzhennye mezhnatsional'nye i regional'nye konflikty: liudskie poteri, ekonomicheskii uschebr i sotsial'nye posledstviia," in Martha Brill Olcott, Valerii Tishkov, and Aleksei Malashenko, eds., *Identichnost' i konflikt v postsovetskikh gosudarstvakh* (Identity and conflict in the post-Soviet states) (Moscow: Moscow Carnegie Center, 1997), pp. 298–321.

16. See Paul Kennedy, *The Rise and Decline of the Great Powers* (New York: Vintage, 1987), on imperial overextension.

17. See Ronald Grigor Suny, *The Revenge of the Past: Nationalism, Revolution, and the Collapse of the Soviet Union* (Stanford, CA: Stanford University Press, 1993).

18. I am indebted to several Azeri and Georgian scholars who discussed this issue with me during my research in Azerbaijan and Georgia in June 1997.

19. Aleksei Zverev, "Etnicheskie konflikty na Kavkaze" (Ethnic conflicts in the Caucasus), in Bruno Koppiters, ed., *Spornye granitsy na Kavkaze* (Disputed borders in the Caucasus) (Moscow: Ves' Mir, 1996), pp. 10–76; Robert J. Kaiser, *The Geography of Nationalism in Russia and the USSR* (Princeton, NJ: Princeton University Press, 1994).

20. The classic statement is Ronald Robinson and John Gallagher, with Alice Denny, *Africa and the Victorians* (New York: St. Martin's Press, 1961). Also see the discussion of "pericentric" theories of empire in Michael Doyle, *Empires* (Ithaca, NY: Cornell University Press, 1986).

21. As with all generalizations, this tripartite distinction overlooks specific differences. Thus the development of civil society in Georgia is far more advanced than in Azerbaijan, especially if one considers the recovery that Georgia has made following Eduard Shevardnadze's assumption of power. Nevertheless, Georgia's simmering ethnic conflicts and the role that one man has played in fostering stability and civil society justify my categorizing Georgian civil society as weak.

22. The annual rates of population growth for the southern Near Abroad are as follows: Armenia 0.3 percent, Azerbaijan 0.8 percent, Georgia −0.4 percent, Kyrgyzstan 0.5 percent, Kazakhstan −1.6 percent, Tajikistan 1.4 percent, Turkmenistan 2.0 percent, Uzbekistan 1.7 percent. Data in Stephen K. Batalden and Sandra L. Batalden, *The Newly Independent States of Eurasia,* 2nd ed. (Phoenix, AZ: Oryx Press, 1997), pp. 94, 106, 120, 138, 151, 162, 174. Note that the relatively low rates of population growth in Kyrgyzstan and Kazakhstan need to be considered in light of the fact that 27 percent of the former's and 47 percent of the latter's population is Slavic/German.

23. See Maxim Sashenkov, "Russia in the Caucasus: Interests, Threats and Policy Options," in Baranovsky, *Russia and Europe,* pp. 433–35.

24. This school of thought, which derives from an intellectual tradition associated with Russian emigré intellectuals in the decades just after the Bolshevik

revolution, regards Russia as historically, culturally, and geographically a hybrid of Asia and Europe. Complicated policy prescriptions and conceptions of identity follow from this. But one theme in contemporary Eurasianist thinking is that Russia ought not to focus principally on the West as a partner in foreign policy but should recognize the critical importance of the former Soviet republics, Asia, and the Middle East.

25. See Oles M. Smolansky, "Russia and Transcaucasia: The Case of Nagorno-Karabakh," in Alvin Z. Rubinstein and Oles M. Smolansky, eds., *Regional Power Rivalries in the New Eurasia* (Armonk, NY: M.E. Sharpe, 1996), pp. 204–08, for a careful treatment of this shift in policy.

26. Russia sought more generous flank limits in the Leningrad military district as well.

27. For an elaboration of this point, see Menon, "In the Shadow of the Bear," pp. 167–74.

28. There is an extensive, well-supported literature showing that democracies do not fight other democracies. Bruce M. Russett's *Seizing the Democratic Peace* (Princeton, NJ: Princeton University Press, 1994), is a good example. But even this body of scholarship does not maintain that democracies are less inclined to resort to war as such. Indeed, some have argued that the process of democratization may increase the chances for war. See Jack Snyder and Edward D. Mansfield, "Democratization and the Danger of War, *International Security* 20, no. 20 (Summer 1995), pp. 5–38.

29. The year 1994 was the most recent one for which I could establish the degree to which the states of Central Asia and the south Caucasus depend on Russia for trade. Data for 1997 were not available as of this writing. For 1995 and 1996, even reasonably accurate trade dependence could not be established because of missing or incomplete data for the imports and exports in the case of the non-Russian countries and the inability to reconstruct a reliable measure of dependence based on the data provided for Russia's trade with these countries. The percentages in the table were calculated from data given in millions of current U.S. dollars. The data for Kyrgyzstan did not provide a breakdown of trade with Russia. The level of dependence had, therefore, to be derived from Russia's imports from and exports to Kyrgyzstan and Kyrgyzstan's worldwide import and export figures. This procedure almost certainly yields a result that overstates Kyrgyzstan's dependence on Russia, but the precise magnitude cannot be established.

30. Economist Intelligence Unit (EIU), *Country Profile: Georgia, Armenia, Azerbaijan, 1996–97* (London: EIU, 1997), p. 61; EIU, *Country Profile: Kyrgyz Republic, Tajikistan, Turkmenistan, Uzbekistan, 1996–97* (London: EIU, 1997), p. 116.

31. EIU, *Country Profile: Georgia, Armenia, Azerbaijan, Kazakhstan, and Central Asian Republics* (London: EIU, 1995), p. 159.

32. Armenia introduced the *dram* (November 1993), Azerbaijan the *manat* (January 1993), Georgia the *lari* (September 1995), Kazakhstan the *tenge* (November 1993), Turkmenistan the *monad* (November 1993), and Uzbekistan the *som* (which became the interim currency along with the ruble in November 1993 and the sole legal tender in July 1994). EIU, *Country Profile: Kazakhstan, First Quarter, 1997* (London: EIU, 1997), p. 45.

33. Calculated from the data in Philip S. Gilette, "Ethnic Balance and Imbalance in Kazakhstan's Regions," *Central Asia Monitor*, no. 3 (1993), p. 21 (Table 2).
34. Sarah J. Lloyd, "Pipelines to Prosperity?" *International Spectator* 32, no. 1 (January-March 1997), pp. 53–55. Lloyd shows that Russian supplies have been erratic.
35. Ibid., pp. 56–57.
36. On Kazakhstan's dependence on Russia for its security-related needs, see Andrei Kortunov, Yuri Kulchik, and Andrei Shumikhin, "Military Development in Kazakhstan: Goals, Parameters, and Implications for Russia," in Roald Sagdeev and Susan Eisenhower, eds., *Central Asia: Conflict, Resolution, and Change* (Chevy Chase, MD: Center for Post-Soviet Studies Press, 1995), pp. 127–37.
37. Interview with a senior official in Turkmenistan's Foreign Ministry, Ashgabat, June 1995.
38. For the official position of Turkmenistan, see the July 5, 1997, statement of its foreign ministry in "Turkmenistan Disputes Russian and Azeri Rights to Caspian Oilfield," British Broadcasting Corporation (BBC), *Summary of World Broadcasts*, SU/WO494/WF, July 11, 1997.
39. On Russia's more flexible conditions, see EIU, *Country Report: Kazakhstan, 1st Quarter, 1997* (London: EIU, 1997), p. 36. Azerbaijan rejected the Russian proposal. I am grateful to Laurent Ruseckas for discussions on this issue.
40. Interview with senior Western oil executive, Baku, Azerbaijan, June 1997.
41. This argument was made to me in Baku in June 1997 during an interview by an individual who served in a leading position in SOCAR, the Azerbaijan state oil company, during the tenure of the country's previous president, Abulfaz Elcibey.
42. For details on the Russian participation in Caspian pipeline and energy consortia, see Rajan Menon, *Treacherous Terrain: The Political and Security Dimensions of Energy Development in the Caspian Sea Zone* (Seattle: National Bureau of Asian Research, 1998).
43. For a succinct account of pipelines planned and under way, see Robert E. Ebel, "Geopolitics and Pipelines," *Analysis of Current Events* 9, no. 2 (February 1997), pp. 2–3. The discussion that follows draws from Ebel as well as the excellent—and more extensive—accounts of John Roberts, *Caspian Pipelines* (London: Royal Institute of International Affairs, 1996); Rosemary Forsythe, *The Politics of Oil in the Caucasus and Central Asia*, Adelphi Paper No. 300 (London: International Institute for Strategic Studies, 1996); and Oumerserik Kasenov, "Russia, Transcaucasia and Central Asia: Oil, Pipelines, and Geopolitics," in Sagdeev and Eisenhower, *Central Asia*, pp. 67–79. I also have relied on interviews conducted in December 1994 and June 1995 with governmental officials, representatives of international financial organizations and Western consulting companies, and U.S. embassy personnel in Almaty and Ashgabat and with scholars, officials, and oil company executives in Baku in June 1997.
44. Richard Hildahl and Laurent Ruseckas, "The New 'CPC': What It Means for the Politics of Caspian Oil," Cambridge Energy Research Associates, *Decision Brief* (July 1996), p. 5.

45. It is true that Kazakhstan has been sending some Tengiz crude to Azerbaijan by barge and then by rail to the Georgian port of Batumi for export. But this is not a viable option for the volume of production expected from Tengiz.

46. The intricacies of the negotiations between Russia and Chechnya on the pipeline are spelled out succinctly in Liz Fuller, "The Great Poker Game," *RFE/RL Newsline*, September 18, 1997, p. 6.

47. Ibid., September 8, 1997, p. 1. On the future relationship between Chechnya and Russia, see Sergei Kovalev, "Russia After Chechnya," *New York Review of Books*, June 17, 1997, pp. 27–31.

48. "Russia to Build Oil Pipeline Bypassing Chechnya," ibid., September 15, 1997, p. 1.

49. Turkey has proposed that oil exported through the northern and western lines should go down the Black Sea to its southern Black Sea port of Samsun and then by pipeline to Ceyhan rather than through the Straits. This idea reflects both its environmental concerns about the Straits and its desire to set the stage for the Ceyhan project as the main conduit for long-term oil production from Azerbaijan.

50. For a thorough analysis of Turkey's Kurdish problem and its prospects, see Henri J. Barkey and Graham Fuller, *Turkey's Kurdish Question* (Latham, MD: Rowman and Littlefield, 1998).

51. See Roberts, *Caspian Pipelines*, pp. 33–43, esp. the map on p. 34.

52. "Gazprom Ready to Give Up on Turkmenistan," *RFE/RL Newsline*, August 1, 1997, p. 3. The head of Gazprom, Rem Vyakhirev, assured Ukraine that his company would supply Ukraine's needs after Turkmenistan's decision to end supplies to it because of unpaid debts.

53. Turkmenistan's quests for pipelines that bypass Russia are described in Ahmed Rashid's excellent articles, "Power Play" and "Pipe Dreams," *Far Eastern Economic Review*, April 10, 1997, pp. 22–24, 27–28.

54. PRNewswire, October 27, 1997; *RFE/RL Newsline*, October 1997, p. 2.

55. The latest mutation of the civil war pits the Pushtun-dominated *Taliban* Islamist movement against Afghan Tajik and Uzbek groups.

56. "Turkey and Iran: It Will Burn Nicely Anyway," *The Economist*, August 2, 1997, p. 30.

57. *Pipeline News*, no. 69, Part I (July-August 1997), p. 5.

58. Laurent Ruseckas, "Caspian Oil: Beyond the 'Great Game,'" *Analysis of Current Events* 9, no. 2 (February 1997), pp. 4–5.

59. I owe much to Michael Mandelbaum's observations here.

60. The best account of the origins of the Nagorno-Karabakh war is Suzanne Goldenberg, *Pride of Small Nations: The Caucasus and Post-Soviet Disorder* (London: Zed Books, 1994), chaps. 6–8. A succinct and judicious analysis is provided in Human Rights Watch/Helsinki, *Azerbaijan: Seven Years of Conflict in Nagorno-Karabakh* (New York: Human Rights Watch, 1994), written by Christopher Panico and based on extensive interviews in Nagorno-Karabakh, Armenia, and Azerbaijan.

61. There is a fierce (I use the term deliberately) debate in the scholarly literature about whether Nagorno-Karabakh was first settled by Azeris or Armenians. Anyone who visits the southern Caucasus will find, as I did, how passionate and diametrically opposed views on these matters are. I

focus here not on the origin of the conflict over Nagorno-Karabakh or on apportioning responsibility for it but on how it affected Russian policy in the region.

62. Armenians and Azeris disagree vehemently about whether Armenian or Azeri civilians were the first to die in clashes between the two ethnic groups that erupted from 1988. Azeris insist that the violence against Armenians in Sumgait was preceded by the deaths of two Azeri men (Ali and Bakhtiar) at the hands of Armenians in Karabakh and that the Sumgait events had been preceded by the outflow of refugees from Karabakh, some of whom, along with criminal elements, launched the assaults on Armenians. Armenians tend to see the Sumgait attacks as a case of unprovoked attacks against innocent civilians.

63. The actual number of killed and wounded remains disputed. See Tadeusz Swietochowski, *Russia and Azerbaijan: A Borderland in Transition* (New York: Columbia University Press, 1995), pp. 205–6; Audrey L. Alstadt, *The Azerbaijani Turks: Power and Identity under Russian Rule* (Stanford, CA: Hoover Institution Press, 1992), p. 216. I have used Swietochowski's estimate.

64. Following the capture of Khojali, a massacre of Azeri civilians ensued that claimed the lives of hundreds of civilians. The 366th Motor Rifle Regiment subsequently was withdrawn, although an undetermined portion of its weapons and personnel stayed behind.

65. These instances of Russian military involvement are described in Human Rights Watch/Helsinki, *Azerbaijan: Seven Years of Conflict,* pp. 5, 88; Thomas Goltz, "Letter from Eurasia: The Hidden Russian Hand," *Foreign Policy,* no. 92 (Fall 1993), pp. 100–1; "The Russian Federation's [sic] Defence Ministry's Military Bases in Georgia," *Georgian Military Chronicle,* Occasional Papers of the Caucasian Institute for Peace, Democracy and Development, 2, no. 6 (October 1995), n.p.

66. Vicken Cheterian, *Dialectics of Ethnic Conflicts and Oil Projects in the Caucasus* (Geneva: Programme for Security and International Studies, Graduate School of International Studies, 1997), p. 28.

67. The estimates of the refugee population and Azerbaijan's territorial losses are based on conversations in Baku (June 1997) with an Azeri scholar who has done considerable research on the refugee question. His figures are lower than those claimed by the Azeri government.

68. Azerbaijan's president, Haidar Aliev, has said that if there is no peaceful settlement of the Nagorno-Karabakh dispute, "we will definitely take back our lands under occupation, whatever this will cost." *RFE/RL Newsline,* May 9, 1997, p. 2.

69. Jim Nichol, "Armenia, Azerbaijan, and Georgia: Political Developments and Implications for U.S. Interests," Congressional Research Service, *CRS Issue Brief,* April 3, 1997, p. 5.

70. For example, just prior to the March 1997 CIS summit, Ivan Rybkin, secretary of Russia's Security Council, called for a "renewed" treaty between Armenia and Russia with a "military component." *OMRI Daily Digest,* March 28, 1997, p. 4.

71. Harry Tamrazian, "Russian, Armenia Committed to Strong Military Ties," *RFE/RL Newsline,* September 3, 1997, pp. 5–6.

72. *RFE/RL Newsline,* September 1, 1997, p. 1.
73. Even before the signing of the treaty, Armenia's president, Levon Ter-Petrossian, described Russia as Armenia's "main strategic partner." Once the treaty was signed, he said that it would make for closer cooperation between Russia and Armenia than existed between Russia and Belarus. *OMRI Daily Digest,* March 28, 1997, p. 4; Tamrazian, "Russia, Armenia," p. 6. For the official Azeri reaction, see the statements of Foreign Minister Hassan Hassanov as cited in *RFE/RL Newsline,* September 4, 1997, p. 2.
74. On these developments, see *RFE/RL Newsline,* September 2, 1997, p. 3; ibid., September 1, 1997, p. 1; ibid., September 8, 1997, p. 2; ibid., September 25, 1997, p. 2; Tamrazian, "Russia, Armenia."
75. *RFE/RL Newsline,* August 11, 1997, p. 3; Liz Fuller, "One State, Two Policies?" ibid., July 23, 1997, p. 6.
76. With the withdrawal of Russian troops from Azerbaijan, the only military facility remaining is a radar station in Gabala that is part of the CIS early-warning network.
77. Aliev's claim was made during a meeting with members of the U.S. Senate in August 1997 and attacked as "an unfounded provocation" by Yuri Yukalov, Russia's representative to the OSCE Minsk Group seeking a settlement of the Krabakh dispute. *RFE/RL Newsline,* August 14, 1997, p. 3; ibid., August 19, 1997, p. 3.
78. Text in *ITAR-TASS* World Service (in Russian) 1235 GMT, July 3, 1997, in *Foreign Broadcast Information Service—Soviet Union,* July 3, 1997.
79. *OMRI Daily Digest,* March 23, 1997, p. 4.
80. There was a previous cease-fire, also arranged by Russia, in February 1994.
81. The $720 million figure excludes transportation costs, spare parts, and fuel supplies. See Lev Rokhlin, "Spetsoperatsiia ili kommercheskaia afera?" (A covert operation or a commercial deal?), *Nezavisimoe voennoe obozrenie* (Independent military review), no. 13 (1997) for the most detailed account of the types and numbers of weapons and their points of origin. Vladimir Yemelyanenko, "Aman Tuleyev: 'Russian Peacekeepers Will Stay,'" *Moscow News,* March 27–April 11, 1997, p. 2; Liz Fuller, "'Yerevangate' Disclosures Leave Key Questions Unanswered," *RFE/RL Newsline,* April 23, 1997, pp. 5–6. Rokhlin puts the amount of arms transfers to Armenia at about $1 billion—a considerable sum, but much less than the 270 billion ruble figure cited by Tuleyev. Rokhlin also asserted that such weapons shipments could not have occurred without the knowledge of former Defense Minister Pavel Grachev and former Chief of Staff General Mikhail Kolesnikov.
82. *RFE/RL Newsline,* July 16, 1997, p. 2.
83. The discussion that follows draws on Human Rights Watch/Helsinki, *Azerbaijan,* chap. 10.
84. On Russia's relationship with the OSCE in the Karabakh dispute, see Carol Migdalovitz, "Armenia-Azerbaijan Conflict," Congressional Research Service, *CRS Issue Brief,* March 3, 1997, pp. 4–6.
85. In February 1997 France and the United States joined Russia as cochairs.
86. Smolansky, "Russia and Transcaucasia," pp. 213–15.
87. In April 1997 fighting between Armenian and Azeri forces in the Qazak sector of northern Azerbaijan erupted in what was described as the worst breach

of the 1994 cease-fire. The Azeris claimed to have killed 13 Armenian soldiers and the Armenians said that they had killed seven Azeris. Each accused the other of starting the skirmish. Lawrence Sheets, "Azeris, Armenians in Worst Fighting for Years," Reuters, April 16, 1997. Another clash occurred in May in the Tauz region of Azerbaijan in which, according to Armenian sources, an Azeri attack on Armenian positions was repulsed and 17 Azeri soldiers killed. *RFE/RL Newsline,* May 14, 1997, p. 2.

88. On the power of, and reasons behind, nationalism in the post-Soviet space, see Anatoly Khazanov, *After the USSR: Ethnicity, Nationalism, and Politics in the Commonwealth of Independent States* (Madison: University of Wisconsin Press, 1995).

89. Ossetians account for two-thirds of the population in South Ossetia; Abkhaz account for only 17 percent in Abkhazia. Most Ossetians live outside South Ossetia; most Abkhaz inhabit Abkhazia.

90. The importance of Orthodox Christianity to the conception of nationhood contained in Georgian ultranationalist rhetoric also made the ethnically Georgian Muslims of Ajaria anxious.

91. See John F. R. Wright, "The Geopolitics of Georgia," and Julian Birch, "The Georgian/South Ossetian Boundary Dispute," in John F. R. Wright, Suzanne Goldenberg, and Richard Schofield, eds., *Transcaucasian Boundaries* (New York: St. Martin's Press, 1996), pp. 134–50 and 151–89 respectively.

92. Ronald Grigor Suny, *The Making of the Georgian Nation,* 2nd ed. (Bloomington: Indiana University Press, 1994), chap. 14; Stephen F. Jones, "Georgia: The Trauma of Statehood," in Ian Bremmer and Ray Taras, eds., *New States and Politics* (Cambridge: Cambridge University Press, 1997), esp. pp. 514–22; Goldenberg, *Pride of Small Nations,* pp. 81–98.

93. Shevardnadze initially sought to co-opt Kitovani (who was made defense minister) and Jaba Ioseliani (who was appointed to the Defense Council). In 1993, Kitovani, who ignited the Abkhaz war by unilaterally sending forces to Abkhazia, was removed from his post. Ioseliani was arrested in November 1995 and charged with a role in the attempted assassination of Shevardnadze, which occurred on August 29, and the Defense Council was abolished.

94. Goldenberg, *Pride of Small Nations,* pp. 109–10.

95. The term "armed forces" is perhaps a misnomer. What Georgia had was more an agglomeration of private armies controlled by charismatic personalities than a professional military.

96. Gamsakhurdia's cooperation with Chechen leader Dzhokar Dudayev had been particularly worrisome to Moscow, as had his vision of an anti-Russian league of Caucasus states.

97. An excellent account of Georgia's disastrous war in Abkhazia is provided in Dodge Billingsley, "The Georgian Security Dilemma and Military Failure in Abkhazia," transcript of a lecture given at the Harriman Institute, Columbia University, October 2, 1997 (and to be published in a future issue of *The Harriman Review*). I thank Mr. Billingsley for permission to cite his paper here.

98. See Fiona Hill and Pamela Jewett, *Back in the USSR: Russia's Intervention in the Internal Affairs of the Former Soviet Republics and the Implications for United States Policy towards Russia,* Strengthening Democratic Institutions

Project, John F. Kennedy School of Government, Harvard University (January 1994), pp. 45–60; Goltz, "Letter from Eurasia," pp. 106–8; Jonathan Aves, *Georgia: From Chaos to Stability?* (London: Royal Institute of International Affairs, 1996), pp. 1, 27–28; Jones, "Georgia," p. 526, while blaming the outcome of the war in Abkhazia on Georgia's military weakness and the unwillingness of its leaders to find a political solution concludes, that "it was just as much a result of the support of the local Russia military and the Russian government for the Abkhaz leaders' uncompromising demands."

99. Hill and Jewett, *Back in the USSR*, p. 54.

100. Arkadii Popov argues that the fighters from the North Caucasus who crossed the Russian border into Abkhazia were provided with substantial amounts of Russian arms. Popov, "Prichiny vozniknoveniia i dinamika razvitiia konfliktov," in Olcott, Tishkov, and Malashenko, *Identichnost' i konflikt*, p. 294. On the closing of the Abkhazia-Russia border, see Open Society Institute, Forced Migration Projects, *Forced Migration: Repatriation in Georgia* (New York: Open Society Institute, 1995), p. 24.

101. Details on the CIS peacekeeping forces and UNOMIG are based on discussions with military officers attached to UNOMIG, Tbilisi, Georgia, June 1997.

102. "The Russian Federation's [*sic*] Defence Ministry's Military Bases," n.p.; Aves, *Georgia*, p. 2; Nichol, "Armenia, Azerbaijan, and Georgia," p. 5.

103. For an example of the hard-line positions adopted by some of these forces, see "Russia Is Arming Abkhazia," *The Georgian Times* (Tbilisi), June 17, 1997, p. 1; *RFE/RL Newsline*, August 20, 1997, p. 2.

104. Susan Caskie, "Georgia: A 'Terrorist War,'" *Transition* 3, no. 6 (April 4, 1997), p. 55.

105. Discussions with UNOMIG officers, Tbilisi, June 1997; Liz Fuller, "Solution to Abkhaz Conflict Continues to Prove Elusive," *RFE/RL Newsline*, July 10, 1997, p. 6.

106. Discussions with UNOMIG officers.

107. I am indebted to UNOMIG officers in Tbilisi for discussing the state of Georgia's military with me during an interview in June 1997.

108. One Russian press report raised the possibility of another (the first occurred in 1995) assassination attempt against Shevardnadze—this time organized by Moscow were he to ask for the removal of Russian troops. It stated that Giorgadze and other exiled Shevardnadze opponents have been meeting regularly in Russia with the former head of military intelligence for Russian forces in the Transcaucasus. Akaky Mikadze, "Damned If You Do and Damned If You Don't," *Moscow News*, August 14–20, 1997, p. 4. In 1998 a second attempt was indeed made to kill Shevardnadze, and Georgian officials made several comments implying Russian involvement.

109. *RFE/RL Newsline*, September 22, 1997, p. 3.

110. In South Ossetia, there are signs of progress. The Ossetian leadership appears willing to accept a confederal status within Georgia, and radicals who pushed for union with North Ossetia have lost influence.

111. Among the best treatments of the civil war in Tajikistan are Sergei Gretsky, "Civil War in Tajikistan: Causes, Developments, and Prospects for Peace,"

in Sagdeev and Eisenhower, *Central Asia,* pp. 217–47; Olivier Roy, *The Civil War in Tajikistan: Causes and Implications* (Washington, DC: United States Institute for Peace, 1993); Shahrbanou Tadjbaksh, "The Bloody Path of Change: The Case of Post-Soviet Tajikistan," *Harriman Institute Forum* 6, no. 11 (July 1993); Tadjbaksh, "National Reconciliation: The Imperfect Whim," *Central Asian Survey* 15, nos. 3–4 (December 1996), pp. 325–48; Barnett R. Rubin, "Tajikistan: From Soviet Republic to Russian-Uzbek Protectorate," in Michael Mandelbaum, ed., *Central Asia and the World* (New York: Council on Foreign Relations, 1994); Rubin, "The Fragmentation of Tajikistan," *Survival* 35, no. 4 (Winter 1993–1994), pp. 71–91; and the many reports of Bruce Pannier in *Transition.*

112. Rubin, "Tajikistan," p. 214.
113. Tajik population figure from *Central Asia Monitor,* no. 3 (1992), pp. 39–40. Tajik activists in Uzbekistan claim that there are in fact many more Tajiks in Uzbekistan.
114. This catchall term has been used by Uzbekistan to justify its undemocratic political system and by Russia to legitimize its intervention in Tajikistan. As applied to the Tajik opposition, an amalgam of groups with distinct agendas and political philosophies, it is misleading in the extreme. See Muriel Atkin, "Tajikistan's Relations with Iran and Afghanistan," in Ali Banuazizi and Myron Weiner, eds., *The New Geopolitics of Central Asia and Its Borderlands* (Bloomington: Indiana University Press, 1994), pp. 99–101.
115. On Yeltsin's warnings about Islamic fundamentalism in Tajikistan, see *New York Times,* August 8, 1993, p. 17. Also see the interview with then–Deputy Foreign Minister Georgii Kunadze, "Tadzhikistan: posledniaia voina SSR ili pervaia voina Rosii?" (Tajikistan: The Soviet Union's last war or Russia's first war?), *Nezavisimaia gazeta,* July 29, 1993, pp. 1, 3.
116. There is a U.N. Mission of Observers in Tajikistan (UNMOT), which monitors cease-fires along the Tajikistan-Afghanistan border. But it has a mere 96 members and repeatedly has been subject to harassment, attack, and kidnapping.
117. Gorno-Badakshan province, home to the Ismaili Pamiri people, declared independence in 1993, and the Tajik government's control of Leninabad is tenuous at best. Bruce Pannier, "Defining the 'Third Force,'" *Transition* 3, no. 5 (March 1997), pp. 43, 45.
118. In my view this is intended to put pressure on the Kulobi-dominated government of Tajikistan by reminding it that Uzbekistan is a key player in Tajik politics. Given the makeup of the opposition—particularly its Tajik nationalist and Islamist elements—it is inconceivable that Karimov would relish the prospect of its taking power in Tajikistan or its having a substantial role in Tajikistan's government.
119. On the cosmetic, public relations–driven character of Uzbekistan's democratization, see, inter alia, Roger Kangas, "Uzbekistan: Press Freedom—On Paper Only," *Transition* 3, no. 6 (April 4, 1997), p. 53; Kangas, "Holding the Course in Uzbekistan," ibid., vol. 3, no. 2 (February 7, 1997), pp. 90–91; "Government-Opposition Relations in Uzbekistan: Dashed Hopes," *CSCE Digest* 20, no. 2 (February 1997), pp. 13, 20–23. The Uzbek leadership's enthusiasm for an arrangement in which the United States does

not make human rights the focus of its policy toward Uzbekistan and instead recognizes Uzbekistan as the dominant regional power in Central Asia that can help offset Russia was apparent in an interview I conducted with a senior official of the Uzbek Foreign Ministry on December 10, 1994, in Tashkent.

120. For a graphic account, see Pannier, "Defining the 'Third Force,'" pp. 43–45.

121. Bruce Pannier, "A Year of Violence in Tajikistan," *Transition* 3, no. 2 (February 7, 1997), p. 97; Jim Nichol, "Tajik Civil War: Recent Developments and US Policy Concerns," *CRS Report for Congress,* January 8, 1997, p. 3; Interfax in English, 1053 GMT, March 8, 1997, in FBIS, *Daily Report—Central Eurasia,* March 8, 1997, n.p., via Internet; *Ekho Moskvy* radio in Russian, 1234 GMT, February 28, 1997, trans. in ibid., February 28, 1997, n.p., via Internet.

122. On the provisions of the accord and its prospects, see Michael Ochs, "Peace Accord Reached in Tajikistan," *CSCE Digest* 20, no. 7 (July 1997), p. 76; Umed Babakhanov and Bruce Pannier, "Peace in Tajikistan or New Stage in Conflict?" *RFE/RL Newsline,* June 27, 1997, p. 6.

123. Carl J. Friedrich, *Constitutional Government and Democracy: Theory and Practice in Europe and America* (Boston: Little, Brown, 1941), pp. 589–90; Friedrich, *Man and His Government: An Empirical Theory of Politics* (New York: McGraw-Hill, 1963), chap. 2.

124. On Kazakh-Russian tensions in Kazakhstan, see Khazanov, *After the USSR,* chap. 5; and Ian Bremmer and Cory Welt, "The Trouble with Democracy in Kazakhstan," *Central Asian Survey* 15, no. 2 (June 1996), pp. 179–99. On actual or emerging conditions that mitigate ethnic conflict, see Jiger Janbel, "When National Ambition Conflicts with Reality," ibid., vol. 15, no. 1 (March 1996), pp. 5–22. I also have benefited from Cynthia Ann Werner's presentation at the Association for the Study of Nationalities (ASN) convention, New York, April 25, 1997.

125. On the growth of anti-Chinese nationalism in Xinjiang in the post-Soviet years, see, inter alia, *Asiaweek,* June 14, 1996, pp. 32–33; *The Economist,* June 13, 1996, p. 33; *New York Times,* February 11, 1997, p. 4, and February 26, 1997, p. 9; and *OMRI Daily Report* (February 17, 1997).

126. Vyacheslav Ia. Belokrenitskii, ed., *Tsentral'naia Aziia: puti integratsii v mirovoe soobshchestvo* (Central Asia: The path to integration in the world community) (Moscow: Institut Vostokovedeniia, 1995), p. 31.

127. For this argument and the evidence, see Rajan Menon, "The Strategic Convergence between Russia and China," *Survival* 39, no. 2 (Summer 1997), pp. 101–25. Also see Michael Gordon, "Russia-China Theme: Contain the West," *New York Times,* April 24, 1997, p. 3.

128. For valuable analyses that discuss the limitations of Turkish and Chinese influence, see Gareth Winrow, *Turkey in Post-Soviet Central Asia* (London: Royal Institute of International Affairs, 1995); Philip Robins, "Between Sentiment and Self-Interest: Turkey's Policy toward Azerbaijan and the Central Asian States," *Middle East Journal* 47, no. 4 (Autumn 1993), pp. 593–610; Mustafa Aylin, "Turkey and Central Asia: Challenges of Change," *Central Asian Survey* 15, no. 2 (June 1996), pp. 157–77; Edmund Herzig, *Iran and the Former Soviet South* (London: Royal Insti-

tute of International Affairs, 1995); Sabri Sayari, "Turkey, the Caucasus and Central Asia," and Seyed Kazem Sajjadpour, "Iran, the Caucasus and Central Asia," in Banuazizi and Weiner, eds., *The New Geopolitics,* pp. 175–96 and 197–215 respectively.

129. Azeri officials have publicly accused Iran of favoring Armenia, and in April and May 1996 they incarcerated members of the Iran-oriented Islamic Party. Iran in turn has criticized what it considers biased Azeri press coverage of its policy in the Azeri-majority northern regions. Elizabeth Fuller, "Azerbaijani Leadership Brooks No Opposition," *Transition* 3, no. 2 (February 7, 1997), pp. 87, 101; *Zerkalo* (Baku), in Russian, March 15, 1997, trans. in *BBC Summary of World Broadcasts,* SU/D2872/F, March 20, 1997.

130. Michael Gordon, "As West Shuns Iran, Russia Pulls Closer," *New York Times,* April 12, 1997, p. 5.

131. Vladimir Lyaporov, "Does Central Asia Still Need Russia?" *Nezavisimaia gazeta,* September 13, 1996, trans. in *Current Digest of the Post-Soviet Press* 48, no. 38 (October 16, 1996), p. 12.

132. In February 1996 Karimov, while noting that some circles within Russia wanted to create an imperial relationship with the ex-Soviet republics, said that Russia "was, is, and will be Uzbekistan's strategic partner." "Russia Remains Uzbekistan's Strategic Partner," ITAR-TASS, February 3, 1996. In October 1996 the leaders of all the Central Asian states except Turkmenistan met in Almaty with Russian Prime Minister Viktor Chernomyrdin to forge a common approach to Afghanistan. The effort did not produce any new initiatives. But what is significant is the turn to Russia.

133. EIU, *Country Profile: Kyrgyz Republic, Tajikistan, Turkmenistan, Uzbekistan, 1996–97* (London: EIU, 1997), p. 92.

134. A case in point is S. Frederick Starr, "Making Eurasia Stable," *Foreign Affairs* 75, no. 1 (January-February 1996), pp. 80–92.

135. For a judicious treatment, see Mehrdad Haghayeghi, *Islam and Politics in Central Asia* (New York: St. Martin's Press, 1995).

136. Anara Tabyshalieva, "Central Asia: Polarization of Religious Communities," *Perspectives on Central Asia* 2, no. 3 (June 1997), pp. 2–4; Georgi Derluguan, "The 'Religious' Factor in Central Asia and the Caucasus," ibid., pp. 1–2.

137. The obvious caveat that needs to be made is that unrealistic expectations by the peoples of the region coupled with the intrusion of objects and ideas of Western origin also could create a backlash—especially if Western policy displays insensitivity, triumphalism, and an ignorance of local history and cultures.

CHAPTER FOUR

Russia and the West

Coit D. Blacker

Some six years after the collapse of the Soviet Union, the struggle to define the essential contours of the New Russia continues its uneven progress. The struggle is most evident at the domestic level, where the contest to determine who does what to whom—*kto kogo*—dominates both the appearance and the substance of Russia's daily political life. Much of the struggle centers on the pursuit of personal power, but it is also—perhaps even primarily—about issues and ideas of enormous consequence; how this struggle concludes will determine nothing less than the kind of state and society that postcommunist Russia will become.

Contemporary Russian foreign policy both reflects and informs the larger debate over the country's future complexion. That this should be the case strikes Western observers as self-evident, given the intimate relationship in democratic societies between domestic politics and the content and the conduct of foreign policy. But it appears to have caught Russian leaders, long accustomed to the de facto separation of the two realms, somewhat by surprise. The leadership's attempts to explain the symmetry between Russian aims at home and Russian purposes abroad—especially in the period since Andrei Kozyrev's dismissal as foreign minister in January 1996—have been accorded a mixed reception internationally. To Western ears in particular, most such efforts have seemed, at best, labored and formalistic; at worst, they have made Russia's leaders seem delusional, if not hallucinogenic.

The failure is only partly one of presentation. At one level, Russian foreign policy in 1998 seeks, in fact, to reconcile the irreconcilable. If, in Alexander Dallin's memorable phrase, it was the tension between "the urge to enjoy and the urge to destroy" that characterized the conduct of

Soviet foreign policy during the Brezhnev era,[1] for today's Kremlin leaders it is the two-part demand that Russia be fully integrated into, while preserving its independence from and autonomy within, key Western institutions that increasingly seems to motivate policy. Whatever its superficial appeal, the strategy is not without risk: What constitutes an appropriate ambition for a great power in its prime can be a dangerous indulgence for a country seeking to recover from decades of political misrule and economic mismanagement.

If the strategy of what might be termed "contingent cooperation," or the promise to cooperate with the West in the furtherance of common goals, coupled with the threat to defect, is in fact risky, why pursue it? The answer comes in several parts. The strategy reveals much, for example, about how Russia's leaders understand the challenges they confront internationally as they, and we, near the end of the twentieth century; and how, in particular, they seek to maximize their leverage as they negotiate the terms of Russia's entry into the international system. In this context, a strategy of "yes, but" would appear to make considerable sense.

The strategy also underscores the extent to which Russia's leaders, like democratically elected leaders everywhere, must try to balance and give voice to competing domestic demands even as they work to advance the country's foreign policy agenda. Since in Russia most of these constituencies have been highly critical of the Yeltsin government's pro-Western stance, the strategy of contingent cooperation has received broad endorsement.

Notwithstanding its tactical utility and popular appeal, however, Moscow's apparent embrace of this strategy is not cost-free. It already has complicated Russia's relations with its Western partners, without whose support it cannot hope to complete the painful process of political and economic transformation. It also risks leading Russia into a series of bilateral relationships designed to "balance" its alleged dependence on the West that, if and when they are invested with real substance, could further alienate its erstwhile supporters, while buying precious little in return. In short, the danger for Moscow is that what began as a series of *tactical* adjustments to policy engineered by Kozyrev's successor at the Foreign Ministry, Yevgeny Primakov, could backfire, generating a host of unwelcome *strategic* consequences.

The purpose of this chapter is to explore what might be thought of as the "deep structure" of contemporary Russian foreign policy—that is, the internal logic and core essence of Kremlin policy toward the world beyond Russia's borders—as suggested by the actual conduct of Russian diplomacy in the period since the recovery of the country's independence late in 1991.

The central argument is that decisions made early on by the Yeltsin leadership, in particular the decision to seek rapid and extensive economic and political integration with the West, were—and remain—enormously consequential, imposing among other conditions important, if mostly implicit, constraints on the leadership's freedom to maneuver internationally. Moreover, as economic conditions for the vast majority of Russian voters went from bad to worse, popular support for the policies of domestic economic reform and global integration—never all that deep or strong to begin with—all but evaporated, further constraining the government and forcing it to retreat rhetorically even as it sought to press ahead substantively. This discrepancy between how Russia's leaders depicted the purposes of policy and how they in fact comported themselves internationally, particularly during the second half of Kozyrev's tenure as foreign minister, strained the government's credibility at home and confused and irritated its Western partners.

The principal foreign policy challenge that President Boris Yeltsin and his ministers confront in 1998 differs in degree, although not in kind, from that with which they have had to contend for the last half decade—namely, how to sustain the essentially integrationist and pro-Western thrust in foreign policy, which they regard, correctly, as indispensable to the restoration of Russia's economic health and political well-bring, in the absence of meaningful domestic support. Under Primakov, they have achieved considerable success against long odds in this difficult and demanding policy challenge through a combination of domestic political legerdemain and (mostly) skillful diplomacy. Regrettably, past performance, however dazzling, is no guarantee of future success.

WHITHER RUSSIA?

Of the Yeltsin government's many ambitious plans to remake Russia, few would turn out to be as contentious as the leadership's decision to jettison the foreign policy bequeathed to it by the Soviet Union. At the time, however, the decision barely provoked comment. By late 1991 Mikhail Gorbachev's efforts to redefine and reconfigure Moscow's relations with the rest of the world had alienated just about everyone active in Soviet political life. The regime's liberal critics, initially effusive in their praise of "the new political thinking," had all but abandoned the policy, terming it a well-intentioned failure, a case of too little, too late; Gorbachev's enemies, hard-line communists and nationalists, thought it treasonous.

Kozyrev and the Logic of Integration

To Russia's young foreign minister, Andrei Kozyrev, the shortcomings of Soviet foreign policy transcended any alleged failure on Gorbachev's part to employ the right formula in pursuit of reform. The real problem, according to Kozyrev, was the nonsensical character of the core assumptions upon which successive generations of Soviet leaders had sought to fashion a coherent policy. Chief among these was the mistaken belief that the appearance of the Soviet Union on the world stage had opened a fundamentally new chapter in international history, one destined to end in the defeat of capitalism and the triumph of the socialist alternative. Since 1945, this fiction continued, the U.S.S.R. had occupied the pole position in something called "the world socialist system," a kind of parallel international order to the one led by Moscow's great rival, the United States.

The truth, according to Kozyrev and other like-minded Russians, was that the Soviet attempt to construct a rival international system had been a colossal blunder—one of a series of tragic miscalculations by the communists—that had cost the Russian people dearly and, in the end, driven the country into bankruptcy; Moscow's allies, especially those whose economies had been linked most closely to that of the Soviet Union, all suffered a similar fate. In Kozyrev's view, the attempt to build socialism, both at home and abroad, had interrupted the process of convergence between Russia and the West that had just begun to bear fruit when the Great October Revolution intervened. With the collapse of the Soviet order, Kozyrev wrote, the way was clear once again for Russia to reclaim its status as a "normal country" and to become "a reliable partner in the community of civilized states."[2]

In the effort to advance both objectives, Russia's new leaders attached the highest possible priority to securing their country's prompt membership in the full array of Western-sponsored institutions—from the International Monetary Fund (IMF) to the Council of Europe—from which the Soviet Union had been excluded or that it had chosen to ignore. Beyond the logical force of such a policy, the strategy held deep appeal to a leadership eager to enhance its own shaky legitimacy and profoundly concerned about a society prone in times of crisis to succumb to the lure of political extremism. Time, Russia's leaders believed, was of the essence. The most urgent threat was believed to be a fascist-inspired bid for power—what Kozyrev characterized as the putative appeal of various "would-be führers," with their promise of "miraculously cheap vodka for all and their grand visions of restoring Russia . . . to the borders of the former U.S.S.R.,"[3]—although given the actual balance of forces in the country in 1992, the more immediate danger to the Yeltsin government was probably a communist-led counterstrike.

Whatever the precise character and dimensions of the threat, Boris Yeltsin and his ministers were only too aware that the political window of opportunity that had opened with the collapse of the communist regime could slam shut with little warning. Indeed, they well understood that their own political survival hinged on their capacity to "deliver the goods," which, in the first months after the Soviet fall in particular, meant the appearance—if not yet the reality—of progress toward a better life for the majority of the Russian people.

They also understood that in the wake of the Soviet Union's unraveling the Russian economy was in disarray and the only way to make good on their ambitious agenda, at least in the near term, was to enlist serious Western support—support that would be forthcoming only if political leaders in the West could demonstrate to their own tight-fisted electorates that Russia had in fact embraced democracy and embarked on the path of radical economic reform.

The interrelationship between what the Russian government hoped to accomplish domestically and what it had to do internationally thus was apparent from the outset, at least to those, like Kozyrev, who believed that the only way to repair the damage inflicted on Russia by seven decades of communist misrule was through the complete reordering of the country's political and economic life. For the Kremlin's new leaders, dismantling the communist order at home and rejoining "the community of civilized states" were mutually reinforcing goals, if not two sides of the same coin.

The ambitious reform agenda advanced by the Russian leadership in the months immediately following its ascent to power struck a positive chord with Western decision-makers alarmed by the potential implications—political, military, and economic—of the sudden collapse of Soviet power, and thus eager to demonstrate their commitment to and support for Russia's dramatic moves toward democracy and market economics. Especially responsive to Russian pleas for assistance were the Kohl government in Germany and the Bush and Clinton administrations in the United States. Both countries scrambled to put in place bilateral assistance programs to help ease the pain of transition, which they coupled with an almost constant stream of requests to other Western countries to lend a hand. Beginning in 1993 Washington and Bonn were also careful to coordinate their approaches to the International Monetary Fund (IMF) to urge the fund's senior managers to work directly—and creatively—with

Russian government officials in the design and implementation of a program to achieve prompt macroeconomic stabilization.

The results of these efforts, while falling short of Russian expectations, were considerable. During the first half of 1993, the Group of Seven countries (G-7) assembled a multilateral assistance program to Russia totaling some $30 billion, including a $6 billion ruble stabilization fund and $4 billion in immediate debt relief. Direct bilateral assistance to Russia (and the new independent states, less the Baltic republics), originally set at $460 million for fiscal year 1993, was increased to $1.6 billion; Congress appropriated another $900 million the following year. In all, between 1992 and 1996 Western countries committed well in excess of $40 billion in aid—through the IMF, the World Bank, the European Bank for Reconstruction and Development, various G-7 mechanisms, and bilateral programs—in direct support of Russia's efforts to reform its economics and democratize its politics.

The developing partnership between Russia and the West also yielded tangible results in the form of greater cooperation on a host of high-profile diplomatic and arms control issues, from the pursuit of security in the new Europe and the search for peace in the Middle East, to the conclusion in January 1993 of a second strategic arms reduction treaty between Washington and Moscow. Under Kozyrev, the Russians also affirmed their support for key U.S. nuclear nonproliferation initiatives, including the indefinite extension of the Nuclear Nonproliferation Treaty (achieved in 1995) and the congressionally mandated program (sponsored by Senators Sam Nunn and Richard Lugar) to assist in the dismantling and destruction of excess long-range Soviet missile systems and nuclear warheads deployed on the territory of the Russian Federation, Belarus, Ukraine, and Kazakhstan.

As Kozyrev had intended, Russia's evident willingness to work closely with Washington and other Western countries on a number of important foreign and security policy issues yielded an unprecedented level of cooperation between the parties and generated enormous, bankable goodwill. Even so, relations between Moscow and the West were hardly stress-free. Differences over two issues—Russian unhappiness with what the leadership regarded as a persistent anti-Serb bias in Western policy toward the ongoing crisis in the former Yugoslavia and Moscow's growing discomfort with Washington's obvious interest in expansion of the North Atlantic Treaty Organization (NATO)—were apparent early on and soon would become major sources of tension between the "partners." For the time being, however, the mood in both Washington and Moscow regarding the development of post–Cold War East-West relations was unmistakably bullish.

For students of international relations, one of the most striking features of the Kozyrev foreign policy line is the extent to which it resembled, particularly at the outset, the posture of a country defeated in war and forced to sue for peace on unfavorable terms. Although not without precedent—Germany and Japan vis-à-vis the United States in 1945, for example—the adoption by Country X of the domestic and foreign policy "script" of its chief rival, Country Y, is a rare event in world politics. What makes it all the more striking is that while it may be appropriate to speak of the Soviet Union's having lost a war, Russia is supposed to have been "liberated" by the defeat of communism and thus freer, at least in theory, to chart its own destiny. Doubtless, the decision by the new Russian government to identify so closely with Western aims and values had much to do with what the leadership thought they were about in the first place—the remaking of Russia into a "normal" country and "rejoining the world." It also may have resulted from the simple act of lending substance to what Michael McFaul has termed the Russian democrats' "ideology of opposition." (Translation: Whatever the Soviet Union stood for both domestically and internationally, the new Russia must stand for the opposite.)[4]

A second important feature of this early Russian posture was the almost complete lack of traction it afforded the leadership as it sought to negotiate the terms of Russia's entry into Western-dominated institutions. At the beginning, the Yeltsin government could do little more than plead for admission on the grounds that having overthrown the communist regime, it deserved to reap the rewards. The West, led by the United States, responded positively to Moscow's requests for assistance (and acceptance), although rather less generously than the Kremlin had hoped; as Russia's leaders were soon to discover, the urgency of one's plight is seldom enough to induce other sovereign states to act, especially in ways that they may regard as inconsistent with their own interests.

It does only modest violence to Kozyrev's legacy to argue, in the vocabulary favored by international relations theorists, that the foreign minister had framed Russian policy by reference to a set of *norms*— "Russia must become more like the West"—rather than by reference to the more familiar concepts of *power* and *interest*—"Russia must be strong enough to defend its vital interests." Critics were soon to charge that in placing the first ambition ahead of the second, the primary architect of Russian foreign policy had gotten it exactly backward, effectively lifting control over the country's future out of its own hands and placing it into the hands of others. Kozyrev argued, both then and later, that to achieve the second goal, the country had first to realize the first.[5]

Kozyrev was right, of course. But as the years passed and Russia's economic and social crises deepened, the government found itself increasingly on the defensive across a broad range of policy issues, foreign as well as domestic. Especially difficult to defend against was the charge that notwithstanding Western economic and financial assistance, the United States and its principal allies were content to let Russia deteriorate, which among its other consequences enabled unscrupulous Western (and Russian) business interests to exploit the country's human capital and buy up its material assets at what critics claimed amounted to bargain-basement prices.

Opponents of the regime also charged—and not entirely without cause—that in placing such a high premium on cooperation with the West, Russia had become inexcusably lax in the defense of many of its historic interests, as demonstrated by the decline of Moscow's influence in such traditionally Russian-dominated regions as the Caucasus and Central Asia; its passivity in the Balkans, particularly Moscow's "betrayal" of Serbia and Serbian interests in Bosnia-Herzegovina; and its "abandonment" of such long-standing (Soviet) allies as Cuba and Iraq.

As Russia's domestic crises deepened, so too did the now-palpable sense of national humiliation and exploitation. In response, the leadership began to amend the rhetoric if not yet the substance of its policies. Having made the case for Russia's integration with the West in such forceful terms, however, it was difficult for the government, especially the foreign minister, to recast policy, however modestly, without seeming to concede the argument to the regime's increasingly vocal critics. Had the Russian economy begun to recover during this period, the pro-Western, integrationist line might have survived as originally formulated; as it was, the persistence of the country's economic malaise was to deal a blow to Kozyrev's policy as well as to the political fortunes of the foreign minister, from which it, and he, were never to recover.

The Eurasian Alternative

At no point in its troubled tenure did the Kozyrev policy of rapid integration with the West enjoy widespread popular support. On the contrary, the policy was controversial from the start. In the early going, however, the opposition was diffuse and disorganized and of relatively little consequence: The people of Russia, as well as much of the leadership, were preoccupied with other, more immediate issues, from keeping their jobs and paying the bills, to generating strategies to guide the country's postcommunist development. The lack of strong public interest in foreign affairs afforded Kozyrev considerable maneuver room for the actual conduct of policy during 1992 and much of 1993, as did the strong support of President Yeltsin, with whom the foreign minister enjoyed a close, if occasionally stormy, working relationship.

Critics of Kozyrev's policy fell along the entire Russian political spectrum—from what might be termed "disaffected centrists" at roughly the midpoint of the scale, to communists and ultranationalists at either extreme. Little united these critics, save their common loathing of Kozyrev, and much divided them. On one issue, however, they were in broad agreement: Russia had gone "too far" in its courtship of, and dependence on, the West.

The charge meant different things to different people. The foreign minister's more responsible critics, such as international relations specialists (and parliamentarians) Alexei Arbatov and Vladimir Lukin, regularly took the government to task for excessive deference to the West, with Lukin, in particular, urging the development of stronger, more cooperative ties with China, India, and Japan—both on the merits and to provide Russia greater flexibility in the conduct of its diplomacy.[6] Less responsible figures went much further in their critiques of policy. Vladimir Zhirinovsky, presidential aspirant and leader of the right-wing Liberal Democratic Party of Russia (LDPR), for example, argued for the virtual suspension of relations with Western countries (except for Germany), the imposition of Russian power throughout much of the former U.S.S.R., and the re-creation of the old Soviet alliance system.[7]

These essentially "Eurasian" alternatives to Kozyrev's strategy of rapid integration with the West reflected the views of an extremely loose coalition of actors, linking only at the most general level those within Russian political life disturbed at the fundamental thrust or direction of the country's foreign policy. (Some of the most effective voices in support of greater "balance" in policy—mid-level officials within Kozyrev's own ministry—were in fact not even represented in this coalition, at least not formally, although they were to play an important role later, when the time came to recast policy under Primakov.) To the extent these critics agreed on anything, it was on the need for Russia to look east and south, as well as west, as it sought friends and partners internationally.

For both communists and extreme nationalists, the denunciations of Russian foreign policy were but one item on the bill of particulars drawn up by each group as it sought to force changes in the government's policies more broadly. (The attacks began within weeks—if not days—of the Soviet Union's disappearance and have continued in one form or another ever since.) Almost totally bereft of content, or at least serious analysis, these assaults sought to draw the sharpest possible distinction between

Russia's sordid present and the Soviet Union's allegedly glorious past—a time when the Kremlin, although seldom loved, was deeply feared. Given that each group of critics drew almost randomly and in roughly equal measure on two ideologically informed schools of thought, communism and fascism, it is hardly surprising that their messages were largely indistinguishable. The practical result was a potent, if slightly incoherent, call to action, which combined in a single concoction leftist-inspired critiques of Western "imperialism" and right-wing, chiliastic testaments to Russia's historic "uniqueness," including its "special mission" as champion and protector of (non-Western) civilization.

Prior to the December 1993 parliamentary elections, in which LDPR candidates garnered almost a quarter of all votes cast, few serious Russians paid much attention to the foreign policy pronouncements of Zhirinovsky. Communists, who also fared well in the elections, were accorded a more serious hearing—owing in large measure to the fact that they were, by and large, more serious people, who until quite recently had run the country and who, despite their having lost power, represented the sentiments of more Russians than any other political party in Russia.

The comparatively strong electoral showing of the communists and Zhirinovsky's nationalists provided each a highly visible platform for its views. It also induced each group to try to refine its basic political message in such a way as to underscore the differences rather than the similarities between them. In light of the backward-looking programs of both political parties, however, the effort at differentiation was only partly successful; in the minds of most Russians, the policy pronouncements of the communists and extreme nationalists were to remain largely congruent, at least for the time being. This was especially true regarding foreign policy, where the deeply anti-Western bias of both parties, coupled with a longing to recover a largely mythical past, constituted the core belief structures of each.

Whatever their prescriptive shortcomings, the attention accorded the foreign policy programs of the communists and nationalists after the 1993 parliamentary elections had important consequences for Russian political life. Most of all, it accelerated the development within the polity of an increasingly bipolar view of Russia's role and place in the world— a division that placed the government's program of rapid integration with West at one extreme and an evocative, if rather fuzzy, "Eurasian" alternative at the other.

The polarization of the debate over Russian foreign policy after 1993 also created a political opening for the government's less radicalized opponents. To take effective advantage of this opening, however, these critics would need to construct a responsible, respectable "third way" in policy terms: a manifestly centrist course, likely to appeal to the great majority of Russians who, while eager to live the good life that closer relations with the West seemed to promise, had come to resent what they saw as excessive deference on the part of the Yeltsin/Kozyrev government to the preferences of Russia's new "partners," particularly the United States.

The handwriting was on the wall. On any number of issues, from what many saw as the less than respectful treatment of Russia's interests in the former Yugoslavia to Washington's unremitting pressure to accelerate the withdrawal of Russian troops from the Baltic republics, centrist critics began to charge that the government simply had been too pliant in its dealings with the West and in so doing had compromised important and long-standing Russian foreign policy interests.

The message was clear. One did not have to be a communist or a fascist to challenge the wisdom of the government's handling of foreign policy. Revisions to policy were essential, and while no one—at least no one of any stature—was calling for a return to Soviet-era solutions, there was clearly room for improvement. The answer, according to people like Lukin, was to balance Russia's relations with the West by intensifying ties with such important regional actors as China and India. The purpose in cultivating better relations with Russia's *other* neighbors was, of course, to realize such direct benefits as mutual gains from trade; it could also, however, provide Moscow much-needed leverage in its dealings with the West by demonstrating the country's willingness to look elsewhere for friends.

As the government's centrist critics developed their case, they sought to separate what they argued informed their own analysis—namely, the defense of Russia's "national interests"—from the "romanticism" of Kozyrev and the nostalgic yearnings of the communists and extreme nationalists. Their motivation for doing so was to discredit their opponents by making both seem weak-minded and disconnected from reality, and thereby poorly equipped to manage anything as demanding and subtle as the conduct of Russian foreign policy.

They were also, however, making a more substantive point: Leaving aside the issue of whether the government's foreign policy made strategic sense for Russia, the tactics were all wrong. In other words, even if Kozyrev was correct in his assessment that partnership with the West was the only way to guarantee Russia's future greatness—which many of his critics suspected he was—one had to be much more willing to "defect" from the norm-generated cooperative "game" that Kozyrev had constructed with the United States and its allies than the foreign minister seemed either able or willing to do. Pleading for help was not the answer.

178 ◆ *Coit D. Blacker*

Rather, what Moscow needed was leverage—in the form of a credible threat to defect—so as to strengthen Russia's bargaining position, extract better terms and more resources from the West, and thereby accelerate the process of economic and political recovery.

In the highly charged environment that characterized Russian political life between the conclusion of the Belovezhkaya accords in December 1991 and the parliamentary elections two years later, such sophisticated critiques of the country's foreign policy only rarely penetrated the public's consciousness. The debate over foreign policy, at least at the popular level, tended to be episodic and much less elevated.

Two unrelated developments in 1994—growing differences between Moscow and Washington over the future shape of security in Europe and late in the year Russia's invasion of Chechnya—served, however, to keep the debate over foreign policy very much alive and, if not much better informed, at least as visible. As pressure mounted on Yeltsin in 1994 and 1995 to take a firmer stand vis-à-vis the Americans and to deal forcefully with the Chechen rebels, the president found himself increasingly on the defensive, unable to silence his domestic critics. As his popularity sagged, while that of Communist Party leader Gennady Zyuganov inched upward, the president, preparing to seek reelection in 1996, realized that something had to give. What gave—although not all at once and not completely—was Andrei Kozyrev and his policy.

THE TURN IN RUSSIAN FOREIGN POLICY, 1994–96

The hardening of the Russian line toward the West began, as indicated, well in advance of Primakov's elevation to foreign minister in early 1996. While the proximate cause was the Russian public's growing disenchantment with the government's domestic policies, the Kremlin's stewardship of the country's international relations also came in for its share of criticism. Most problematic for the regime was the U.S.-Russia relationship, which despite repeated denials from senior officials on both sides, had begun by 1994 to show unmistakable signs of wear.

Russia and the United States

Some erosion was probably inevitable, given the hyperbole that accompanied the first meeting between Bill Clinton and Boris Yeltsin in Vancouver in April 1993 and the relentlessly upbeat assessment of the relationship's prospects issued by officials in both capitals in the months immediately following. Even allowing for the predictable deflation of expectations, however, by mid-1994 relations between Washington and Moscow had taken a manifest turn for the worse, complicated by disagreements over the pace and character of economic reform, arms control, and the situation in the Balkans. The real culprit, however, was growing tension between the two sides over the complex question of security arrangements for post–Cold War Europe.

By the fall of 1994, senior U.S. officials had reached broad agreement on the need to press ahead, forcefully, with NATO enlargement. Achieving consensus on the issue had proven to be something of a challenge, with such administration heavyweights as National Security Advisor Anthony Lake (an unabashed proponent of expansion) and Deputy Secretary of State Strobe Talbott (supportive, but deeply concerned over the possible effects of enlargement on Russia and U.S.-Russian relations) pulling in somewhat different directions. In the end Clinton's senior advisors composed their differences and settled on a strategy by which the United States would affirm its support for a policy of gradual and deliberate expansion, while redoubling efforts to engage the Russians on the subject of Europe's evolving security "architecture." As part of this initiative, Washington made clear its eagerness to consider an agreement with Moscow to define and regularize NATO-Russia relations.[8]

Serious discussions regarding enlargement had been under way within the administration, as they had been within NATO circles more broadly, for more than a year by the time Richard Holbrooke returned to Washington from his posting in Bonn in September 1994 to help coordinate the government's NATO policy. Although U.S. officials had gone to considerable lengths to try to keep the outcome of the administration's deliberations confidential, word leaked almost immediately. The Russian leadership, fully aware that such discussions were under way, appears nonetheless to have been caught by surprise. Its response was sharply, and uniformly, negative.

For months Kremlin officials had been warning their U.S. counterparts that the Russian public, agitated by the anti-American fulminations of such figures as Zhirinovsky, had come to believe that NATO expansion was directed against Russia, whatever the justifications offered by the West. The gathering force of public opinion already had led the government to abandon its laissez-faire attitude toward enlargement, which had been in evidence as recently as Yeltsin's visit to Poland in August 1993.[9] The talk about enlargement could only further complicate relations, they warned, notwithstanding their own strong preference to continue the policy of cooperation with the West. By the time of Yeltsin's state visit to Washington in September 1994, speculation in the press that relations were nearing an impasse had grown so widespread that the Russian president felt the need to rebut such charges directly. "Some people in the world and some people in Russia," Yeltsin thundered, "say that our dialogue with Bill Clinton will prove hard and will show no results. I would like to state explicitly . . . that this dialogue we are going to have will make great progress."[10]

Although hardly the disaster that some had predicted, the September 1994 meetings were not without tension, as the two presidents (and their foreign ministers) wrestled with the thorny issues of Bosnia, Moscow's compliance with the Conventional Forces in Europe (CFE) treaty, arms transfer policies, and the withdrawal of Russian military units from the Baltics. On European security, the two sides "exchanged views" and agreed to keep working the issue. The personal chemistry that had begun to develop between Clinton and Yeltsin was again in evidence at the Washington summit, a feature of the relationship that was to prove of enormous consequence in the difficult days to come.

The formula for dealing with the complex question of European security first employed at the September 1994 summit—in essence, quiet agreement to kick the can down the road—enabled the two sides to avoid an open break over the issue. It could not, however, prevent the exposure of a deep fissure running through the middle of the relationship that was to widen over time. The deliberate pace of the enlargement process allowed the two sides to straddle the divide for longer than otherwise would have been the case, but the unresolved character and high visibility of the issue drained the relationship of much of its residual energy.

The low point in relations came six weeks later, precipitated by three quick Russian shocks. On December 1, in Brussels, Kozyrev balked at the signing of the draft Partnership for Peace agreement between Russia and NATO that had been in the works for months, citing as his reason the endorsement of enlargement contained in the North Atlantic Council communiqué released earlier in the day.[11] Four days later, at a Conference on Security and Cooperation in Europe (CSCE) heads-of-state session in Budapest, a clearly agitated Yeltsin cautioned against efforts "from a single capital" (read: Washington) to determine "the destinies of whole continents and the world community as a whole" and warned darkly of Europe's "plunging into a cold peace."[12] Finally, less than a week later, Yeltsin ordered Russian troops into Chechnya, in a costly and ultimately unsuccessful effort to crush the restive republic's bid for independence. Formally, the United States took no issue with Moscow's move, declaring it an internal matter of the Russian Federation, but privately the news came as something of a thunderbolt. The gnashing of teeth in Washington was almost audible.

The combined effect of these developments was twofold. The first was to induce a kind of pause in U.S.-Russia relations that was to last for months as policymakers on both sides sought to assess the damage and plot next steps. (The pause ended with Clinton's visit to Moscow in May 1995 to commemorate with Yeltsin and others the fiftieth anniversary of the end of World War II in Europe—a visit that passed amicably enough but did little to reenergize the bilateral relationship.)

The second effect, which was not unrelated to the first, was to have much more lasting consequences for Russian policy. It was during this interregnum in the development of relations between Moscow and Washington that the Yeltsin government began in a serious way to play the "Eurasian" card by seeking to cultivate much closer relations with various non-Western actors, most especially China. The strategy also, and more alarmingly from Washington's perspective, involved the intensification of relations with Iran, to which the Russians were already supplying several kinds of conventional military equipment, including, as of January 1995, two Kilo-class attack submarines.

Making New Friends

The United States welcomed the improvement in Sino-Russian relations that began in earnest with Kozyrev's first official visit to China in March 1992. Notwithstanding the sale of billions of dollars' worth of Russian military equipment to the People's Republic of China (PRC), Washington's generally positive assessment of the rapprochement between Moscow and Beijing continued well into 1994. It was not until Chinese President Jiang Zemin's visit to Russia in September of that year, which ended with the call for the development of a Sino-Russian "partnership," that some in the U.S. government began to express misgivings about the content and direction of Russia's China policy—misgivings that were to intensify over the course of the next several years as the "partnership" between Moscow and Beijing acquired greater content.

The comparatively relaxed U.S. posture regarding the development of relations between Russia and China stood in sharp contrast to Washington's reaction to the news that Russia's Ministry of Atomic Energy (MINATOM) had entered into a long-term arrangement with the corresponding ministry in Iran to complete the construction of at least one, and possibly two, 1000-megawatt, light-water nuclear reactors (begun by a German engineering firm but abandoned in 1979 following the ouster of the Shah of Iran) and to begin work on two smaller, 440-megawatt reactors of Russian design at some future date.[13] The deal, estimated to be worth at least $800 million to $1 billion to the

Kremlin, deeply alarmed U.S. policymakers on the grounds that such an agreement, which also provided for the extensive training of Iranian scientists and technicians in Russia, would facilitate Tehran's acquisition of nuclear weapons. Of at least equal concern to the United States, however, was what it seemed to suggest about Russia's interest in cultivating friendly relations with what Washington regarded as the mother of all pariah states.

Administration officials were even more distressed to learn that, as part of the reactor deal, the Russians apparently were contemplating the sale to Iran of *both* enrichment and reprocessing facilities. The Russian commitment in May 1995 to bar the transfer of any such "sensitive" equipment or know-how to Iran partly—but only partly—assuaged Washington's fears, and the reactor deal between Moscow and Tehran remained a substantial irritant in U.S.-Russia relations during this period (as, indeed, it did through 1997).[14]

In an important sense, then, well in advance of Primakov's installation as foreign minister, the Russian government had begun to steer the country's foreign policy in a new direction, and one not entirely to Washington's liking. What this apparent shift actually meant, however, was extremely difficult to discern during the second half of 1995, as Yeltsin—the *sole* authoritative voice on Russian policy as American officials had come to learn—all but disappeared from public view in July 1995 and then again in November (within two days of his meeting with Clinton at Hyde Park, New York), both times because of heart trouble. Further clouding the issue were Kozyrev's periodic, if rather anemic, affirmations of the essential continuity of Russian foreign policy during this period, which seemed to fly in the face of available evidence.

The results of the Russian parliamentary elections in December 1995—which saw the communists, Agrarians, and extreme nationalists capture 50 percent of the seats in the State Duma—eliminated any lingering doubts about the authenticity of the turn in Moscow's foreign policy. The dismal showing of the political parties directly supporting the government, such as *Nash Dom Rossiya*, as well as those allied with it, all but forced Yeltsin's hand and led the president to formalize what had been under way in practice for well over a year. In a move designed to signal the end of one era and the opening of another, on January 5, 1996, the Kremlin announced Kozyrev's resignation and Primakov's appointment as foreign minister of the Russian Federation.

THE PRIMAKOV SOLUTION

Primakov wasted little time in setting out his vision for Russian foreign policy after Kozyrev. In his first press conference on January 12 and in an appearance before the International Affairs Committee of the State Duma a month later, Russia's new foreign minister previewed virtually all the key themes that Western policymakers and analysts have come to associate with his stewardship of policy. At the center of this vision was—and is—Primakov's contention that despite its current travails "Russia . . . remains a great power" and that the country's foreign policy "should correspond to that status."[15]

Since his appointment Primakov has gone to considerable lengths to remind his audiences, both at home and abroad, that the overarching purpose of Russian foreign policy is to protect and advance the country's "interests," suggesting, for example, in his appearance before the Duma in February, that his predecessor had somehow lost sight of this seemingly elementary formulation.[16]

The better to meet this requirement, Primakov has argued, Russia, like any great power, needs a "diverse" foreign policy—one that, in addition to promoting good relations with the United States and the countries of Europe, also should seek to cultivate strong ties with China, India, Japan, and "the countries of the Near and Middle East."[17] Such a strategy, Primakov has insisted, is not directed against the interests of any country or group of countries, including Russia's Western partners; rather, its purpose is to restore a degree of "balance" to Moscow's policies, thus helping to create an external environment favorable to "economic growth and the development of democratic processes in Russian society."[18]

Primakov's pursuit of greater "balance" in Russian foreign policy is intimately connected to the concept of leverage, which in Moscow's case means the ability to improve one's relative standing in the international system by setting up a kind of bidding war between or among rival suitors. Such a strategy can work, however, only if a player's threat to jump ship, or to defect from one camp to another, is seen as credible by the other players—which itself depends on whether the player threatening to defect can still hope to realize its ambitions in the event it switches sides. This, in turn, requires that capabilities within the system in question be diffuse and not concentrated in the hands of any one player. It is for this reason above all others that in setting forth the tasks of contemporary Russian foreign policy, Primakov has gone out of his way to depict the international system within which these tasks must be accomplished as "multipolar," rather than "unipolar," in character.

Whether Primakov actually believes the world to be multipolar is difficult to determine. The evidence cuts both ways. On the one hand, he has pressed hard to build up Moscow's relations with a host of would-be non-Western "partners," most notably China. Yeltsin's visit to the PRC

184 ◆ *Coit D. Blacker*

in April 1996, during which the sides underscored the strategic character of their relationship, seems to have gone well from the Russian perspective, as did Primakov's trip the following November and Chinese Premier Li Peng's three-day stay in Moscow at the end of 1996. The most recent round of high-visibility Sino-Russian diplomacy, which ended in April 1997 with Jiang Zemin's state visit, must have been particularly satisfying to Primakov. Barely one day into the meetings, the two governments released a joint statement in which they characterized the world as multipolar and expressed their opposition to any country seeking to practice "power politics" or to "monopolize international affairs." (Lest anyone miss the point, at a joint press appearance with Jiang Yeltsin remarked that "someone is longing for a single-polar world. He wants to decide things for himself.")[19]

With considerably less fanfare, Primakov has also been instrumental in reenergizing relations between Russia and India, which had fallen into disrepair following the Soviet collapse; in keeping the diplomatic lines open to Japan, which had all but closed down in the aftermath of Yeltsin's abrupt cancellation of his scheduled trip to Tokyo in September 1992 but which, since mid-1997, have a taken a decided turn for the better; and in pressing ahead with Iran, despite intense U.S. pressure to cease and desist. He has devoted as well considerable attention to relations with Moscow's 11 partners in the Commonwealth of Independent States (CIS)—his first trips as foreign minister took him to Ukraine, Belarus, Kazakhstan, and Uzbekistan, in fact—although it is clear that Russia's heightened level of interest in the affairs of the other Soviet successor states has constituted something of a mixed blessing from the perspective of many CIS leaders.[20]

On the other hand, Primakov also has invested considerable time and energy in the further development of Russia's *Westpolitik*, and from all indications is the primary architect of Moscow's policy toward the United States and the major countries of Europe. He was Secretary General Solana's primary Russian interlocutor on NATO expansion between October 1996 and the conclusion of the NATO-Russia Founding Act in May 1997, and carried much of the bilateral negotiating burden on this contentious issue with his Western colleagues, including Warren Christopher and Madeleine Albright. He has consistently underscored—and just as consistently acted as if he accepts—the central importance to Russia of maintaining the best possible relations with Moscow's former Cold War adversaries, both to help safeguard regional and international stability and to assist Russia's own economic and political transformation.

The modest disconnect between Primakov's rhetorical emphasis on "balance" and "multipolarity" and the actual practice of Russian diplomacy in the period since his appointment has both an objective and a subjective component. Objectively, the Russians are constrained from doing more to signal their independence from the West by the actual distribution of power within the international system. While certain kinds of capabilities have become more diffuse in recent years—for example, the capacity to inflict human suffering—along other dimensions, such as the ability to mobilize significant monetary and economic resources, power remains as concentrated as ever.

As Primakov understands as well as anyone, among outside actors it is only the West and its associated institutions that have the means to help defray the enormous costs of Russia's transition to a market economy. The roughly $30 billion that the international financial institutions (IFIs) have provided to Moscow since 1993 to assist in stabilizing the country's economy has been instrumental in bringing inflation under control, ensuring the ruble's convertibility, and attracting foreign investment. The $10 to $15 billion in direct support that leading Western countries have supplied both bilaterally and multilaterally also has been important, primarily in underwriting the costs of various technical assistance programs without which the pain of transition would be even greater. In all it is estimated that Russia has been the recipient of $40-plus billion in Western grants, credits, and low-cost loans since 1992 and that well in excess of an additional $100 billion, much of it in the form of hard-to-attract investment capital, could be placed at the country's disposal if the government should succeed in its efforts to convince the Duma to pass appropriate enabling legislation.

Trade statistics tell a very similar story. Two-way trade between Russia and China totaled approximately $5.6 billion in 1996, most of it in commodities, semifinished goods, and, from Russia to China, a long list of weapons, weapons systems, and various kinds of military equipment. The comparable figure for Russia and the Organization for Economic Cooperation and Development (OECD) and its 29 countries approached $70 billion in 1996, with much of the traffic into Russia made up of high-technology goods and services, such as computers, telephone systems and the like, industrial machinery, and consumer products.[21]

The larger point is that the ability to mobilize resources on this scale and to supply the kinds of goods and services needed to underpin the reform process in Russia is uniquely Western. Moscow's largest and most important non-Western partners, China and India, in fact compete with Russia for investment capital. They also stand largely outside the IFI structure and have no foreign assistance budgets to speak of. Even assuming a desire to do so, in other words, they and other developing countries are simply incapable of providing anything like the level of assistance that the West has made, and can make, available to Russia.

Such economic facts of life notwithstanding, the Russians could still, of course, decide to reverse course economically; they could, for example and most dramatically, jettison the macroeconomic stabilization program negotiated with the IMF. While the consequences, particularly over the short term, could be catastrophic (as discussed later), it is well to remember that Russia is in many ways a rich country, with abundant natural resources, a well-educated population, a long history of scientific and technological achievement, and a demonstrated ability to produce world-class goods and services.

The Russians could choose, as they have at previous junctures, either to go it alone economically or to decrease their dependence on the West by forging the closest possible ties with important, non-Western actors. (They also could seek to pursue a differentiated policy toward the West—intensifying relations with the member countries of the European Union, for example, while downgrading relations with Washington, much as the Soviet Union did at several points during the Cold War.) That such a strategy would complicate, and in all likelihood retard, Russia's recovery goes without saying. It also might be beside the point. Political leaders in many parts of the world have engineered equally abrupt shifts in policy in response to political and social pressures that pale in comparison to those operating on Russian leaders in 1998.

The point, in any event, is that in the absence of such a decision, the economic facts of life with which Russia currently has to contend—courtesy of the IMF and international financial markets, in particular—severely constrain over the near to medium term its freedom to maneuver internationally, in deeds certainly, if not always in words.

The other major constraint is subjective, but probably just as important: Boris Yeltsin remains at heart an integrationist. At any number of critical junctures in the conduct of Russian foreign policy, Yeltsin has intervened to resolve issues in ways that underscore his commitment to overcoming Russia's isolation from the West. At the May 1995 Clinton-Yeltsin meeting in Moscow, for example, the Russian president personally authorized Moscow's accession to a draft joint declaration on the future of security in Europe that the Foreign Ministry had declined to sanction in advance of the summit session.

At Hyde Park five months later, in response to a request from Clinton, Yeltsin again overruled his advisors and approved Russia's military participation in the NATO Implementation Force (IFOR), the multinational, NATO-led peacekeeping force for Bosnia. More recently, during his meeting with German Chancellor Helmut Kohl in April 1997, Yeltsin undermined the bargaining position of his own foreign minister when he announced to the press that Russia and NATO would conclude their negotiations on a draft charter (the Founding Act) in time for a scheduled "16 Plus 1" heads-of-state meeting in late May, even though important issues had yet to be resolved.[22]

The strongest evidence that Yeltsin remains a committed integrationist, however, was his government reshuffle in March 1997 in which he elevated two of Russia's most market-oriented reformers, Anatoly Chubais and Boris Nemtsov, to the rank of first deputy prime minister and either fired or demoted a score of mid- and senior-level officials whom Western governments had come to regard as obstacles to reform. That Yeltsin did so in the face of strong Duma opposition—and despite the Russian public's loathing of Chubais, whom many Russians hold personally responsible for the perceived excesses of the privatization program in 1992 and 1993—indicates the depth of his commitment to keep Russia moving in the direction of political and economic integration with the West.

None of this is to suggest that Russia's president is above seeking to extract whatever advantage he can in his dealings with Western counterparts by threatening either to stop doing something they regard as essential or to start doing something they regard as destructive. It is to suggest, however, that Yeltsin has a well-honed sense for knowing how hard, how often, and in which directions to press the West without endangering the pursuit of his larger policy goals.

Yeltsin's clear determination to keep Russia on a (mostly) pro-Western course begs the obvious question of how the president's inevitable passing from the political scene will impact the direction and content of Russian foreign policy. It is impossible, of course, to answer the question with any certainty, given the vagaries of Russian politics. It is worth noting, however, that with the exception of Chubais, who is unlikely to succeed Yeltsin in any event, none of Russia's leading political actors and/or presidential aspirants has rushed to embrace the integrationist banner. The strongest claimants—Zyuganov, Zhirinovsky, former National Security Advisor Aleksandr Lebed, and Moscow Mayor Yuri Luzhkov—are all associated in the public mind at least with much more nationalistic postures, in foreign and well as domestic policy terms. How any of these political figures actually would comport themselves once installed in the Kremlin's offices is a different matter.

For the time being, however, the combination of objective and subjective constraints just outlined militates against the adoption by the Russian government of a full-blown "Eurasian" alternative to policy—assuming for purposes of argument that some within the leadership would in fact opt for such a departure, given half a chance. And, indeed, the government has refrained from doing so, content to let Russia's higher diplomatic profile in East and South Asia, in particular, speak for itself.

To date the strategy of driving west while feinting east has cost Russia very little. Relations with the United States and its allies remain productive, if less intimate than they were between 1992 and 1994, and assuming the two sides can manage the small but stubborn collection of issues over which they find themselves at loggerheads—NATO enlargement, Russia's nuclear cooperation with Iran, and differences over Bosnia and the implementation of the Dayton peace accords—the prognosis for the further development of relations would seem to be favorable. The real issue is whether Primakov can keep his balance as he walks what amounts to a political and diplomatic tightrope—that is, continue to pursue good relations with the West, especially the United States, while simultaneously cultivating important ties with powerful states beyond the effective reach of Washington's influence.

PATHWAYS AND PITFALLS

This chapter began with a series of propositions about the interconnectedness of domestic politics in Russia and the country's foreign policy. Given the thrust of the analysis, it also seems the appropriate point on which to conclude.

Boris Yeltsin did not dismiss Andrei Kozyrev in January 1996 because of some consequential mistake in the latter's conduct of policy. Throughout his tenure, Kozyrev faithfully executed the strategy that he and Yeltsin, together with other leading members of the president's official family, developed jointly. Yeltsin fired Kozyrev because by 1995 the government's foreign policy, much like its domestic policies, had become deeply unpopular with a Russian electorate disillusioned with reform and eager to assign blame to those in positions of responsibility; Kozyrev, with few in high places to fight for his retention, was an obvious candidate to offer up for sacrifice. In the baldest of terms, Yeltsin released Kozyrev from his official duties because the foreign minister had become a political liability to his president, who himself was struggling against considerable odds to preserve his hold on power.

Yevgeny Primakov was held in very high regard by many in Russia's foreign policy establishment at the time of his appointment, having spent most of his professional life either involved in the making of policy or advising those who did. He had earned a reputation as a careful, thoughtful analyst of global politics, one of the country's premier geostrategists, an excellent negotiator, and a skilled bureaucrat. Yeltsin did not tap Primakov to succeed Kozyrev, however, because he was the best that

Russia had to offer—although he may well have been. Rather, Yeltsin appointed the experienced Soviet-era foreign policy professional because he was seen to be a "centrist" in policy terms, and thus likely to appeal to a broader cross-section of the Russian political class than his predecessor, who was considered—and rightly so—an unrepentant Westernizer.

There is nothing unusual, or even particularly unhealthy, about democratically elected leaders hiring and firing aides to signal their responsiveness to popular concerns about the content and direction of policy. Effective governance requires, among other things, a certain level of public confidence that those whom the voters have chosen to advance their interests will faithfully represent the broad, if inexact, collection of preferences that defines public opinion at any given time. The danger arises when elected officials allow these mostly inchoate preferences not just to influence policy but to determine it, which not only constitutes an a priori leadership failure but which can, and often does, eventuate in a series of policy disasters.

The turn in Russian foreign policy detailed in the preceding analysis was the manifest result of a decision on the part of Yeltsin and those closest to him politically to accommodate a shift—away from reform and away from integration—in Russian public opinion. To date, no disasters have befallen Russia, and the president's foreign policy team has demonstrated considerable skill in the actual, day-to-day management of Russia's complex relations with the outside world.

Whether the Russian leadership can avoid becoming hostage to its own rhetoric about the need for a more "balanced," less Western-oriented foreign policy will turn, ironically, on the extent to which the United States, together with its principal allies in Europe and Asia, ignores the messages coming out of Moscow and elects to remain deeply engaged with Russia, both economically and politically. Six years into the reform process, Russia has yet to put in place many of the institutions essential to the functioning of a market economy. Such direct Western support as the IMF's Extended Fund Facility has been, and remains, critically important to this process of institutionalization. In many ways, however, it is the less obvious kinds of support—working with Russian authorities to design and implement sensible economic policies, for example—that will determine, at least in part, the success or failure of the Russian reform effort.

Were the West to disengage from Russia economically, the consequences would be immediate and profound. At a minimum, such a Western retreat would very likely precipitate a run on the ruble, which could rapidly deplete the Kremlin's hard-currency reserves and spark a new round of hyperinflation. In a worst-case scenario, the government could move to suspend convertibility of the currency, which would lead both

Western and Russian investors to look elsewhere for places to park their money. Subjected to such massive and sudden pressures, the economy could very well implode.

Should such a catastrophe overtake Russia, the narrow political base on which the government relies to pursue its policies would further contract, if not evaporate altogether. The one other—perhaps the only other—predictable consequence would be the strengthening of those parties and political interests most opposed to the government and its policies, namely the communists and extreme nationalists. The radicalization of Russian domestic politics would inevitably radicalize the country's foreign policy, which could drive the government—desperate to keep pace with public sentiment—to assume an explicitly anti-Western posture and to seek allies among those states similarly inclined.

There is nothing inevitable, or even very probable, about this nightmare scenario.[23] It is not impossible, however, and therein lies the problem. Russia's current flirtation with an alternative foreign policy, designed both to mollify the regime's domestic critics and to provide the government greater leverage in its dealings with the West, could set in motion a process over which Russia's leaders could lose control, thereby generating a host of long-term, strategic, and wholly unwelcome consequences.

Three factors give rise to modest optimism that the worst can be avoided. First is the government's own keen awareness of the stakes, coupled with its determination *not* to lose control over events. Russia's leaders remain deeply engaged with and responsive to their Western counterparts on the full range of issues of interest and importance to both. They have gone to great lengths to keep faith with the IMF to ensure that the funds continue to flow and that the stabilization program remains on track. And with the exception of relations with Iran (and, most recently, Iraq), they have been careful not to cross any of the red lines that Washington has drawn around various "pariah states."

Second is the manifest interest of those in the new Russia who have profited most from the liberalization of the economy to preserve the integrationist tilt in foreign policy, primarily to ensure their continued access to Western markets and capital. The emergence of private economic interests in Russia, in particular the rise of a handful of extremely powerful banks and bank-led "financial industrial groups," has resulted in the establishment of a kind of informal integrationist lobby in Moscow whose pro-Western policy preferences have precious little to do with sentiment.[24]

It is, moreover, a lobby with unrivaled access to the country's decision-makers—some of whom, such as former Deputy National Security Advisor Boris Berezovsky, are themselves members in good standing of Russia's new capitalist class (and most of whom have profited in one way or another from their association with it). The extremely close relationship that has developed between "the party of power" in Russia and the country's leading business interests—a relationship that serves the interests of each—would seem to suggest that, absent a change in regime, the drive to secure Russia's full integration into the U.S.-led and Western-dominated international economic system will continue, more or less unabated. It also suggests, at least to this author, that where Moscow's economic interests lead it, its political interests are likely to follow.

The third factor is the willingness of the West to stay the course with Moscow, despite a tendency on the part of the Russians to signal in highly public ways their opposition to any number of Western policies and initiatives. That the leading Western countries have been sufficiently disciplined to resist the temptation to respond in kind to this steady stream of mostly minor, but nonetheless annoying, provocations is a testament to the patience, sophistication, and maturity of their leaderships. The consequences of a policy failure are understood to be enormous, and, for once at least, all Western leaders seem to have reached essentially the same conclusion.

The combined force of these three factors strongly suggests that for the near to medium term, the Russian leadership will hew to a broad middle course in the conduct of foreign policy. As indicated, such a posture is likely to entail continued and substantial engagement with the West on such high-end policy issues as the maintenance of international peace and security, regional affairs, nuclear nonproliferation, and the struggle to combat terrorism, combined with continuous efforts to forge stronger and better relations with key regional actors from the Middle East to East Asia.

To do otherwise at this juncture—to renounce engagement in favor of a more confrontational posture vis-à-vis the West or, alternatively, to abandon the pursuit of greater "balance" in Russian policy by deemphasizing relations with China and India, for example—could prove, in fact, costly to the Kremlin. The Russians can ill afford, and have no compelling reason, to confront the West, given the importance they attach to Western economic assistance and political support; assuming skillful handling and prudent management on Moscow's part, they also have no incentive to turn their backs on their non-Western friends with whom they have begun to develop significant political and economic ties. In other words, Russia's current (and prospective) foreign policy strategy is basically sound in terms of content, although it is—and will remain—difficult to implement. Expressed differently, the risks inherent in Moscow's current course reside less in the design of policy than in its execution.

The one note of caution amid all this optimism is, of course, the state of the economy. If material conditions begin to improve in Russia and the population has reason to look toward the future with at least a modicum of hope, Russia's leaders will have sufficient political room within which to operate, in foreign as well as domestic policy matters. Maintaining a "balanced" foreign policy—one that feints east but continues to drive west—under such conditions is a manageable task. Should the economy fail to recover, however, and the decline in living standards with which the majority of the people has had to contend continues unabated, all bets are off, and not just in Russian foreign policy.

Notes

I am grateful to Alexander Dallin, Sherman Garnett, Gail Lapidus, Michael Mandelbaum, Michael McFaul, Michel Oksenberg, and Steve Sestanovich, in particular, for their many helpful comments and suggestions on successive drafts of the manuscript. I also learned much and profited greatly from the authors' review conference, held in May 1997 at Council headquarters in Washington, D.C.; my thanks to all who took an active interest in my work. I am indebted to Sarah Harrigan, of Stanford University's International Policy Studies program, for her research assistance.

1. I first heard Dallin use the phrase at a conference on the future of U.S.-Soviet relations in May 1977, at Belmont House, Maryland. Dallin, in turn, attributes the thought that informs the phrase, if not its precise wording, to George Kennan.
2. Andrei Kozyrev, "Russia: A Chance for Survival," *Foreign Affairs* 71 (March/April 1992), pp. 9–10.
3. Ibid., p. 5.
4. Michael McFaul, "The Sovereignty Script: Red Book for Russian Revolutionaries," Paper prepared for a conference on problematic sovereignty, sponsored by the Institute for International Studies, Stanford University, February 1998.
5. See, for example, Andrei Kozyrev, "Harmony or Cold Peace," *Cleveland Plain Dealer,* July 24, 1995, p. 9B.
6. See, in particular, Alexei G. Arbatov, "Russia's Foreign Policy Alternatives," *International Security* 18 (Fall 1993), pp. 5–43; and Vladimir Lukin, "Russian Realities: U.S., Ex-Rival Must Discard Delusions," *Phoenix Gazette,* April 14, 1994, p. B7.
7. Lee Hockstader, "Who Is Zhirinovsky? Mysteries Surround Russian Nationalist," *Washington Post,* December 18, 1993, p. A1; see also Vladimir Kartsev, *Zhirinovsky!* (New York: Columbia University Press, 1995), pp. 89, 95, and 97.
8. James M. Goldgeier, "U.S. Security Policy toward the New Europe: How the Decision to Expand NATO Was Made," Paper presented at the 1997 annual meeting of the American Political Science Association, August 1997.
9. Jane Perlez, "Yeltsin 'Understands' Polish Bid for a Role in NATO," *New York Times,* August 26, 1993, p. A3.

10. "Remarks by President Clinton and Russian President Boris Yeltsin at Arrival Ceremony," *White House Press Release,* September 27, 1994.

11. Daniel Williams, "Russian Minister Balks at NATO's Expansion Plans," *Washington Post,* December 2, 1994, p. A33.

12. "A Common Security Space: Speech by Russian Federation President Boris Yeltsin at the Budapest Meeting of the Conference on Security and Cooperation in Europe," *Rossiiskaya gazeta,* December 7, 1994, as reported in *Current Digest of the Post-Soviet Press* 46, no. 49 (1994), pp. 1, 6.

13. "Nuclear Developments," *The Nonproliferation Review* (Spring/Summer 1995), p. 111.

14. Maryam Aharinejad and Greg J. Gerardi, "Report: An Assessment of Iran's Nuclear Facilities," *The Nonproliferation Review* (Spring/Summer 1995), pp. 207-13.

15. Press Conference with Foreign Minister Yevgeny Primakov, *Kremlin International News Broadcast,* January 12, 1996.

16. Remarks by Foreign Minister Yevgeny Primakov at the Duma Committee for International Affairs, *Kremlin International News Broadcast,* February 8, 1996.

17. Press Conference with Foreign Minister Yevgeny Primakov.

18. Ibid.

19. Michael R. Gordon, "Russia-China Theme: Contain the West," *New York Times,* April 24, 1997, p. A3.

20. "Primakov Starts with the CIS," *Moskovskiye novosti* 2 (January 14–21, 1996), p. 13, as reported in *Current Digest of the Post-Soviet Press* 48, no. 2 (1996), p. 12.

21. *Directory of Trade Statistics Yearbook* (Washington, DC: International Monetary Fund, 1997), pp. 380–81.

22. See Alan Cowell, "Yeltsin Now Seems Ready to Accept NATO at His Borders," *New York Times,* April 18, 1997, p. A3.

23. Russia's weathering of the fall 1997 economic crisis in Southeast Asia is encouraging, even hopeful, in this regard. Although by Kremlin estimates the crisis in Asia led nervous investors to withdraw some $4 billion to $6 billion from Russian capital markets in November and December, by early 1998 the situation had largely stabilized. The central bank's willingness to spend hard currency to defend the ruble, combined with the increase in short-term rates, calmed international financial markets and enabled Russia to avoid, at least for the moment, a Korea-like meltdown.

24. As Michael McFaul writes, ". . . [t]he normative impetus for pursuing liberal, integrationist foreign policies faded as Russian expectations concerning Western assistance were not and could not be met, while euphoria for the markets, democracy, and the Western way ended. Even by the end of Russia's first year of independence, foreign policy appeared to be drifting back to more anti-Western, illiberal patterns of the Soviet period. Support for maintaining a liberal policy orientation was reinvigorated, however, when emergent economic interest groups with tangible interests in peaceful relations with other states, and especially peaceful relations with Western democracies, began to assert their influence in foreign policy matters." See Michael McFaul, "A Precarious Peace: Domestic Politics in the Making of Russian Foreign Policy," *International Security,* in press.

ABOUT THE AUTHORS

Leon Aron is a Resident Scholar at the American Enterprise Institute in Washington D.C. and Director of the Emergent Russian Market Seminar for senior executives of U.S. corporations. Born in Moscow, Dr. Aron came to the United States as a refugee. He received an M.A., M.Phil, and Ph.D. in political sociology and media sociology from Columbia University. Prior to joining the American Enterprise Institute in 1992, he was Senior Policy Analyst in Soviet Studies at the Heritage Foundation. Dr. Aron taught the graduate seminar on postcommunist Russia's politics and society at Georgetown University and was awarded the Peace Fellowship at the U.S. Institute of Peace. In addition to numerous articles, he is the author of the first full-scale, scholarly biography of Boris Yeltsin, which will be published in the fall of 1998. He co-edited and contributed to *The Emergence of Russian Foreign Policy* (1994).

Coit D. Blacker is Senior Fellow and Director for Special Projects at the Institute for International Studies and, by courtesy, Associate Professor of Political Science at Stanford University. In 1995 and 1996, he served as Special Assistant to the President for National Security Affairs and Senior Director for Russian, Ukrainian, and Eurasian Affairs at the National Security Council. Professor Blacker received his A.B. from Occidental College and his A.M., M.A.L.D., and Ph.D from the Fletcher School of Law and Diplomacy at Tufts University. In 1993 he was awarded an honorary doctorate by the Russian Academy of Science's Institute of Far Eastern Studies. He is the author of several books, including *Hostage to Revolutions: Gorbachev and Soviet Security Policy, 1985–91* (1993) and *Reluctant Warriors: The United States, the Soviet Union, and Arms Control* (1987); with Gloria Duffy, he edited *International Arms Control: Issues and Agreements* (1984).

Sherman W. Garnett is a Senior Associate at the Carnegie Endowment for International Peace, where he has been since 1994. He directs the Project on Security and National Identity in the Former U.S.S.R. as well as the Endowment's project on Russian-Chinese relations. Dr. Garnett spent eleven years in the government before joining the Endowment, most recently serving as Deputy Assistant Secretary of Defense for Russia, Ukraine, and Eurasia. He was a staff member of the Directorate for Multilateral Negotiations on chemical and biological weapons from 1984 to 1988 and was the Secretary of Defense's Personal Representative to the Negotiations on Conventional Armed Forces in Europe from 1988 to 1989. Dr. Garnett received his B.A. in Political Philosophy from Michigan State University, his M.A. in Russian and East European Studies from Yale, and his Ph.D. in Russian literature from the University of Michigan. He is the author of the book *Keystone in the Arch: Ukraine in the Emerging Security Environment of Central and Eastern Europe.*

Michael Mandelbaum is Director of the Project on East-West Relations at the Council on Foreign Relations. He is also the Christian A. Herter Professor of American Foreign Policy at the Paul H. Nitze School of Advanced International Studies at the Johns Hopkins University in Washington, D.C. He has taught at Harvard University, Columbia University, and the U.S. Naval Academy. Professor Mandelbaum received his B.A. from Yale University; M.A. from King's College, Cambridge University; and Ph.D. from Harvard University. He is the author of numerous articles and books and is the editor of nine volumes published by the Council on Foreign Relations Press, most recently *Sustaining the Transition: The Social Safety Net in Postcommunist Europe* (1997); *Postcommunism: Four Perspectives* (1996); *The Strategic Quadrangle: Russia, China, and the United States in East Asia* (1995); and *Central Asia and the World* (1994).

Rajan Menon is the Monroe J. Rathbone Professor and Chairman, Department of International Relations, at Lehigh University. He is also an Adjunct Professor at the Harriman Institute, Columbia University, and taught for many years at Vanderbilt University. He has published extensively on Soviet and Russian foreign policy and the international relations of Central Asia, the Transcaucasus, and Northeast Asia. He is the author of *Soviet Power and the Third World* (1985) and co-editor of *Limits to Soviet Power* (1989). His articles have appeared in numerous journals and edited volumes. From 1989 to 1990 he served, while an International Affairs Fellow at the Council on Foreign Relations, as Special Assistant for National Security and Arms Control to former congressman Stephen J. Solarz (D-NY).

INDEX

Abdullojonov, Abdumalki, 145, 146
Abkhazia, 36–38, 41, 44, 58*n*72,
    108–9, 138–43
Adenauer, Konrad, 42
Afghanistan, 8, 106
Africa, 10, 113
Agriculture, 79
AIOC (Azerbaijani International
    Operating Company), 46, 132
Albright, Madeleine, 184
Algeria, 113
Aliev, Haidar, 110–11, 130
Apartheid, 27, 81
Arbatov, Alexei, 102, 175
Ardzinba, Vladislav, 41, 140
Armenia, 6, 8, 44, 153, 158; and
    Caspian oil, 118–25; and the Kara-
    bakh conflict, 126–34; power in-
    dices for, 105–6; and trade, 114–17
Ataturk, Mustafa Kemal, 4, 20*n*6
Atlantic Alliance, 6, 82–83
Atlanticism, 101
Authoritarianism, 48–49, 72, 76
Azerbaijan, 10, 109, 150–53; and the
    Karabakh conflict, 126–34; oil ven-
    tures in, 36, 46, 111, 114, 118–25,
    132; power indices for, 105–6
Azerbaijani International Operating
    Company (AIOC), 46, 132

Baltics, 7–9, 24, 77–85, 110, 177. *See
    also specific countries*
Belarus, 26, 64–99, 130; and the
    Grand Compromise, 38; and nu-
    clear weapons, 28; and the tactics
    of "integration," 36, 38–39
Belavezh Accords, 35, 46–47
Belgium, 11
Berezovsky, Boris, 45, 191
Black Sea, 135, 158*n*49; Consortium,
    149; Fleet, 86, 88, 90
Bolskevik revolution, 4, 15, 22*n*22,
    170
Borders, 31, 80–81, 108–9

Bosnia, 24. *See also* Yugoslav crisis
Brezhnev era, 168
Britain, 2, 14–15, 112
Bush, George, 23, 171

CAEU (Central Asian Economic
    Union), 116
Canada, 19
Capitalism, 153, 170
Caspian Sea, 8, 46, 118–25, 132, 134
Caspian Pipeline Consortium, 46,
    121, 123
Catherine the Great, 62*n*94, 65
Catholicism, 15, 23. *See also* Chris-
    tianity
Caucasus, 5, 8, 9–10, 26, 100–166.
    See also Near Abroad
Central America, 10, 113
Central Asia, 6, 8–10, 26, 100–166.
    See also Near Abroad
Centrism, 175, 189
Ceyhan project, 112–13
CFE (Treaty on Conventional Forces
    in Europe), 84, 112, 130
Chechnya, 27, 38–39, 111, 137; and
    the Karabakh conflict, 131; 1997
    peace accord with, 45; and nuclear
    weapons, 28; and the oil industry,
    45–46, 112; and power differen-
    tials, 106; and Yeltsin, 6, 12, 178,
    180; Yushenkov on, 39
Chernomyrdin, Viktor, 41, 45, 76,
    118
Chevron, 46
China, 7, 12–14, 69, 177, 180–84,
    191; exports to, 50; Kozyrev's visit
    to, 180; militant nationalism in, 49;
    and the southern Near Abroad,
    100–101, 104, 114, 116, 119, 121,
    124, 148–49; and Yeltsin, 13, 14,
    183–84
Christianity, 4, 8, 15, 23, 151
Christopher, Warren, 184
Chubais, Anatoly, 39, 75, 187